"Franks, Burgundians, and Aquitanians" and the Royal Coronation Ceremony in France

Fol. 75v of the *Ordo* of Paris, Bibliothèque nationale, Lat. 14192. Photograph by author.

of the

American Philosophical Society

Held at Philadelphia for Promoting Useful Knowledge

VOLUME 82 Part 7

"Franks, Burgundians, and Aquitanians" and the Royal Coronation Ceremony in France

Elizabeth A. R. Brown

Brooklyn College and The Graduate School
The City University of New York

THE AMERICAN PHILOSOPHICAL SOCIETY

Independence Square, Philadelphia

1992

Library of Congress Catalog Card No.: 92-70404
International Standard Book No.: 0-87169-827-7
US ISSN: 0065-9746

To the memory of Charles Holt Taylor

CONTENTS

End of inventory of sources used by Jean du Tillet for his chapter on French royal coronation in the first recension of his *Recueil des Roys*. Paris, Bibliothèque nationale, fr. 2854, fol. 144r.

ACKNOWLEDGMENTS

This study developed from a paper that I presented at the International Conference on Medieval Coronations held in Toronto in February 1985 in memory of John Brückmann. I thank János Bak, Jane Couchman, and Patricia Brückmann for their invitation to the conference and their hospitality, and the participants in the conference for their questions and comments.

Harvey Stahl first called my attention to the *ordo* of Paris, Bibliothèque nationale, lat. 14192, when, some years ago, he was working on the scriptorium of Saint-Denis; he has subsequently given me invaluable counsel. I also owe special thanks to François Avril, Marie-Noëlle Baudouin-Matuszek, George T. Beech, the late John F. Benton, Uta Renate Blumenthal, Pierre Bougard, the late Jacques Boussard, Leonard E. Boyle, Walter Cahn, Françoise Gasparri, Ralph E. Giesey, Sarah Hanley, Natalie Zemon Davis, Donald R. Kelley, Marie-Pierre Laffitte, Andrew W. Lewis, Susan Lowry, Susanne Roberts, Mary A. Rouse, Richard H. Rouse, Alfred Soman, Robert Somerville, Patricia Danz Stirnemann, Daniel Traister, Thomas G. Waldman, Paul L. Ward, and Ian P. Wei. François Avril, Walter Cahn, Françoise Gasparri, Susan Lowry, Mary Rouse, Richard Rouse, and Patricia Stirnemann furnished welcome instruction and advice on points connected with the provenance and dating of the manuscripts that I treat, and I profited exceedingly from (and have, I hope, used responsibly) the suggestions that they gave. Richard E. Sullivan provided a close reading and a host of useful criticisms of an early version of this study. I am particularly grateful for the encouragement and advice of Richard A. Jackson (who is completing his long-awaited edition of the French coronation *ordines* and who has generously shared with me the wealth of material that he has collected) and Hervé Pinoteau (whose knowledge of French royal ceremonial and heraldry is unrivaled). Guy Lanoë played an especially important role in the evolution of the study. Thanks to Patricia Danz Stirnemann, his colleague at the Institut de Recherche et d'Histoire des Textes in Paris, I learned of his research on the manuscripts of Beauvais. He kindly sent me a summary of an unpublished paper on the *ordo* of BN, lat. 14192, which he delivered in October 1990, and, subsequently, the text of an article on liturgical manuscripts of Beauvais that will soon be published. In January and February of 1992 I was fortunate enough to be able to work with him in Paris and discuss the important implications of his research for my own. His findings and our conversations have prompted substantial revision of my conclusions. Although we do not agree on every point, this study owes much to his generous counsel.

As in the past, it is a pleasure to acknowledge the kind assistance of the staffs of the Bibliothèque municipale of Arras; the Bibliothèque municipale of Rouen; the Cabinet des livres of the Musée Condé at Chantilly; the Archives nationales, the Bibliothèque de l'Arsenal, the Bibliothèque de l'Institut de France, the Bibliothèque Mazarine, and the Bibliothèque nationale in Paris; the Biblioteca Apostolica Vaticana; the Avery Architectural and Fine Arts Library, the Graphic Arts Collection of the Library of the School of Library Service, the Law School Library, and Butler Library of Columbia University; the Yale University Library; and the New York Public Library. I am indebted as well to the staffs of the Library of Caius College, Cambridge; the Bibliothèque publique et universitaire in Geneva; the Bibliothèque de l'Assemblée nationale (Chambre des députés) in Paris; the Henry Charles Lea Library and the Rare Book Collection, Department of Special Collections, Van Pelt-Dietrich Library Center, University of Pennsylvania, in Philadelphia; and the National Library of Russia in Saint Petersburg. Thanks too to Peter Harriss and Wayne D. Geist of the City University of New York for generous help with photographs.

Research for this study was made possible by grants from the Academy of Sciences of Russia, the American Council of Learned Societies, the International Research and Exchanges Board (IREX) (with funds provided by the National Endowment for the Humanities and the United States Information Agency, none of which is responsible for the views that I express here), the National Endowment for the Humanities, and the PSC-CUNY Research Award Program; by sabbatical leaves from Brooklyn College and the Graduate School of the City University of New York; and by my colleagues at Brooklyn College—particularly Teofilo F. Ruiz and Christine Farrell. I extend to all these individuals and institutions my thanks, as I salute Carole N. Le Faivre and Susan M. Babbitt, two of the finest, most astute, and most sympathetic editors ever.

ABBREVIATIONS

AN—Archives nationales
BAV—Vatican City, Biblioteca Apostolica Vaticana
BIF—Paris, Bibliothèque de l'Institut de France
BM—Bibliothèque municipale
BN—Paris, Bibliothèque nationale
BPU—Geneva, Bibliothèque publique et universitaire
MGH—*Monumenta Germaniae Historica*
MPL—*Patrologiæ cursus completus . . . Series prima . . . ecclesiæ latinæ,* edited by J.-P. Migne
SS—Saint Petersburg, National Library of Russia (formerly the M. E. Saltykov-Shchedrin State Public Library)

Full references to all works used for this study appear in the Bibliography. In the notes the works are cited by the first words of their titles.

PREFACE

Most medieval coronation *ordines* have no special relevance to the lands where they were used or the kings at whose coronations they were intoned. Barren of references to specific kings and kingdoms, they stand outside time and space as cryptic witnesses to the loftiness of the royal state and glory. A few rare ceremonials are more personalized and include references to particular peoples and places associated with the lands where the *ordines* were confected[1]; such ceremonials were naturally most often copied in the realms where they originated. But at least one such *ordo*, which referred to the peoples who inhabited and a saint who was especially venerated in the kingdom where it was composed, was adopted and adapted in a realm for which it was never intended. There, despite its alien origin, the *ordo* gained authoritative status and profoundly influenced the contents and terminology of the kingdom's later coronation services.

In France, from at least the thirteenth (and probably the twelfth) century through the reign of Louis XVI, the royal consecration prayer expressed the hope that the king would never abandon the scepters of the Saxons, Mercians, and Northumbrians (or, more precisely, in garbled form, "North Cimbrians").[2] As John Selden aptly remarked in 1631, "The Negligence or Forgetfulnesse that left these names in it, were almost incredible, if we saw it not. . . . For what had euer any of the *French*

---

[1] The impulse to particularize the coronation *ordo* greatly increased after the fifteenth century: Jackson, *Vive le Roi!*, 232-33 n. 26 (Fr. ed., 37 n. 26); and also Ecles, *Coronation Service*, esp. 66, 78 (the *ordo* observed at the coronation of George VI of England in 1937). See Schramm, "Krönung," 182-90; revised in idem, *Kaiser*, 2: 192-99 ("Die Krönung im 9. und 10. Jahrhundert"). See also 14 n. 47 below.

[2] Jackson, *Vive le Roi!*, 229-30 n. 19 (Fr. ed., 25 n. 19); idem, "*Ordines*," 64; Chéruel, *Histoire des institutions*, 1120 (Louis XVI). The formula "Saxonum, Merciorum & Nordan, Cimbrorum" (translated as "des Saxons, des Merciens, des peuples du Nord et des Cimbres") was considered an integral part of the consecration prayer in 1825: Alletz, *Cérémonial*, 107; Ménin, *Cérémonies*, 58. The official record of the coronation of Charles X, however, does not indicate that the formula was actually included in the prayer of consecration: *Prières et cérémonies du sacre de S. M. Charles X*, 64-65; I am grateful for this reference to Hervé Pinoteau; see also *Cérémonial*, ed. Millon, 67. Cf. Garnier, *Le Sacre de Charles X*, 85-86; Hohler, "Some Service-Books," 67; Elze, "Ein Krönungsordo," 325.

Kings to doe with these people?"[3] By the seventeenth century explanations had been devised, but if Selden knew them, he said nothing, perhaps because they involved antiquated French claims to England. Strikingly esoteric, the phrase apparently did not disturb those who employed it in medieval times, who must have had more respect for tradition than for political reality—unless "negligent or forgetful," as Selden put it, they simply copied mechanically what they found (or what they thought they saw) in their sources. This was certainly true of one fourteenth-century scribe, whose reading of the phrase produced incomprehensible gibberish as he transformed "Saxonum" into "saxorum," "Merciorum" into "in etate," and "Nordam chimbrorum" into "normam cymbrorum"—as well as "uidelicet" into "uidens" and "sceptra" into "scepta."[4] Nor did the audience or those who were crowned, it would seem, attend very closely to the prayers and benedictions recited at the ceremonies.[5]

---

[3] Selden (*Titles of Honor,* 222, 235) correctly hypothesized that the survival of the phrase indicated the *ordo*'s ultimate dependence on "some Saxon Ceremoniall"; he judged the MS of the Saxon service book that he knew to be six centuries old (ibid., 151, 172-75). He published the version of the *ordo* of Charles V of 1364-65 from the copy in Sir Robert Cotton's library (now London, British Library, Cotton Tiberius B. viii) because of its "authentique" quality: ibid., 221, cf. 175; the text of the *ordo* is found on 222-55; see *Coronation Book,* ed. Dewick. Selden carefully collated the text of the *ordo* with a similar version in *Decretorum Ecclesiæ Gallicanæ,* ed. Bouchel, 701-16, which Richard A. Jackson has identified as a recension of the copy of Charles V's *ordo* deposited at Saint-Denis. See Nelson, "Ritual and Reality," 333. In 1611 Valladier (*Paranese royale,* 178) heatedly disputed Selden's assessment and offered his own imaginative explanation of the phrase, which he associated with Pope Stephen IV's consecration of Louis the Pious at Reims in 816: see the following note.

[4] ". . . ut regale solium uidens saxorum. in etate. normam. cymbrorum. scepta non deserat": BAV, lat. 4733, fol. 62v. Marlot (*Le Theatre d'Honnevr,* 658 n.) records the curious variant found in a MS of Reims, "Saxon, Noricorum, Nordinambrorum, Danorum, & Cimbrorum." In his translation of the coronation *ordo,* published in 1575, Benoist, curate of Saint-Eustache in Paris, rendered the phrase "Saxons, Merciers, Phrisons, & Cymbres": *L'Ordre et les Ceremonies,* 27v. In 1611 Valladier gave it as "Saxonum, Noricorum, Nordmannorum Danorum & Cimbrorum" (in French, "des Saxons de Bauiere, des Normans, Phrisons ou Danois, & des Cimbres") and argued that Pope Stephen IV used the phrase when he consecrated Louis the Pious in 816. Thereafter, he said, it was inserted in the Roman Pontifical for general use, to encourage kings to convert "ces nations Barbares": *Paranese royale,* 74-77. In 1643 Marlot examined Valladier's ideas; he also commented on the theory of Hubert Meurier that the phrase was included in the *ordo* because the Saxons were subject to the French in the eighth century: *Le Theatre d'Honnevr,* 658-59, 667. Meurier's book (*De sacris Unctionibus Liber tres, in quibus de sancta Ampulla, & Regum Francorum consecratione disseritur*) was published in Paris in 1593; the only surviving copy of this rare book is owned by the BM of Reims, and I have unfortunately been unable to consult it: Lelong, *Bibliothèque historique,* 2: 705, no. 25969; Quéant, *Etude sur le Sacre,* 328, no. 28.

[5] The formula "Saxons, Mercians, and Northumbrians" appears in the *ordo* prepared for the coronation of Emperor Henry VII in Milan in 1311. In the prayer of consecration (*Extendat omnipotens Deus*) Saint Ambrose replaced the English apostle, Saint Gregory, and a reference to *regimen Italicorum* was introduced. Nonetheless the *ordo* retained "Saxons, Mercians, and Northumbrians" (with the addition of *aliorumque populorum sibi subditorum,* complementing an earlier reference to *plebibus sibi annexis*), as it did the inappropriate ref-

This study deals with two unusual French *ordines* in which relevance took precedence over tradition.[6] In both the pregnant phrase "Franks, Burgundians, and Aquitanians" appeared in the prayer following the king's unction in the place traditionally occupied by the alien triad "Saxons, Mercians, and Northumbrians." The ceremonials were thus transformed and made fully appropriate for the ruler of France. Percy Ernst Schramm drew attention to the significance of *ordines* featuring Franks, Burgundians, and Aquitanians, but he did not know the twelfth-century *ordo* in the Bibliothèque nationale's manuscript lat. 14192 (hereafter the *ordo* of lat. 14192), which contains the formula. Nor did he make clear how rarely the formula appeared in coronation *ordines*. Nonetheless, he instinctively (and, I think, quite correctly) believed that an *ordo* with this formula would most likely have originated in twelfth-century France.[7] When and why such an *ordo* should have come into being he did not hypothesize, but the twelfth-century manuscript that I shall consider offers evidence which suggests possible answers to these questions.

A much longer and more elaborate *ordo* with Franks, Burgundians, and Aquitanians, first published in the late sixteenth century, has received far more attention than the twelfth-century ceremonial. This *ordo* appeared in French translation in the *Recueil des Roys de France* that, in 1566, was offered to Charles IX of France (1560-74) by Jean du Tillet, prothonotary and secretary of the king, and civil clerk (*greffier civil*) of the Parlement of Paris from 1530 until his death in 1570.[8] Printed in the editions of the *Recueil* that were published between 1578 and 1618,[9] it has aroused the interest and curiosity of scholars for four centuries.

---

erence to *utrorumque horum populorum*. See MGH, *Legum*, 2: 506 (esp. n. p), 507; *Quellensammlung*, ed. Eichmann, 2: 69-78, esp. 74; Schramm, "Krönung," 187; idem, *Kaiser*, 2: 195-96. See also 14 n. 47 below.

[6] Nelson, "Rites of the Conqueror," 381.

[7] Schramm, "Krönung," 186-88; idem, *Kaiser*, 2: 195-96; idem, "Ordines-Studien II," 22, 32 (on which see idem, *Kaiser*, 4[1]: 284); idem, *König*, 1: 182.

[8] Du Tillet's life and writings are discussed in Brown, *Du Tillet and his* Recueils, and eadem, *Du Tillet and the French Wars of Religion;* a summary listing of his writings is found in Brown and Famiglietti, *The* Lit de Justice.

[9] Two pirated eds. appeared in 1578 under the title *Les Memoires et Recerches;* because of the vagaries of sixteenth-century printing, the *ordo* published in these eds. contains many readings that differ from those in later eds. of Du Tillet's works, and in all surviving MSS; the eds. were not as carefully corrected as Parent (*Les métiers du livre*, 122–24) indicates sometimes happened. In 1579/80 Jacques du Puys published the first officially sanctioned ed. (rprt. 1586 and 1587), which included, in a second part paginated continuously with the first, Du Tillet's *Recueil des honneurs et rangs des grands*, presented to Charles IX *ca* 1567; in 1588 Du Puys published Du Tillet's *Recueil des Angloys*, a work on relations between France and England since the Norman Conquest that Du Tillet presented to Henry II in February 1558. In 1601/2 other Parisian publishers brought out an expanded ed. of Du Tillet's work (including the *Recueil des Roys*, the *Recueil des honneurs et rangs des grands*, and

As Du Tillet presented it, the *ordo* was the first complete ceremonial that could be linked to a specific French coronation. Du Tillet assured Charles IX that Louis VII (1137-80) had commissioned its composition in 1179 for the consecration of his son and heir, Philip, later dubbed Augustus (1180-1223). Fully as important, Du Tillet invoked the *ordo* as evidence that in 1179 Louis VII had designated Reims as the site of royal coronation, instituted the twelve peers of France, and assigned them their offices at the ceremony. These are weighty claims, calculated to magnify the importance of the *ordo*, which was, and remains, intriguing for other reasons. Du Tillet presented it not in Latin but rather in a French translation whose date he did not specify but which has been linked on substantive and linguistic grounds to the fourteenth and fifteenth centuries.[10] Further, aside from saying that the *ordo* had been registered in the Chambre des comptes, Du Tillet did not identify his source, thus inviting speculation. Both the *Recueil des Roys* of 1566 and an earlier recension of the work that Du Tillet had presented to Henry II (1547-59) contain clues

---

the *Recueil des Angloys*); in the ed. of 1606/7 (rprt. 1618) inventories of documents that Du Tillet prepared for the first recension of the *Recueil des Roys* were added to the *Recueil*. In *Du Tillet and his* Recueils, I discuss the different eds. and their relationship to one another.

[10] Schramm summarizes the debate on the *ordo* and gives a guide to bibliography, in "Ordines-Studien II," 31; 38-39, no. 18; idem, *König*, 2: 4, no. 18. In "Ordines-Studien II," 38, he presents the ceremonial as one of the "Übersetzungen des 'letzten Kapetingischen Ordo' (des sog. Ordo von Sens), nachweisbar seit dem 14. oder 15. Jahrh. (angeblich der Ordo Ludwigs VII., bzw. der für die Krönung Philipps II. August im Jahre 1179 benutzte)." Under this heading, Schramm's first three references, to MS sources, are inaccurate; he candidly acknowledged that systematic examination of the texts might well alter his conclusions: "Ordines-Studien III," 388. As he himself points out, the first MS that he cites (from the library of Charles V, briefly described in a catalogue of the collection) has disappeared, and hence its contents cannot be established: "Ordines-Studien II," 38, 41-42. His second source (London, British Library, Add. MS 32097) contains, as Richard Jackson has kindly informed me, translations of the *ordo* of Reims (1226-50) and the *ordo* of Charles V of 1364-65; on the date of the *ordo* of Reims, Jackson, "Manuscripts, Texts," 53–55. The third source (a treatise giving detailed prescriptions for the coronation, written in 1478 by Jean Foulquart, clerk of the *échevinage* of Reims) includes an *ordo* apparently prepared for the coronation of Louis XI in 1461, which has many similarities to the Latin *ordo* at the end of Register *Croix* of the Chambre des comptes (which Schramm does not analyze, and which will be discussed below); however, it differs in important respects from that *ordo*, as does that *ordo* from Schramm's "last Capetian *ordo*": *Archives administratives de la ville de Reims*, ed. Varin, 2^1: 559-79 n. 1 (esp. 576-75) (and ibid., 528-30 n. 2, for the *ordo* of Reims); Schramm, *König*, 2: 5, no. 24; Jackson, *Vive le Roi!*, 36-37; 223, no. 8 (Fr. ed., 40-41, 209, no. 8). Thus the only relevant source for the *ordo* that Schramm numbered 18 is the text in Du Tillet's *Recueil des Roys* (which Schramm cites from the 1580 ed.) and in the Godefroys' *Le Ceremonial François*. Schramm does not note that Du Tillet's *ordo* was first published in 1578, and he wrongly assumes that the text published in 1580 was simply reprinted by Denys Godefroy in 1649. Pinoteau, "Tenue de sacre de saint Louis," 467 n. 20 (continued from 466) believed that the translation was made in the fourteenth or, more likely, the fifteenth century; Jackson, *Vive le Roi!*, 230 n. 19, identifies it as fifteenth-century. In 1817 Pastoret, "Louis VII," 86, correctly said that the French of the *ordo* was sixteenth-century; in 1911 Halphen, "Histoire de France," 136-37, calling the translation "très libre" and dating it to the sixteenth century, judged it Du Tillet's work.

to the *ordo*'s provenance, which, if followed, could have resolved the mysteries surrounding the ceremonial and exposed the hollowness of Du Tillet's pronouncements. Without attending to these clues, however, Du Tillet's contemporaries overlooked the problems that the *ordo* posed and either unquestioningly accepted his assertions or implicitly endorsed his dating of the *ordo* by repeating his assertions regarding Louis VII, Reims, and the peers of France.

One of the first to adopt Du Tillet's conclusions was Bernard de Girard, lord of Le Haillan (1535?-1610), commonly known as Du Haillan. The first edition of his impressive study *De l'estat et succez des affaires de France* appeared in 1570, the year of Du Tillet's death, just four years after Du Tillet had presented his *Recueil des Roys* to Charles IX, and eight years before the work appeared in two pirated printed editions. Although Du Haillan did not cite Du Tillet in his brief list of sources,[11] two years later, in 1572, in a revised edition of the work, he paid lavish homage to the *greffier* for the extent of his research, his "admirable diligence" and "no less great expenses." The work that had most aided him, from which he had taken "les plus belles antiquitez" found in the third and fourth books of his work, was, Du Haillan declared, "ce beau & laborieux Œuure que fit Iean du Tillet." "In many places," he frankly announced, "my work will serve as an abridgment of his."[12] In the edition of 1570, as in later recensions, Du Haillan maintained, following Du Tillet virtually verbatim, that Louis VII "had the *ordo* of consecration and coronation composed for his son and his successors, and assigned to the peers of France their office at the said consecration." He went on to cite other of Du Tillet's remarks, including the observation that the *ordo* was

[11] Girard, *De l'estat* (1570 ed.), a vij[3]v. In "L'historien Du Haillan," Bonnefon presents useful information concerning Du Haillan.

[12] "Mais l'ouurage qui m'a le plus seruy & aidé, & duquel i'ay tiré les plus belles antiquitez que vous trouuerez au bastiment du Troisiesme & Quatriesme liure, c'est de ce beau & laborieux Œuure que fit Iean du Tillet, Greffier en la Court de Parlement de Paris, lequel auec une incroyable peine, une admirable diligence, & liaison de diuerses pieces ramassées, & non moins grande despence, il à [*sic*] tiré de tous les plus precieux papiers, Monuments, & Tiltres qui se retreuuent és Courts des Parlemens, Chambres des Comptes, & autres lieux publicqs, & des Chartes des Eglises de ce Royaume. Ie dois veritablement, Lecteurs, le plus grand honneur du Troisiesme & Quatriesme liure au labeur dudict du Tillet, & veux bien vous dire qu'en plusieurs endroicts, mon Œuure pourra seruir d'vn abregé du sien": Girard, *De l'estat* (1572 ed.), e iiij[7]r. The passage is slightly modified in the ed. of 1580, where Du Haillan describes Du Tillet's book as "imprimé despuis deux ans": *De l'estat* (1580 ed.), e ij[9]r. In the dedication to his *Histoire de France* (dated July 1576) (1576 ed., [9]v; 1577 ed., [20]r), Du Haillan acknowledged that "[l]es diligens & laborieux labeurs de feu Iean du Tillet greffier Ciuil en la Cour de Parlement de Paris m'ont beaucoup serui en la description des Estats & constitutions de France, comme i'ay cy deuant dit en la preface de mon liure de l'Estat & succez des affaires de France."

"registered in the Chambre des comptes at Paris" and that after 1179 the coronation had only been held at Reims, with the peers in attendance.[13] In the edition of *De l'estat* published in 1572, Du Haillan revised his account of the establishment of the peers of France to accord with Du Tillet's views, declaring that of all the hypotheses regarding the time of their creation, "la plus certaine" was that they had been instituted by Louis VII.[14] These conclusions, without explicit references to Du Tillet, appeared in Du Haillan's *Histoire de France,* published in successive editions between 1576 and 1615.[15]

Writing on the affairs of Reims (to 1584), and again relying on Du Tillet, Antoine Colard, canon of Reims, associated with 1179 and Louis VII the confection of an *ordo* for consecrating the kings of France at Reims, and the establishment of the peers of France who were to attend the ceremony.[16] So too did Nicolas Vignier, who declared in 1587 that Du Tillet did not seem to have reached his conclusions "sans bon garant." Vignier relied primarily on medieval historians for his account of Philip Augustus' coronation; he was particularly influenced by one source, which he did not identify but which he said testified that young Henry of England attended the ceremony "comme Pair de France." He was

[13] " . . . ce fut luy, qui voulant faire sacrer & couronner son fils le Roy Philippes Auguste, donna ceste prerogatiue à l'Eglise de Rheims, & fit escrire l'ordre du sacre & couronnement, tant pour sondit fils que ses successeurs, & departit aux Pairs de France leur office audit sacre. Cest ordre enregistré à la chambre des Comptes à Paris a tousiours esté gardé, ensemble auec la prerogatiue, & n'a ledit sacre & couronnement esté depuis fait qu'à Rheims, ny sans lesdits Pairs": Girard, *De l'estat* (1570 ed.), 96r. Du Haillan slightly modified the passage in successive editions; his addition of "lors creez" to his first reference to the peers increased the similarity of his text to Du Tillet's: (1572 ed.), 66; (1580 ed.), 186r-v; (1596 ed.), 346. In his work on the counts of Champagne, published in 1572, Pithou declared it "bien vray semblable" that dukes and counts attended the coronation of Philip Augustus as peers; his account of the ceremony (which he declared could be said to have been "l'vn des actes plus solennels qui se remarquent en nos histoires") was based solely on reports of contemporary historians: *Le premier Livre,* 55; in *Opera,* 498.

[14] Girard, *De l'estat* (1572 ed.), 99-100; see also ibid. (1580 ed.), fols. 208r-9r; cf. ibid. (1570 ed.), fols. 108r-11r (where, on fol. 109r-v, rejecting Charlemagne's creation of the peers, he declares it most likely the work of Hugh Capet).

[15] For the creation of the peers by Louis VII, the award of the prerogative of coronation to Reims in 1179, and the attendance of peers at that coronation, Girard, *Histoire de France* (1576 ed.), 162-65, 386-88, 464; (1577 ed.), 1: 263-68, 624-25, 749-50; *Histoire generale des Roys de France* (1615 ed.), 1: 147-49, 337-38, 400.

[16] "Ludovicus VII. Rex francorum præscribit formulam Regum Franciæ Remis inaugurandorum, simulque instituit Pares Franciæ qui coronando Regi adstarent, eisque titulos attribuit": BN, Mélanges de Colbert 46, part 2, fol. 395r; cf. Du Cange, *Glossarium,* 5 (1734): 143; Lelong, *Bibliothèque historique,* 3: 318, no. 34232. Colard also said that at the same time the archbishop of Reims was made first of the ecclesiastical peers and elevated to the rank of duke; given his affiliation with the church of Reims, it is understandable that he attributed the assignment of the privilege of coronation not to Louis VII but rather to Pope Alexander III. In the notes for his *Annalium libri septem, quibus antistum urbis Rhemorum gesta explicantur* (1575) (BN, Champagne 33, fol. 16v), Colard cites in full the title of the second ed. of Du Tillet's *Memoires et Recerches,* published in Troyes in 1578.

somewhat wary about Du Tillet's position, saying that some ("aucuns") were convinced that "it could have been" in 1179 that the twelve peers were instituted. Although he had not investigated the question himself, he cited Du Tillet's statement ("à ce qu'il dit") that the *ordo* prepared for the ceremony had been registered in the Chambre des comptes in Paris and thereafter been observed.[17] In 1609 André du Chesne endorsed Du Tillet's stance (without explicitly invoking him) in his *Antiquitez et Recherches de la Grandeur et Maiesté des Roys de France.* There he linked with Louis VII the designation of Reims as the site of coronation and with "the *ordo* of 1179" the assignment of offices to the peers at the ritual.[18] In his *Histoire de Navarre,* published in 1612, André Favyn cited Du Tillet as his authority for dating the prerogative of Reims to 1179.[19] Dealing a year later with the vexed issue of the origin of the peerage, Favyn denounced the testimony of Turpin and the notion that Charlemagne created the peers; he cited Du Tillet (whose "laborious research" he praised) as one who attributed their institution to Louis VII, but opted himself for King Robert (996-1031).[20] Seven years later he capitulated, saying that although Robert had created numerous peers, Louis VII had reduced the number to twelve for Philip Augustus' coronation; elaborating on Du Tillet, he declared that this had been determined "by a decree of the general Parlement held in the *Grand Salle* of the bishopric of Paris on Pentecost in 1179"—which had also assigned the privilege of consecration to Reims.[21]

Favyn's myth was persuasive because of its precision, and later historians embraced it. Guillaume Marlot (1596-1667), prior of Saint-Nicaise of Reims, confidently associated Du Tillet's *ordo* with Louis VII in a work on Reims and the coronation that appeared in 1643. Imaginatively embroidering Favyn's statement, he described the ceremonial as an "Ordonnance" or "arrêt" that King Louis had "solemnly ratified" or "decreed" ("rendu") in the episcopal palace in Paris. He endorsed its importance in

---

[17] Vignier, *Bibliotheqve Historiale,* 3: 166-67.

[18] Du Chesne, *Antiqvitez,* 386, 448. Du Chesne was not punctilious about citing his sources: Brown and Famiglietti, *The* Lit de Justice.

[19] Favyn, *Histoire de Navarre,* 999; see Leber, *Des cérémonies,* 377.

[20] Favyn, *Traictez des premiers officiers,* 235-47, 250-51; ibid., 237, 263 (on Du Tillet). In *Le Theatre d'Honnevr,* 1: 569, published in 1620, Favyn cited as his source for the idea that Robert created the peers "vn vieil Roman faict par vn Roy d'Armes dit Braban, escrit du temps de Philippes de Valois Pere de la Cheualerie."

[21] ". . . par Arrest du Parlement general tenu en la Grand Salle de l'Euesché de Paris, à la Feste de Penthecoste Mil cent Soixante et Dix-Nevf": Favyn, *Le Theatre d'Honnevr,* 1: 496. See also ibid., 1: 301 (reference to twelve peers in an act of July 1216), 569 (respective roles of Robert and Louis VII).

establishing the office of the twelve peers at the coronation. As an ardent defender of the antiquity of Reims' prerogative, however, Marlot was reluctant to see Louis' act as constitutive of the archbishop's rights and presented it as confirming a privilege that was far older. He believed that the presence of the Franks, Burgundians, and Aquitanians in the *ordo* demonstrated that the Saxons, Mercians, and Northumbrians had been inserted in the prayer of consecration by some later king.[22] These positions were affirmed in the second volume, posthumously published in 1679, of Marlot's great *Metropolis Remensis Historia* to 1606.[23] In 1663 Père Anselme threw the weight of his authority behind Du Tillet's hypotheses, and the *greffier*'s ideas were endorsed in Anselme's prestigious (and much used) genealogical history of the French royal house.[24]

A poor Latin translation of Du Tillet's *ordo* appeared in the condensed version of the *Recueil des Roys,* rendered into Latin by Lotarius Philoponus, which was published in Germany in 1579.[25] In this form the *ordo* was accorded special stature through its inclusion in the fourteenth volume of Abraham Bzovius' *Annales ecclesiastici,* published in 1618; following Du Tillet, Bzovius said that the *ordo* had been "prescribed" ("præscriptum") by Louis VII.[26]

---

[22] Marlot, *Le Theatre d'Honnevr,* 193-94 ("par Arrét solenellement rendu en la Salle de l'Evéché de Paris, conserua le droit de Sacrer à l'Archeuéque de Reims, ainsi que ses predecesseurs en auoient vsé de temps immemorial"; "cette Ordonnance"), 662 ("le formulaire dressé par l'ordre de Louys 7. rapporté par du Tillet"), 679. Confusing Favyn's position with Du Tillet's, Marlot attributed to Du Tillet (ibid., 672-73) the position that King Robert established the twelve peers in 1020 and invoked Favyn in arguing that Louis VII did so; see n. 20 above. In ibid., 229-31, Marlot states that Louis VII reduced the number of peers to twelve for his son's coronation, and made the archbishop of Reims the first ecclesiastical peer and his county a duchy because of the archbishop's privilege of consecration. An anonymous seventeenth-century notice in Latin on Saint-Remi of Reims and the coronation associates with an "edict" of Louis VII the bestowal of the prerogative of consecration on Reims: BN, Duchesne 74, fols. 57r-70r, at 62v.

[23] Marlot, *Metropolis Remensis Historia,* 2: 412 ("in Mauritij Parisiensis Episcopi palatio Pares Franciæ institutos à Ludovico VII. qui & ordinem, ac ceremonias sancivit, singulis in præsenti, futurisque inaugurationibus proprias"). See also the French version of the *Historia* (to 1663), 3: 460-61; and Reims, BM, MS 1770, fol. 230r.

[24] Anselme, *Le Palais de l'Honnevr,* 215-16; idem, *Histoire genealogique,* 1: 78; 2: 3 (the first ed. appeared in 1674). See also Ménin, *Traité,* 34-35, 36, 91 (with the false date 1175, rather than 1179), 91-94. The editors of *Gallia Christiana,* 9: 96, 732, implicitly endorsed Du Tillet's conclusions; see n. 75 below.

[25] Du Tillet, *Commentariorum . . . libri duo,* 104-11, esp. 106-7 (the consecration prayer). Philoponus' translation omits many of the specific historical references found in the *Recueil des Roys.*

[26] Bzovius, *Annalivm,* 14: 256-62; see Pastoret, "Louis VII," 86. Bzovius introduced the *ordo* as follows: "Cum autem verum officium Regum Reginarumque coronationibus ceremoniisque sacrorum & coronationis exponatur, placet in hunc locum ordinem a Ludouico iuniore præscriptum inserere." Under the year 1314 Bzovius included not only the *ordo* but also, preceding it, Philoponus' translation of Du Tillet's account of royal funerals (ibid., 14: 252-56; see Du Tillet, *Commentariorum . . . libri duo,* 135-40); they appear as appendages to his notice on the death of Philip the Fair (1285-1314) and the consecration of

A condensed version of the Latin translation was included in a collection of sources relating to French history that was published in Lyon in 1626[27]; in 1776 a modernized and slightly edited rendition of Du Tillet's own French version of the *ordo* appeared in an anthology of pieces relating to French inaugural ceremonies, where it was identified with Louis VII.[28] Most important in promoting the validity of Du Tillet's assertions about the *ordo*, as well as its authenticity, was, however, its publication (in carefully revised form) and its assignment to 1179 in *Le Ceremonial François*, the premier collection of material relating to French royal celebrations compiled by Theodore Godefroy and published by his son Denys in 1649.[29]

The authority attributed to Du Tillet's *ordo* commanded respect well into the twentieth century. True, beginning in the mid-seventeenth century some scholars raised their voices against Du Tillet's pronouncements. In the different editions of his voluminous *Histoire generale de France*, first published in 1621, the royal historiographer Scipion Dupleix expressed admiration for Du Tillet, "bon François & vray Catholique," but he was skeptical about the possibility of determining precisely which king was responsible for creating the twelve peers. "Most modern historians," he said, attributed the establishment of the institution to Louis VII (which was of course Du Tillet's position, although Dupleix did not mention him by name). Dupleix, however, judged that they did so "by conjecture" rather than on the basis of solid evidence, even though he seemed prepared to admit that Henry of England attended the consecration of Philip Augustus as both vassal and peer.[30]

Louis X (1314-16), which he correctly assigned to the feast of Saint Stephen Protomartyr (3 August), saying that this fell on a Sunday but failing to note that the ceremony took place in 1315; see Brown, "Kings Like Semi-Gods." Bzovius included no reference to the *ordo* in his comments on the coronation of Philip Augustus in *Historiæ Ecclesiasticæ . . . Annalibvs*, 2: 362.

[27] *Regum et Reginarum Coronatio*, published without attribution in *Respublica sive Status*, 579-606 (omitting the consecration prayer, where the formula "Franks, Burgundians, and Aquitanians" appears); the translation ends with the termination of the queen's *ordo*. Earlier in the volume (ibid., 135-381), properly attributed to Du Tillet, are found, again in Latin translation, selected chapters of the second part of Du Tillet's *Recueil des Roys*, excluding the chapter on coronation; see ibid., 226 (chapter on the peers, with Du Tillet's references to 1179, the prerogative of Reims, and the creation of the peers).

[28] Bévy, *Histoire des inaugurations*, 198-224.

[29] *Ceremonial*, ed. Godefroy, 1: 1-12; on the Godefroys and their ed., see below, 80–85, 87–88.

[30] Dupleix, *Histoire generale*, 1 (1621): a iiij[3]v (assessment of Du Tillet), 407-8 (discussion of the institution of the twelve peers, contesting the "fable" that Charlemagne had created them; cf. 1: 400-403, attacking the "fables" of Turpin); in treating the coronation of Philip Augustus (ibid., 2 [1624]: 186), Dupleix refers to Henry of England simply as duke of

Doubts and hesitations soon grew stronger and more pronounced. In 1636 the historian Coste, who wrote the narrative accompanying Jacob Bie's engraved portraits of the kings of France, made clear that although he accepted Du Tillet's interpretation of Philip Augustus' coronation, others questioned the appearance of peers at the ceremony since no contemporary historian mentioned this.[31] In one of his posthumously published works Henri, count of Boulainvilliers (1658-1722), indicated that he had read Du Tillet's book, and he gave shaky support to his conclusions (although he linked the reduction of the number of peers to twelve with Louis VII's rather than with Philip Augustus' coronation).[32] In another work, however, he declared that the first evidence for the existence of the peers of France was a document of 1216 (which cast doubt on Du Tillet's date).[33] Writing in the first two decades of the eighteenth century, François de Camps, abbot of Signy, was bothered by the same problem that had concerned Jacob Bie's collaborator almost a century earlier. Camps, to be sure, recounted Louis VII's conference in the episcopal palace in Paris, said that the young king Henry of England attended Philip Augustus' coronation as a peer, and approved the date of 1179 that Du Tillet (and the Godefroys) assigned to the *ordo*.[34] He admitted surprise, however, that no contemporary historian alluded to Louis VII's "reglement" and "ordonnance." Nicolas Brussel was more outspoken. In 1727, without mentioning Du Tillet, he attacked those who associated the establishment of the twelve peers of France with 1179, emphasizing the irrelevance to this question of the acquisition of the county of Langres by the city's bishop in that year. Du Tillet had indeed considered this event a terminus post quem for the creation of the peers, and

---

Normandy and royal vassal and remarks that neither Rigord nor Guillaume le Breton mentions peers in describing the ceremony. Dupleix made no changes in these passages in the third and fifth eds. of his work.

[31] Bie and Coste, *Les vrais Portraits*, 212.

[32] *Abregé chronologique*, 1: 360.

[33] Boulainvilliers, *Histoire de l'ancien gouvernement*, 1: 345 (fifth letter on the Parlements of France, written in 1708); see Vic and Vaissete, *Histoire generale* (1730-45 ed.), 3: 576; (1872-93 ed.), 7: 75-76. Although none of Boulainvilliers' works was published during his lifetime, they circulated in MS copies. Boulainvilliers was generally vague regarding the date when the peers were instituted, thus revealing the influence of Jean Le Laboureur's *Histoire de la Pairie* (12-29, esp. 14, for 1216), which he utilized but which has often been wrongly attributed to him. See Simon, *Henry de Boulainviller*, 94-100, esp. 95-96; 184-94, 254-55, 265; eadem, *A la recherche*, 13-14, 19, 34-35; Prevost, "Boulainvilliers, Henri de." Curiously, the abridgment of the history of France by Mezeray (1610-83), published in 1690, associates the fixing of the number of peers at twelve with the coronation of Louis VI at Reims in 1131: *Abregé*, 1: 467-68; Simon discusses Boulainvilliers' criticisms of Mezeray's work, in *A la recherche*, 13, 35.

[34] *Dissertation historique*, 52-53, 56-61, 66-68.

Brussel says that those who accepted the date of 1179 had misguidedly invoked the event to give "un air de vrai-semblance" to their position.[35] In 1734 the Maurist editors of Du Cange's *Glossarium*, citing the descriptions of the coronation of Philip Augustus by Roger of Howden and Rigord, indirectly attacked Du Tillet when they contested the views of Antoine Colard and declared that Louis IX, not Louis VII, had instituted the twelve peers.[36] In 1737 the Benedictines Vic and Vaissete invoked Boulainvilliers' self-contradiction and Du Cange's *Glossarium* in questioning the date and provenance that Du Tillet had assigned to the ceremonial; they did not mince words, making it clear that Du Tillet was the object of their attack.[37] Dom Brial raised serious, well-articulated doubts about the *ordo* in 1817[38]; so too did the academician Bernardi, in a paper read posthumously before the Académie des Inscriptions et Belles-Lettres on 21 March 1827.[39] In 1883 Achille Luchaire[40] and in 1894 Ferdinand Lot and

---

[35] Brussel, *Nouvel examen*, 1: 648-49; for the charter of donation of the county of Langres, *Gallia Christiana*, 4: 586 (dated 1179); ibid., *Instrumenta*, 187-88, no. LXXI (dated 1178); and also 188, no. LXXII (a royal charter of 1179 relating to Langres). Marlot (*Le Theatre d'Honnevr*, 673) rehearsed the arguments of Pithou (*Le premier Livre*, 49; expanded in *Opera*, 494-95) regarding the ducal status of Reims and of Langres, said to have been granted in 1179; see also Camps, *Dissertation historique*, 58-59. In *Les Olim*, 1: xliii-iv, Beugnot endorsed Brussel's position.

[36] Du Cange, *Glossarium*, 5 (1734): 143.

[37] Vic and Vaissete, *Histoire generale* (1730-45 ed.), 3: 575-76; (1872-93 ed.), 7: 74-75 n. 26; and Molinier, ibid., 78-79 n. 1.

[38] In "Anonyme. Auteur du formulaire," 22-26, Brial noted the lack of evidence for the existence of the twelve peers before 1216 and suggested that the *ordo* might have been created for the coronation of Louis VIII in 1223. His position was endorsed in 1875 in Camille Rivain's index to the first fifteen volumes of the *Histoire littéraire de la France* (542), although an article by Pastoret ("Louis VII," 86-87) that appeared in the same volume as Brial's associated the *ordo* with 1179. Pastoret fully recognized that the *ordo* posed problems, but he suggested that such anachronistic elements as the presence of the twelve peers (who, he thought, were not established until 1202) and the role as guardian of the regalia assigned to the abbot of Saint-Denis (who Du Tillet himself said received the paraphernalia only in 1260) were in all likelihood later interpolations: see Du Tillet, *Recveil des Roys*, 186 (cited here and below, unless otherwise noted, from the ed. of 1580). In 1827, following Pastoret, Bernardi ("Mémoire," 612) emphasized the problem posed by the abbot of Saint-Denis and the regalia but dismissed the possibility of interpolation.

[39] "Mémoire," 611-12, 621, 631, 653. Having analyzed the development of the peerage and the role played by Philip the Fair in the process, Bernardi insightfully suggested (ibid., 653) that "ce réglement qui porte la fausse date de 1179, et qui fixe le cérémonial du sacre" was actually composed after Philip's reign; similarly, in 1911 Halphen ("Histoire de France," 137) linked the *ordo* with what Schramm later termed the last Capetian *ordo* and with the fourteenth century; see n. 208 below. Citing others who accepted 1179 as the date of the *ordo*, Bernardi ("Mémoire," 612) mentioned Henri-François d'Aguesseau, chancellor of France (1668-1751). I have been unable to find any endorsement of the date in Aguesseau's works, although he was acquainted with Du Tillet's writings; in 1696 he gently mocked (*Œuvres*, 3: 702) the "Dissertations plus curieuses qu'utiles" that had been dedicated to determining whether the twelve peers were established under Louis VII, Philip Augustus, or Saint Louis, and refused to take any position on the issue himself.

[40] *Histoire des institutions*, 1: 68-69 n. 1, 306; 2: 294-95; followed by Cartellieri, *Philip II August*, 1: 44 n. 1; and by Holtzmann, "Prozeß," 35-36 n. 4.

Charles-Edmond Petit-Dutaillis[41] impugned the *ordo*'s authenticity. Nonetheless, other scholars accepted Du Tillet's testimony and his *ordo*.[42] A heated debate took place in Germany in the second decade of this century, with Maximilian Buchner defending the *ordo*, and Hans Schreuer attacking Du Tillet's dating and maintaining (quite rightly) that the *ordo* included in the *Recueil des Roys* must have been composed between 1223 and 1365.[43] Although Schramm supported Schreuer,[44] he did not determine where Du Tillet had found his *ordo*.

The heated and ultimately futile controversy over Du Tillet's *ordo* would never have occurred had Du Tillet fully identified the source of the ceremonial that he included in his *Recueil des Roys*—or had his critics turned to the manuscript copies of his first recension of the *Recueil*, where Du Tillet mentioned the source that he later exploited. As I shall show, it was a fourteenth-century ceremonial transcribed in Register *Croix* of the Chambre des comptes, which Du Tillet subtly modified. The most important of the changes that he made was his substitution of "Franks, Burgundians, and Aquitanians" for "Saxons, Mercians, and Northumbrians." The second portion of my study considers the circumstances under which Du Tillet resurrected the phrase and

---

[41] Lot, "Quelques mots," 40, 53 (who wrongly states that Godefroy simply reproduced Du Tillet's *ordo*); Petit-Dutaillis, *Etude sur . . . Louis VIII*, 222 n. 1 ("qui nous paraît à nous-même plus que suspect").

[42] See, e.g., Leber, *Des cérémonies* (1825), 200, 204, 315, 377, 378-79, 384, 415; MPL 182 (1854): 446 n. 667; Quéant, *Etude sur le Sacre* (1868), 52, 65-66, 117, 119, 177, 199, 318 n. 292, 327, no. 13 (declaring the question of the origin of the twelve peers "assez obscure," but holding that the institution "parut dans tout son éclat au siècle de Philippe-Auguste," and that "dans son Formulaire" Louis VII had "réglé d'une manière définitive l'exercice de leurs fonctions par rapport au sacre," established the form of the coronation oath, and awarded Reims its prerogative). In an article published in 1870-71 ("Essai sur l'origine," 45-46), Anatole de Barthélemy invoked the *Dictionnaire de Trevoux* in declaring that an ordonnance of Louis VII issued in 1179 "règle le détail de la cérémonie du sacre de son fils." I have found no explicit reference to any such "ordonnance" (clearly the *ordo* that Du Tillet dated 1179) in the *Dictionnaire*, although its compilers accepted Du Tillet's account of the coronation: *Dictionnaire de Trevoux*, 2: 331 (Du Tillet as an authority on coronation); 4: 445-46 (Louis VII's probable institution of the peers of France); 4: 1914 (the first use of *fleurs de lis* "sans nombre" for decorations at the consecration of Philip Augustus in 1179). It seems clear that Barthélemy relied on Du Tillet's own work rather than the *Dictionnaire* for his reference to "la dalmatique et les bottines de soie azurée semée de fleurs de lis"; see 120 below. In 1894 Lot ("Quelques mots," 40 n. 3) expressed surprise that such a scholar as Barthélemy could have accepted the *ordo*'s authenticity. Péré presents a useful review of the evidence in *Sacre et couronnement*, 11-15.

[43] See the Bibliography, s. v. Buchner and Schreuer. In 1911 Ernst Mayer approved Buchner's position and went so far as to suggest that Du Tillet's *ordo* might have been used for the coronation of Louis VI in 1108: "Pairs," 443-44 (esp. 444 n. 2). E.-A. Goldsilber, however, argued that Buchner's thesis was far from being established: "Courrier allemand," 232. In "Histoire de France," 136-37, Louis Halphen presented a brilliant critique of the hypothesis.

[44] "Krönung," 187; idem, *Kaiser*, 2: 196 n. 112; see also Halphen, "Histoire de France," 136-37.

fashioned his *ordo*, the tactics he used in doing so, and the failure of his *ordo* to exercise the practical influence for which he seems to have hoped.

Du Tillet's responsibility for crafting the *ordo* featured in his *Recueil des Roys* can be securely established. The creator of the twelfth-century *ordo* and the circumstances under which he fashioned it are far more elusive. These questions I examine in the first part of this study. The name of the person who adapted a hallowed but foreign *ordo* to the needs of the French monarchy will in all likelihood never be surely known. I suspect, however, that it was Suger, royal councilor and abbot of Saint-Denis from 1122 to 1151, chronicler and student of his abbey's and his kingdom's past, adept at employing, exploiting, and sometimes creating historical evidence to serve France and Saint-Denis. He had many traits in common with Jean du Tillet, who also admired, recorded, and analyzed the history of France, and whose concern with current issues and desire to find in the documents what he thought they should say sometimes jeopardized commitment to strict historical accuracy and meticulous analysis—although he was more restrained than Suger, who was capable of blatant forgery.[45]

My conclusions and hypotheses depend on the words and structures of a number of texts, the most important of which I present here. The mid-twelfth-century *ordo* of BN, lat. 14192, is fundamentally important. Although it has been studied before,[46] its variants from other texts have been of primary concern, and its unique text has never been edited apart from others to which it is related. Of even greater interest are the *ordo* that Du Tillet fashioned and the source from which he created his ceremonial; the latter, for reasons that I shall explain, I designate the *Ordo maior* of Register *Croix* of the Chambre des comptes. This *ordo* has never been published. Nor has Du Tillet's ceremonial been edited from the three most important extant manuscript copies of his *Recueil des Roys* for Charles IX. Those who have studied this *ordo* have relied on the versions found in the published editions of the *Recueil*, but these texts provide more information about

---

[45] On Suger, see *Abbot Suger*, ed. Gerson, esp. the contributions of Benton, Bournazel, Hanning, Lewis, Rezak, Spiegel, and Stahl; and Brown and Cothren, "Twelfth-Century Crusading Window." Bournazel ("Suger and the Capetians") exaggerates Suger's propensity to fabricate, but Waldman ("Abbot Suger") demonstrates that he tampered shamelessly with the evidence in order to gain control of the abbey of Argenteuil; see also Brown, "Saint-Denis and the Turpin Legend," 53–54 esp. n. 9, 59.

[46] Ward presents many of the text's variants in "Early Version," 345-61. Significant variants in all known MSS are analyzed in Richard A. Jackson's forthcoming edition of French coronation *ordines*.

sixteenth-century compositors' grammatical and orthographical idiosyncrasies than they do about Du Tillet's own intentions. Additional sources included in the appendix cast further light on Du Tillet's use of the *Ordo maior* of *Croix*. Another appendix focuses on the *Ordo maior* itself and considers its relationship to earlier and later French *ordines*.[47]

---

[47] Lanoë ("Un *ordo*") and Elze ("Ein Krönungsordo") have recently edited two important and remarkably similar medieval *ordines*, which consist essentially of five key prayers of the so-called Burgundian *ordo*: see Elze, "Königskrönung"; the date of Lanoë's MS suggests that this *ordo* was composed earlier than has hitherto been assumed. Strikingly, each specifies in the prayer of consecration (*Omnipotens eterne Deus*) the peoples and realms whom the king was to rule. Lanoë's northeastern French MS of *ca* 1000 (a fragment of a Gregorian sacramentary) names the Franks and Aquitanians ("in regem francorum et equitanorum," "Ecclesiamque ecquitanam et frantiam," "francorum regnum"); Elze's thirteenth-century pontifical from the province of Braga cites the Franks, Burgundians, and Spanish ("in regem Francorum et Burgundionum Yspanorum," "ecclesiamque Francie vel Yspanie"). Like the Burgundian *ordo*, Elze's lacks the references to paternal inheritance found in the Ratold *ordo* (see 91 ["paternę apicem glorię"], 96 below), and also in the tenth-century *ordo* of Eleven Forms (see Jackson, "Manuscripts, Texts," 44) to which his, the Burgundian, and Lanoë's *ordines* are closely related. Lanoë's *ordo*, in contrast, refers to "*paternum* decenter solium" in the prayer of consecration and includes in the admonition *Sta et retine* the phrases "paterna successions" and "hereditario iure." As Elze makes clear, his *ordo* was probably never used. Lanoë hypothesizes that his ceremonial was composed for the coronation of Charles the Bald at Orléans in 848: see Levillain, "Le sacre"; Bautier, "Sacres," 34–35; Nelson, *Charles the Bald*, 154–55. It seems curious, however, that the *ordo* mentions only two of the different peoples whom Charles ruled: cf. ibid., 135; *Recueil des actes de Charles le Chauve*, 1: 484, no. 182; Tessier, in ibid., 3: 150 n. 3; 34 below. Further, the *ordo* used for Charles' coronation as king of Lorraine in 869 alludes to no specific peoples: MGH, *Legum Sectio II. Capitularia*, 2^2: 337–41, no. 276; 456–58, no. 302; cf. as well, ibid., 461–62, no. 304 (coronation of Louis the Stammerer, 877); see Bautier, "Sacres," 38–39. Finally, until his imperial coronation Charles' diplomas regularly entitled him simply "gratia Dei rex": Tessier, in *Recueil des actes de Charles le Chauve*, 3: 150–51. Two unique diplomas of 849 for Saint-Martin of Tours designate him "Francorum et Aquitanorum gratia Dei rex," but they survive only in late copies and contain many anomalies: ibid., 1: 300–305 (esp. 301, 304), nos. 113–14. Like similar additions to other of Charles' diplomas (ibid., 2: 25, no. 236bis; 371, no. 389), the references to Franks and Aquitanians seem likely to me to be interpolations: cf., however, Tessier, in ibid., 3: 150–51; Levillain, "Le sacre," 40–41; Nelson, *Charles the Bald*, 155. For whatever purposes Lanoë's and Elze's *ordines* were written and copied, they furnish additional evidence of the impulse to particularize the consecration ceremonial during the Middle Ages.

I. "FRANKS, BURGUNDIANS, AND AQUITANIANS" IN THE TWELFTH CENTURY

1. The *Ordo* of Lat. 14192

The first known appearance of the phrase "Franks, Burgundians, and Aquitanians" in a royal coronation ceremonial occurs in the twelfth-century *ordo* of lat. 14192.[48] This is closely related to the first (A) version of two surviving recensions of the tenth-century second English coronation *ordo*, whose earliest extant witness is the *ordo* preserved in the sacramentary of Ratold, abbot of Corbie (972-86).[49] Some nineteen other known manuscripts, all continental in origin, contain more or less similar ceremonials.[50] But of these only the *ordo* of lat. 14192 has the formula "Franks, Burgundians, and Aquitanians." There is no convincing evidence that it appeared in any other medieval *ordo*,[51] and the surviving exemplar is important as the earliest—and arguably the sole—extant witness to a medieval ceremonial featuring the Franks, the Burgundians, and the Aquitanians.

---

[48] BN, lat. 14192, fols. 73r-83v; in the Appendix, I A, 89-98 below. Like Schramm, the person who annotated the seventeenth-century copy of the BN *ordo* made for the princes of Condé believed the *ordo* appropriate to the twelfth century, assigning it to Louis VII: see n. 50 below and, for Schramm, n. 10 above.

[49] Ward, "Early Version," 347-49, 352 (esp. n. 6); Schramm, *Kaiser,* 2: 200-201, 244-48; Hohler, "Some Service-Books," 80; Bouman, *Sacring,* 158; Nelson, "Earliest Surviving Royal *Ordo,*" 341-60; eadem, "Second English *Ordo,*" 361-74; see also n. 107 below. On Ratold, Delisle, "Recherches sur l'ancienne bibliothèque de Corbie," 412.

[50] In "Early Version," 347-49, Ward described the 18 MSS that he knew; I exclude from my reckoning his F (later French *ordines*) and Ox (seventeenth-century copies from a MS of French provenance). In his forthcoming ed. of the French coronation *ordines* Richard A. Jackson lists 19 MSS, excluding Ward's F, G, K and Ox, and adding three late-medieval pontificals, as well as two seventeenth-century copies, one of Ward's Re (Reims, BM, MS 342, fols. 69v-80r; in BN, lat. 11743, fols. 75r-84r) and one of the *ordo* of lat. 14192 (Chantilly, Institut de France, Musée Condé, Cabinet des livres, MS 1149 [XIX D 17], fols. 4r-9r); see Jackson, "Manuscripts, Texts," 45 n. 58. The copy at Chantilly was made for the princes of Condé, who served as *grands-maîtres* of France. The copyist remarked on fol. 4r, "L'on à dict que ce formulaire est du Roy Louis le Jeune"; his transcription is filled with errors, and incorporates into the text the material on fol. 81v (originally part of an old pontifical; see 16–17, 20, 96 n. 1 below) concerning the consecration of a church. See Chantilly, *Le Cabinet des livres, Manuscrits,* 3: 296, 299, 304.

[51] In Appendix, I B, 98-100 below, I consider and reject the possibility that transcriptions of *ordines* with "Franks, Burgundians, and Aquitanians," made by Adrien de Valois and Pierre Delalande in the seventeenth century were taken from different MSS. See also 21–22 below (a copy of the *ordo* of lat. 14192 in the library of Saint-Lucien of Beauvais).

The only direct evidence regarding the circumstances under which this formula was included in the *ordo* of lat. 14192 comes from the manuscript itself, which is a laconic and challenging witness. The clues that it offers are sparse, but, as will be seen, they support the possibility that the *ordo* was confected for actual use and that it was copied and decorated in or near Paris before 1150. As I shall show, it was in Beauvais by the fifteenth century (and in all likelihood much earlier), but it left the cathedral library for Paris in the late sixteenth or early seventeenth century, and except for a brief sojourn in Clermont in the mid-seventeenth century it has subsequently remained there.

The *ordo*, copied in an independent booklet or *libellus* of eleven leaves, has three parts: the ceremony for the coronation of a king (fols. 73r-81r); the queen's *ordo* (fols. 82r-v); and the *Benedictio vexilli* (82v-83r).[52] It consists of a gathering of four bifolia (fols. 73-80) and three individual leaves, tipped in (fols. 81-83). The gathering and the first leaf (fols. 73r-81r) contain the king's *ordo*, the next two pages the queen's *ordo* and the blessing of the *vexillum* (fols. 82r-83r). The reverse of the final folio is blank. Since the late seventeenth century if not before, it has been bound as the last in a collection of eight *libelli* dating from the tenth through the mid-seventeenth century.[53]

The king's *ordo* terminates on the obverse of the first of the single leaves (fol. 81). Curiously, this is a reused folio, taken from an early-eleventh-century pontifical.[54] It contains the beginning of an *ordo* for the consecration of a church and is decorated with two handsome initials in a style associated with Saint Gall[55]; before its incorporation into the *ordo* the other side was blank. Such deco-

[52] Cf. Ward, "Early Version," 349, but also 358 nn. 8, 9, 11. The BN *ordo* does not contain the *Missa pro regibus* found in other MSS: ibid., 359-61, and cf. 349. The history of the *oriflamme* is discussed in Hinkle, *The Fleurs de Lis*, s.v. in index; and Lombard-Jourdan, *Fleur de lis*, 129-76; see also below, 76-78, 135-38. *Libelli* are discussed in Robinson, "The 'Booklet,' " 46-69; Schimmelpfennig, *Zeremonienbücher*, 9-12; Rasmussen, "Le 'Pontifical,' " 414-15.

[53] Carozzi lists the contents of the MS in his ed. of Adalbero of Laon, *Poème au roi Robert*, cli-iii. Nebbiai-Dalla Guarda cautiously suggests that the first part ("la première partie") of BN, lat. 14192, "provient peut-être de l'abbaye de Saint-Denis": *Bibliothèque de Saint-Denis*, 306. I consider more fully the history of the collection below, 26-30.

[54] Lanoë ("Quelques manuscrits") assigns the leaf to the late tenth century and associates it with Saint Gall, although he does not give the reasons for his conclusions. François Avril kindly informed me that although he concurs in linking the page to Saint Gall, he is more inclined to date it to the early eleventh century.

[55] See, in general, Nordenfalk, "Miniatures ottoniennes," 44-59. MSS of Saint Gall that offer useful comparisons are discussed and illustrated in Merton, *Buchmalerei in St. Gallen*, esp. 74, 76, 80-81, and pls. LXXIV, LXXXI (no. 2), LXXXII, LXXXIII (no. 2), LXXXIV (no. 2), LXXXVI (Saint Gall, Stiftsbibliothek, MSS 338, 341, 374, 376, 560); Duft, *Hochfeste im Gallus-Kloster*, esp. pls. II, V-VIII; and, for a ninth-century prototype of this style of decoration, Landsberger, *St. Gallen Folchart-Psalter*, esp. 26, 31, and pls. II, IV.

ration as is found on fol. 81v was beginning to be employed in France in the early eleventh century, and its use is connected particularly with the monastery of Fleury.[56] Manuscripts linked to Fleury, such as the Evangeliary of Gaignières (BN, lat. 1126) and the Sacramentary of Beauvais,[57] do not, however, contain such lavishly decorated minor initials as are regularly found in texts from Saint Gall and as appear on this page. It thus seems unlikely to be French in origin, but it (or, more likely, the book from which it was detached) could easily have found its way to France from the Empire.[58]

The use of the leaf as the final page of the king's *ordo*, as well as the addition of two separate pages for the queen's ceremonial and the blessing of the *vexillum*, suggest that the *ordo* was prepared in some haste, and that the scribe, having readied a single quaternion for his work and running short of parchment, appropriated other material that was conveniently available to complete the booklet. The parchment of the leaf from the pontifical proved less than suitable for the use to which the twelfth-century scribe put it. Its reverse was too smooth to retain over the centuries the red ink used for the final rubric of the king's *ordo*, and, doubtless after his return to France from exile in 1570, Pierre Pithou (1539-98) transcribed the partly effaced section interlinearly.[59] Nonetheless, for the moment the page served two purposes: its decorated side as a de luxe back cover for the king's *ordo*, its blank side as space for the final segments of the ceremonial, copied on eleven lines. The leaves of the booklet, approximately equal in size, vary in width from 155 to 163 mm. and in length from 214 to 218 mm. The dimensions of the page from the pontifical (fol. 81) are 156 by 205 mm. Thus, unless fortuitously the dimensions of the page precisely matched the size of the parchment that the scribe had been using, its size was probably reduced; it seems hardly likely that the scribe knew from the beginning that he would be employing the single page and fashioned his quaternion accordingly.

The variation in the number of lines on one bifolium (fols. 74 and 79) and on the final page (fol. 83) again indicates that the scribe may have been pressed for time. These folia are ruled, respectively, in seventeen lines, 9.5 mm. apart (fols. 74, 79), and in

---

[56] Nordenfalk, "Miniatures ottoniennes," 49-53.

[57] Malibu, J. Paul Getty Museum, MS Lud. V 1; see Von Euw and Plotzek, *Handschriften der Sammlung Ludwig*, 1: 219-22, figs. 137-41.

[58] The decoration bears no resemblance to that of an early-eleventh-century missal from Saint-Denis (BN, lat. 9436).

[59] See 23-27 below.

nineteen lines, some 10 mm. apart (fol. 83). Aside from the reused page (ruled for 16 lines), the rest of the sheets are ruled (in drypoint, on the hâir side) in eighteen lines, approximately 9 mm. apart. The errors that were let slip also indicate haste—although three mistakes were in fact corrected.[60]

Whatever the pressure under which the scribe was working, he produced a legible, attractive booklet. The script of the *ordo* is strong, large, and clear, suggesting that the ceremonial might have been prepared for actual use. The *ordo* was simply decorated with alternating red and blue, plainly-ornamented initials. Walter Cahn characterizes some as fairly fluidly rendered, others as more meticulously formed.[61] In the king's *ordo* the blue initials are often touched with red and the red with blue; they are generally more elaborate than those of the final pages containing the queen's *ordo* and the *Benedictio vexilli*. The rubrication throughout is unassuming but complete, although again more attention was paid to the king's *ordo* than to the queen's. At least at the beginning, the scribe made some attempt at variety and elegance. The four lines of the rubric that introduces the king's *ordo* and the initial rubric of the next page (fol. 73v) were written, alternately, in blue and red; they contrast with the simpler rubrication at the end of the king's *ordo* (fol. 81r) and the beginning of the queen's (fol. 82r), executed simply in red. There are red touches on several letters on fol. 76r and green touches on some letters on two facing pages (fols. 79v, 80r), which are otherwise decorated only with a single rubric and plain red initial "E".

The physical evidence provided by the *libellus* is not easy to decipher. Date is less difficult to hypothesize than provenance, since neither the script nor the simple decoration is extraordinary enough to permit them to be linked to a specific site. Analogous decoration appears in a number of twelfth-century manuscripts from northern France—Normandy, Reims, and Saint-Maur-des-Fossés. There are clear similarities between the *ordo* and a commentary on the Psalms (BN, lat. 12006) that probably came from

[60] On fol. 78r (see 93 n. q below), *tueri* was written above *taturi*, apparently by the same scribe who copied the text; on fol. 80r (see 95 n. h below) *pertinates* was corrected to *pertinaces* in the text itself. Note too the correction by erasure (with a red line drawn through the abraded letters), before *merearis* on fol. 77v (see 92 n. m below). On fol. 78v (in *Accipe sceptrum*), the text reads *pacificas*, rather than *pacifices;* on fol. 79v, in the rubric *Hic datur ei uirga, datur* should be *detur;* on the same fol., *reueles* should be *releues;* on fol. 80r, *sui* (in the phrase *a peccato sui gladio*) should be either *seu* or *siue*, and *pacem diebus tuis* should read *pace in diebus tuis;* on fol. 81r, *atilli* should be *ut illi*. On fol. 82v, *tribue* is written *tribuę*^{n}, although elsewhere it is correctly transcribed. See 94, 95, 96, 97 below.

[61] I am grateful to Walter Cahn for the letter of 30 October 1984 in which he made these comments.

Saint-Maur-des-Fossés and in all likelihood dates from the first third of the twelfth century. A manuscript of the letters of Ivo of Chartres (d. 1116), whose provenance is as yet unknown, is also important because of its analogous script (BN, lat. 2893). Similar secondary decoration is found not only in a twelfth-century collection of the works of Saint Augustine (BN, lat. 1930), which has a fifteenth-century ex libris from Saint-Etienne of Caen, but also in a twelfth-century missal from Saint-Remi of Reims (Reims, BM, MS 225).[62] In comparison with these manuscripts, the *ordo* of lat. 14192 is remarkable chiefly for its simplicity. In the absence of detailed comparative analyses of twelfth-century northern French manuscripts, the most that can be said of the *ordo*'s provenance is that it seems to have been produced in northern France, and that it could have been written and decorated in the region of Paris.

According to Walter Cahn,[63] the carefully-formed shapes and foliate ornamentation of certain initials suggest a conservative attitude toward script and decoration consonant with a date before the mid-twelfth century. Precisely such a date is suggested by the absence of lining in plummet and the consistent use of drypoint, features that would soon change. Some elements of the script indicate a date toward the middle of the twelfth century, but the extended final *s*, formed with two strokes, possesses the same archaizing quality as some of the colored initials. If the manuscript was prepared in the region of Paris, the precocious aspects of the script could be explained by the innovative styles of Parisian copyists. They regularly established norms that others followed, which filtered slowly into the hinterlands. All things considered, it seems perfectly possible that the *ordo* was copied in the 1130s in or near Paris.[64]

In the fifteenth century the *ordo* of lat. 14192 was in the cathedral library of Beauvais. Its presence there is recorded in the catalogue of the library prepared in 1404-17 and again in that of 1464-72, but it had disappeared before Claude Joly drew up his inventory in 1664.[65] To judge from the descriptions in the catalogues, it was a striking book, and the significance that the cathedral chapter attributed to it is witnessed not only by the fact

[62] Garand, "Manuscrits monastiques," 9-33, esp. pl. 4, facing p. 21.

[63] Again, I thank Walter Cahn for these comments.

[64] Richard H. Rouse has consistently favored a date in the late 1130s for the MS, and Françoise Gasparri believes that, "à la limite," this is possible. Largely because of the script of the *ordo*, François Avril considers a date in the 1120s or 1130s appropriate. Cf. Ward, "Early Version," 349.

[65] Omont, "Recherches," 33, no. 129; 41, no. 72; for the catalogues, ibid., 5, 9, 84-85; Lanoë, "Quelques manuscrits," who in 1990 ("Définition du pouvoir royal") identified the *ordo* of lat. 14192 as the volume described in the inventories of Beauvais.

that it was separately shelved (rather than being grouped with other booklets) but also by its binding, which won it a place alongside the library's most elegant volumes. In the inventory of 1404-17 it was described as a coronation ceremonial, "in a small volume gilded on the exterior, with one margin, in antique script," and was valued at 15 s.[66] This sum is not strikingly high, although several manuscripts (generally lacking bindings) were appraised at 2 s. or 4 s.; it was, however, the least precious of the five elaborately bound codices among which it was grouped (and presumably shelved).[67] Two of these were the Canons of Saint Jerome on the four Gospels, one bound "in ivory and silvered copper," the other "in ivory and silver"; the first was appraised at 5 l. and the second at 6 l. Of two liturgical volumes the first was bound in silver and ivory (and valued at 40 s.); the second was "a small text with silver on the exterior, with images of Saints Peter and Paul," and was estimated to be worth 16 s.[68]

The description of the *ordo* in the inventory of 1464-72 is far more detailed than the one in the earlier catalogue, and it suggests that in the intervening years the ceremonial had received a more luxurious binding than the gilded one it had possessed at the beginning of the century. In the later inventory the book is described as "a small volume, between two boards, one covered in brass with the inscription above, 'Jhesus Nazarenus, rex Judeorum,' and on the other cover two images of ivory, each holding a crozier"; it was said to contain the consecration of the king and "a manner of pontifical," doubtless because of the extraneous leaf used for the end of the king's service.[69] As Danielle Gaborit-

[66] "Item consecratio Regis, in parvo volumine aurato exterius, in una margine, de antiqua littera; incipit in secundo folio: 'victorie feliciter', et in penultimo, in rubro: 'ad benedicendam Reginam'; precii xv. solidorum": Omont, "Recherches," 33, no. 129. Those responsible for the catalogue often stipulated that a MS had one or two *margines*, perhaps distinguishing those copied in long lines from those copied in two columns. Gaborit-Chopin ("La plaque," 287) reproduces this description but omits the valuation.

[67] Omont ("Recherches," 13-14) discusses the various prices assigned to the volumes in the library.

[68] Omont, "Recherches," 33, nos. 127-28, 130-31 ("copertus ebore et argento"; "copertus ebore et argento"; "coperto argento et ebore"; "in uno parvo textu exterius argentato, cum ymaginibus Petri et Pauli"). The inventory of 1404-17 describes the first two volumes as, respectively, "quatuor Euvangelia" and "quidam alius textus Euvangeliorum." The catalogue of 1464-72 identifies them more precisely as containing "les Canons de saint Jherosme sur les IIII. Euvangilles"; it shows that they were identically bound. The first is said to be "entre deux ais bien ouvrés par dehors," the second "entre deux ais ouvré[s] comme l'autre par dehors." See ibid., 40, nos. 67, 67 [*bis*]; in Desjardins, *Histoire de la cathédrale*, 167.

[69] "*Item* ung volume petit, entre deux ais, desquels l'ung est couvert de leton et par dessus escript *Jhesus Nazarenus, rex Judeorum*, et par dessus l'autre ais sont deux ymages d'ivoires, chascune tenant une croce, commençant ou IIe feuillet *victorie feliciter* et ou penultième *ad benedicendam reginam*, et contient la consécration du Roy et une manière de Pon-

Chopin has suggested, the first cover must have showed a crucifixion, with the inscription on the *titulus*. She convincingly argues that the "ivory" plaque on the second side was one confected of whale-bone which was discovered at Beauvais when the house of the cathedral's canons was being reconstructed in 1767, and which was subsequently acquired by the Louvre.[70] The plaque's dimensions (159 mm. by 89 mm., 8 mm. thick) mean that it could have been comfortably mounted on a cover made for the *ordo*, whose largest sheet (fol. 82) measures 215 mm. by 165/161 mm. Gaborit-Chopin dates the plaque *ca* 1100 and shows that the two bishops depicted on it (identified by the inscriptions *Hervevs* and *Rogervs*) must be Hervé (*ca* 987-98) and his successor Roger (d. 1016), two of the most eminent bishops of Beauvais.[71] Maintaining that the author of the earlier inventory "n'accorde guère d'importance à la reliure," she suggests that the binding described in the inventory of 1464-72 was the same as the one recorded in the catalogue of 1407-13.[72] She may possibly be correct, although she underestimates the attention paid to bindings in the first inventory. The first cataloguer carefully designated manuscripts that were unbound or that had only one cover, and he described the ivory decoration of three of the volumes with which the *ordo* was grouped in 1407-13, as well as the images of Peter and Paul on another. It seems likely that he would have noted similar features of the *ordo*'s binding and not have described it simply as "gilded on the exterior." The cathedral considered the volume an important possession in 1407-13 and might well have given it a more luxurious casing in the ensuing half century. But even if the *ordo* did have the same covering in 1407 as it did in 1472, this does not mean that it was thus bound at the time it was written, in the second quarter of the twelfth century; nor is there any reason to think that the plaque was specially confected for the *ordo*, an impossibility if Gaborit-Chopin's date of *ca* 1100 is correct.

Given the *ordo*'s small dimensions and simplicity, the luxurious binding which it possessed in the fifteenth century indicates that it was valued for its contents, testimony to the association

tifical": Omont, "Recherches," 41, no. 72; see also Desjardins, *Histoire de la cathédrale*, 168, no. 72, and 159 (the location of the volume in a cabinet in the upper chamber of the treasury). The two finely bound liturgical MSS listed in the inventory of 1404-17 (Omont, "Recherches," 33, nos. 130-31) do not appear in the catalogue of 1464-72.

[70] "La plaque," 279-80, esp. 280-82 n. 10.

[71] "La plaque," 280, 282, 286-87; *Gallia Christiana*, 9: 704-7.

[72] "La plaque," 287.

of the cathedral and its bishop with royal consecration. This is suggested as well by the presence of an apparent duplicate of the ceremonial in an episcopal ordinary once owned by the church of Saint-Lucien of Beauvais, which was described in detail in the seventeenth century by a canon of the cathedral, probably Godefroy Hermant (1617-90).[73] His comparison of the *ordo*'s text with the version of the Ratold ceremonial edited in 1642 by Hugues Menard[74] reveals that the copy at Saint-Lucien contained the phrase "Franks, Burgundians, and Aquitanians" and other variants found in the *ordo* of lat. 14192. There is no way to determine the date of the ordinary of Saint-Lucien, but it seems possible—and likely—that its *ordo* was copied from the exemplar in the cathedral library precisely because that ceremonial was considered a particularly venerable text.

Although the *ordo* of lat. 14192 was at Beauvais in the fifteenth century, it is impossible to determine when it entered the cathedral's library. Is it likely to have been prepared or copied by someone in the entourage of a bishop of Beauvais in the early twelfth century, for use at a royal coronation? This seems hardly conceivable, since bishops of Beauvais are not known to have attended royal consecrations before the late twelfth and early thirteenth centuries. Even if they were present among the crowd of ecclesiastics that chroniclers delight in saying graced such occasions, they attracted no special notice and apparently played no special role.[75] Eudes II was the incumbent between 1133 and 1144, the period when the *ordo* of lat. 14192 was copied, and he is remembered chiefly because of his contacts with Abbot Suger of

[73] In "Quelques manuscrits," Lanoë gives the text of the canon's description. Quignon discusses the catalogues of the library of Saint-Lucien, in *La Bibliothèque de Beauvais*, 8-9; on Hermant, ibid., 11, 15-16, 18 n. 2.

[74] Ward, "Early Version," 346 n. 3.

[75] Loisel (*Memoires*, 146-47) states that Philippe of Dreux attended the coronation of Philip Augustus in 1179 and was the first bishop of Beauvais to be present at a royal consecration; he is followed by Anselme, *Histoire genealogique*, 2: 260; see also *Gallia Christiana*, 9: 732 ("adfuit inter pares apud Remos coronationi Philippi-Augusti regis"). Loisel cites no evidence and is likely to have been relying on Du Tillet's *ordo*, whose authenticity Anselme also accepted: see n. 24 above. Rigord and Guillaume le Breton only refer generally to the clerics present in 1179: *Œuvres de Rigord et de Guillaume le Breton*, 1: 12; 2: 21, lines 347-48; cf. ibid., 16, lines 224-25. The English chronicle *Gesta Regis Henrici secundi* (1171-*ca* 1192), 1: 242, says that Philip Augustus was crowned by the archbishop of Reims with the assistance of the archbishops of Tours, Bourges, and Sens, "et fere omnibus episcopis regni"; Roger of Howden (d. post 1201) included this passage, in *Chronica*, 2: 193-94. According to Anselme (*Histoire genealogique*, 2: 260-61), Philippe was at the coronation of Queen Ingeborg at Arras in 1193, and his successor Milon of Châtillon-Nanteuil at the consecrations of Louis VIII in 1223 and Louis IX in 1226; for Milon, see also *Gallia Christiana*, 9: 740-41. Discussing the establishment of the peerage, Du Tillet noted the absence of the bishop of Beauvais from the coronation of Philip in 1059: see 58 (esp. n. 226) below.

Saint-Denis.[76] These ties, I believe, may well account for the appearance of the manuscript in Beauvais.[77]

Until 1672 the later fortunes of the *ordo* of lat. 14192 are difficult to trace with precision. After the fifteenth-century inventories the next evidence regarding its fate must be deduced from the annotations in the hand of Pierre Pithou found on the manuscript. As has been seen, on fol. 81r, Pithou transcribed the partially effaced final rubric of the king's ceremonial; on fol. 82r, in the margin of the queen's *ordo* he wrote *Chlotild,* and on fol. 82v, *Oriflambe,* opposite the commencement of the *Benedictio vexilli.*[78] That Pithou should have been interested in the *ordo* is not surprising. Lawyer, political activist, and scholar, he sought out and edited records of the past, and he was particularly concerned with texts that supported the liberties of the Gallican church.[79] How he gained access to the *ordo* of lat. 14192 before his death in 1596 is a matter of conjecture, but he may possibly have seen it through his intimate friend Antoine Loisel (1536-1617), with whom he had studied law under Cujas.[80] Loisel was born in Beauvais and retained close ties with his native city; his *Memoires* on Beauvais and the Beauvaisis were published in the year of his death. He knew the cathedral library well and took pride in the manuscripts it possessed, particularly its collection of conciliar texts, capitularies, and "la forme du Sacre de nos Roys" (of 1059), which he noted Jean du Tillet had published in a French translation.[81] In 1617 Loisel bemoaned the fact that the library was not well maintained ("bien entretenuë"), but he himself had contributed to the dispersal of its holdings, which in 1631 Pierre Louvet declared had caused

[76] *Gallia Christiana,* 9: 721-22; Suger, *Œuvres complètes,* 223, 233, 237, 333-41, no. VII (Suger's testament, for which see n. 140 below); 349-60, no. X (Suger's *Ordinatio* of 1140, for which see n. 140 below). As the editors of *Gallia Christiana,* 9: 722-23, point out, the "Odo" who attended the consecration of Saint-Denis in 1144 may be "Odo III," who succeeded "Odo II" sometime in 1144.

[77] See 50-51 below.

[78] I appreciate the advice of Marie-Pierre Laffitte regarding these notations. Other examples of Pithou's script are found in BN, fr. 16924, fol. 261r; and Paris, Bibliothèque de l'Arsenal, MS 2590; see also Turner, "Jean du Tillet," 63 n. 1.

[79] The biographical sketch by Foisset aîné in Michaud, *Biographie universelle,* is particularly useful; so too is Franklin, *Les anciennes bibliothèques,* 2: 249-51 n. 7; and Delisle, *Cabinet des manuscrits,* 1: 207-8, 422; 2: 8 n. 3, 43, 133, 256. To buttress his contention "que le Roy ne reconnoist aucun superieur au temporel de son Royaume, sinon Dieu seul," Pithou included in his posthumously published *Preuves des libertez de l'eglise gallicane,* 1: 94-95, a copy of the memorandum of Archbishop Gervais of Reims on the coronation of Philip I in 1059. The text is said to be taken from "un ancien livre de la Bibliotheque de Monsieur Petau" (now BAV, Ottobon. lat. 811, fols. 113r-14r; see n. 150 below), but Pithou gave the name of the abbot of "Sanctus Wingaloeus" (which is left blank in ibid.) as "Guarinus."

[80] Labouderie and Dellac discuss Loisel's life and writings, in Michaud, *Biographie universelle.*

[81] Loisel, *Memoires,* 61-62; in Omont, "Recherches," 8.

"its total ruin."[82] Loisel certainly borrowed manuscripts from the library; how many manuscripts he failed to return or appropriated is unclear. He is, however, known to have taken at least four, including one of the finely bound evangeliaries grouped with the *ordo* of lat. 14192 in the catalogue of 1404-17.[83] Loisel's interest in the cathedral's manuscripts and in royal coronations could have led him to bring the *ordo* of lat. 14192 to Pithou's attention—and even to have removed it from its binding and sent it to him in Paris for study. Alternatively, Pithou could have seen it in Beauvais and taken it himself: he, Loisel, and the Jesuits were those whom Louvet explicitly charged with "borrowing" manuscripts from the library and contributing to its decline.[84]

These hypotheses assume that the *ordo* of lat. 14192 was in Beauvais and available to Loisel and Pithou when they worked there. There is, of course, no guarantee that this is the case. Had Loisel known the ceremonial, he might well have mentioned it in enumerating the library's treasures, although his failure to do so does not mean that the manuscript was not still there. Another scholar who was interested in coronations had, however, worked in the cathedral's library in the 1550s, and he might possibly have expropriated the *ordo* and taken it to Paris. This scholar was Jean du Tillet, whose interest in coronations is beyond doubt. A receipt of 4 November 1558 shows that he had borrowed eleven

---

[82] Louvet, *Histoire et Antiqvitez*, 1: 362-63 ("de laquelle ont esté tiré les Capitulaires de Charlemagne, à present mis en lumiere, & vne infinité de rares Manuscripts, tant par les feus sieurs Pithou, Loisel, que Iesuites, les empruns desquels secondez de l'Imprimerie luy ont apporté sa totalle ruine"); see Omont, "Recherches," 8 n. 3. Louvet dedicated the first volume of his work to Augustin Potier, bishop of Beauvais, to whom Loisel had dedicated his *Memoires;* on Potier, Quignon, *La Bibliothèque de Beauvais*, 11.

[83] Omont, "Recherches," 7-8 (MSS borrowed on 12 September 1588); 9 n. 2; 15-16; 33, no. 127; 77; Delisle, *Cabinet des manuscrits*, 1: 431 (esp. n. 3). Loisel's collection passed to his grandson Claude Joly, canon and chanter of Notre-Dame of Paris (who prepared the catalogue of the cathedral library of Beauvais in 1664); Joly, who took some MSS himself, gave his collection to Notre-Dame in 1680, and from there it passed to the BN: ibid., 1: 288, 431; 2: 340; Quignon, *La Bibliothèque de Beauvais*, 16; Franklin, *Les anciennes bibliothèques*, 1: 32-35. One of the MSS appropriated by Loisel was a seventh-century copy of the *History of the Franks* by Gregory of Tours (BN, lat. 17654): Omont, "Recherches," 77. Adrien de Valois (1607-92) used it in his *Rervm Francicarvm . . . Libri VIII* (2: [3]r); so too did Thierry Ruinart in his ed. of Gregory's works, published in 1699: MPL, 71: 97-98. Both Valois and Ruinart also used a MS of Gregory's *History* that Loisel had taken from Corbie.

[84] See n. 82 above. Before his death in 1596 Pithou is known to have acquired six of the cathedral's MSS, whose ex libris, according to Omont, show that they had belonged to the library established by the Jesuits at the Collège de Clermont in Paris between 1564 and 1594: Omont, "Recherches," 15, 74-75. Franklin discusses the Jesuits' collection (although he mentions no books from Beauvais), as well as the pillaging of the library that occurred when the Jesuits were expelled from France in 1594; when the library was reestablished in 1618 it was enriched by a bequest from Cardinal François de Joyeuse, archbishop of Rouen, who had bought the books of Pierre Pithou and who left the Jesuit library half of his collection: Franklin, *Les anciennes bibliothèques*, 2: 245-46, 248-49.

manuscripts from the library, at least two of which he had not returned.[85] This was not Du Tillet's first visit to the library at Beauvais. Although he did not include a full translation of Gervais' famous memorandum on the coronation of 1059 in the *Recueil des Roys* for Henry II that he finished by early 1555, he referred there to "vng liure contenant la vieille forme du sacre et couronnement du Roy, escript du temps du Roy Henry premier," and used for Philip I, which was "en la librairye du chapitre de Beauuois."[86] He utilized the manuscript in discussing Reims' privilege, the election of rulers by the estates, and the origin of the peerage.[87] When he expanded this *Recueil* for Charles IX ten years later, Du Tillet presented a complete translation of the memorandum (to which Loisel referred in 1617). The editions of the work that appeared between 1578 and 1618 ensured the text's renown.[88] Du Tillet may well have seen the *ordo* of lat. 14192 in the cathedral library (and possibly the copy of the ceremonial in the library of Saint-Lucien). Perhaps he was responsible for taking the *ordo* to Paris. Pithou could have consulted it while it

[85] Omont, "Recherches," 7; curiously, the entry says that he had returned some at the beginning of Lent in 1556/57. One of the books that Du Tillet borrowed (and apparently returned) was a collection of conciliar acts and constitutions (now BAV, Reg. lat. 3827) which contains Pope Hadrian's letter to Charlemagne regarding the veneration of images. Du Tillet's brother and homonym did not know this MS when he prepared his edition of the *Libri Carolini* (which was published in 1549), and this suggests that neither brother had worked in the library at Beauvais in the 1540s: MPL, 98: 991-92. The *greffier* is the first known early-modern scholar to refer to Hadrian's letter, which he cited in his *Institvtion dv Pere Chrestien a ses Enfans*, 84-85, published in 1563. In *Du Tillet and the French Wars of Religion*, I give background and further information.

[86] SS, Fr. F. v. IV, No. 8/1, fol. 129v; BN, fr. 2854, fol. 141v; BN, fr. 18653, fol. 69r.

[87] SS, Fr. F. v. IV, No. 8/1, fols. 127v-28r, 129v, 213v; BN, fr. 2854, fols. 139v, 141v, 234r-v; BN, fr. 18653, fols. 67r, 69r, 97r-v; see 60-63 below.

[88] Du Tillet, *Recveil des Roys*, 183-85. The attention that Du Tillet drew to the memorandum may have led the cathedral chapter to take special care to preserve it. Loisel's reference to it in 1617 (see 23 above) suggests that it was still in the library at that date. It appears to have been acquired by the Jesuit Jacques Sirmond (1559-1651), who, like Etienne Baluze, knew the holdings of the cathedral because of his work on the capitularies: see Omont, "Recherches," 49, no. 9; 65, no. 50; and n. 82 above (Louvet's complaints about Jesuits); in his prefatory note to readers in his ed. (1623) of the capitularies of Charles the Bald and his successors, Sirmond refers to MSS from the libraries of Du Tillet, de Thou, and the churches of Beauvais, Laon, Metz, and Liège: *Opera varia*, 3: eiij [6] r. The ed. of the memorandum that the Jesuits Philippe Labbe (1607-67) and Gabriel Cossart (1615-74) prepared some fifteen years after Sirmond's death was based on his MS ("Auctior ex MS. Sirmondi"). This text, reproduced in subsequent conciliar collections, differs in a number of respects from the one in BAV, Ottobon. lat. 811, fols. 113r-14r (once owned by Paul Petau; ed. in *Historiæ Francorum scriptores*, 4: 161-62; and *Recueil des historiens*, 11: 32-33); in *Etude sur le Sacre*, 164, Quéant incorrectly states that Du Tillet translated the act from this MS. Comparison of the text ed. by Labbe and Cossart with Du Tillet's translation shows that the Sirmond MS was the Latin source on which Du Tillet drew in the 1550s. The first ed. of the work of Labbe and Cossart appeared in 1671-72; in the ed. of 1728-33 (*Sacrosancta Concilia*), the text is found on 12: 55-58. I am grateful to Richard A. Jackson for sharing with me his research on the sources and eds. of the memorandum of 1059.

was part of Du Tillet's collection. Pithou might have acquired it from Du Tillet; it could have passed into the library of Paul Petau (1568-1614), *conseiller* of the Parlement of Paris between 1588 and his death and an avid collector of manuscripts, some of which he acquired from Du Tillet's heirs.[89]

Pithou could also have seen and annotated the ceremonial in Petau's library, which contained at least one of the *libelli* with which the *ordo* is now bound. Notes in Pithou's hand also appear on the back cover of the third *libellus* now in BN, lat. 14192, a letter of a Count Etienne (probably of Blois) to his wife Ada (fols. 24r-26v), which Luc d'Achery first published in 1661.[90] Tempting as it is to conclude that Pithou wrote on both this booklet and the *ordo* when Petau owned them, there is no sure proof that either was in Petau's possession—although evidence of the company in which the *ordo* found itself shortly after Petau's death, soon to be discussed, strongly supports this possibility. That Petau at some time owned the first booklet now in BN, lat. 14192, is unquestioned. His distinctive signature ("Pa Petauius") and library mark (S. 51)[91] appear on the initial folio. The *libellus* contains the only extant copy of the *Life of Suger* by Guillaume of Saint-Denis,[92] a circular letter on Suger's death and a poem honoring him, a letter of Guillaume to his fellow-monks (in one twelfth-century hand, fols. 1r-15v), and a circular letter on the death of Abbot Ivo of Saint-Denis (1169-72) (in a second contemporary hand, fols. 15v-16v). The second booklet contains a collection of Suger's last letters (in a third twelfth-century hand, fols. 17r-23v). These texts are evidently closely linked to one another, and, as will be seen, Petau must have owned the second *libellus* as well as the first.

---

[89] Delisle discusses Petau's collection, in *Cabinet des manuscrits,* 1: 287-88; see also Pellegrin et al., *Les manuscrits classiques latins,* 1: 437-38; 2^1: 23-26. Of fundamental importance is Meyier's study of the Petau collection; *Paul en Alexandre Petau,* esp. 4, 79-80, 218 (Paul Petau's acquisition of MSS owned by Du Tillet's brother and homonym); see also 196 n. 88, 212 (MSS acquired by Petau's son Alexandre [d. 1672] from the Du Tillet estate in the mid-seventeenth century). Pithou used a legal MS that once belonged to Du Tillet's brother and homonym, which was owned by Paul Petau's son Alexandre when he sold many of their MSS to Queen Christina of Sweden in 1650. Whether it was part of the Du Tillets' collection or was in Paul Petau's library when Pithou consulted it cannot be determined. See Turner, "Jean du Tillet," 58, 63 n. 1; in "Bibliography," Turner gives additional information regarding the publications and MSS of Du Tillet's brother. Pithou is also known to have used a MS of Suetonius in Petau's collection: Meyier, *Paul en Alexandre Petau,* 11.

[90] *Spicilegium,* 3: 430-31; as the table of contents shows, in the first ed. the letter appeared in 4: 257. See n. 101 below (Adrien de Valois' communication of the letter to Achery).

[91] Meyier studies the marks of Petau's ownership and gives examples of his script, in *Paul en Alexandre Petau,* 24-31, esp. the pl. following 28.

[92] Lecoy de La Marche, ed., Suger, *Œuvres complètes,* xv-xvii.

They probably came to him from Saint-Denis, from which both he and Pithou acquired manuscripts after the Huguenots devastated the abbey in 1567.[93]

Sometime after Petau's death in 1614, his copy of Suger's *Life* "with his letters" was acquired by the house of the Discalced Carmelites of Clermont. An inventory of the Carmelite library compiled in the first half of the seventeenth century shows that three other works now in BN, lat. 14192, were bound with the *Life* and letters; in all likelihood they traveled to Clermont together.[94] From our standpoint the most important of these three booklets is the "Formula observed in the coronation of the king," the last item in the inventory, which also lists letters of Ivo of Chartres and of "a certain bishop of Mainz," "Adalbero's verses to King Robert," "an old cartulary of a certain church," and a work by "Augustinus the librarian" dedicated to Pope Paul III (1534-49). It is surely no coincidence that the fourth booklet of BN, lat. 14192, is a fragment of a collection of Ivo's letters (in a twelfth-century hand, fols. 27r-31v);[95] that the fifth is Adalbero of Laon's *Carmen ad Rotbertum Regem* (in three early-eleventh-century hands, fols. 32r-43v, with an appended bifolium, fols. 44r-45v, containing an

---

[93] Carolus-Barré, "Pillage et dispersion," 97-101, esp. 100; Meyier, *Paul en Alexandre Petau,* 113-16, 206-7 (Dyonisian MSS acquired by Paul and Alexander Petau). Since the ex libris at the bottom of the initial folio of the first folio has been excised, the original owner's identity cannot be known, but the position once occupied by the ex libris is consistent with (although unfortunately not demonstrative of) Dyonisian origin; as Meyier shows (ibid., 113-16), many of the MSS of Saint-Denis that came into Paul Petau's hands retained their ex libris and shelfmarks. More important, a marginal note opposite the beginning of the circular letter on Suger's death (fol. 11r) states that "it is to be read on the anniversary of lord Suger abbot" ("legenda in anniuersario donni suggerij abbatis"). Such a note might have been inserted at any house affiliated with Saint-Denis, but it would be particularly appropriate in a MS belonging to Saint-Denis itself.

[94] "Vita Sugerii Abbatis cum eiusdem Epistolis: Iuonis Carnotensis Episcopi Epistolæ, &c. Versus Adalberonis Episcopi ad Robertum Regem. Formula obseruata in Coronatione Regis": Labbe, *Nova Bibliotheca,* 207, no. 38. The catalogue of the Carmelite library was shown to Labbe by the Carmelite Louis-Jacques de Saint-Charles of Chalon-sur-Saône: ibid., 206 ("Idem . . . exhibuit mihi perhumaniter alterum Catalogum mss. ex quo didici in Bibliotheca Carmelitarum Excalceatorum Claromontensium in Aruernia latere inter cæteros hosce mss."). Labbe did not publish the catalogue until 1653, when, as will be seen, the codex was again in Paris. Charles Le Tonnelier recopied the inventory in fuller form in 1675: Lanoë, "Quelques manuscrits." His transcription shows that the codex contained "Volumen in quo sunt Vita Suggeri abbatis, Epistolae ejusdem, Epistolae Ivonis Carnotensis et cujusdam episcopi Moguntini, Versus Adalberonis episc. ad Robertum regem, Vetus cartularium cujusdam ecclesiae, Augustini bibliothec. de via Pauli et defunct. etc. ad Paulum III PP. et Forma observata in coronatione regis": Carozzi, ed., Adalbero, *Poème,* cli-ii (from Paris, Bibliothèque de l'Arsenal, MS 4630, fol. 259v). Carozzi (ibid., clii) identifies the author of the penultimate work, Agostino Stenco, and gives its title, "Ad Paulum III Pont. Max. Augustini Bibliothecarii de via Pauli et de fontibus inducendis in eam."

[95] The fragment begins toward the end of Ivo's letter numbered 204, and contains the letters numbered 205-12 and 214, and most of the letter numbered 216 in MPL, 162: 259-71.

account of a plea of 898 and a saints' passion);[96] and that the seventh is Agostino Stenco's account of navigation on the Tiber, written for Paul III and published in Rome in the mid-sixteenth century (fols. 63r-72v). The Carmelite inventory does not refer to the letter of Count Etienne to Ada that Pithou annotated, but the letter was copied on only two folios and could have been skipped by the cataloguer. Nor does the inventory mention the sixth booklet now in BN, lat. 14192, a register of the Parisian confraternity of the church of Saint-Maur-et-Saint-Fiacre (fols. 46r-62r), whose latest entry is dated 1637. On the other hand, when the Carmelites possessed the codex, it contained letters of a bishop of Mainz and a cartulary, of which there is no trace in BN, lat. 14192, but which, as will be seen, were still parts of the codex in 1672 and 1648, respectively.

By at least 1648 (and perhaps as early as 1640)[97] the collection of booklets was back in Paris, in the library of Antoine Vyon d'Herouval (1606-89). Auditor of the Chambre des comptes of Paris and an avid collector of manuscripts, he was the friend of such scholars and bibliophiles as Du Cange, Jacques Sirmond, Luc d'Achery, Roger de Gaignières, Claude Joly, and the royal historiographer Adrien de Valois, to all of whom he freely communicated the documents and manuscripts he knew and possessed.[98] It was in his library that Adrien de Valois first saw the codex containing Adalbero's *Carmen,* which he edited and which was published in 1663.[99] He dedicated the work to Vyon, heaping praise on him for his generosity to scholars and thanking him particularly for having brought the codex to his attention "abhinc annos XIV."[100] In the preface to his notes on the *Carmen*

[96] Carozzi, ed., Adalbero, *Poème,* clii-v. The plea (on fol. 44r) may be original; the saints' passion (fols. 44v-45v) was copied in the eleventh century. Oexle ("Adalbero," 629-38, esp. 635-36) shows, as Carozzi (cliii) and the BN's catalogue suggest, that the two folios following Adalbero's poem were originally attached to it. Oexle convincingly hypothesizes that a Cluniac monastery of northern France, possibly in or near Laon, originally owned the booklet: "Adalbero," 632, 636-37.

[97] See nn. 101 and 105 below.

[98] "Eloge de Monsieur Vion"; Moréri, *Le Grand Dictionnaire Historique,* 10: 654-55; Bruel, "Notes," 609-11; Delisle, *Catalogue des actes de Philippe-Auguste,* xlvi-vii; idem, *Cabinet des manuscrits,* 1: 324, 347, 440-41; 2: 45, 233, 234; Brown and Famiglietti, *The* Lit de Justice.

[99] The testimony of many contemporaries regarding Valois' life and works is collected in *Valesiana,* esp. [7]v-[15]. In 1658 Valois acknowledged the help that Vyon had given him with sources for the second volume of his *Rervm Francicarvm . . . Libri VIII* (a a iij[22]r).

[100] Valois, ed., *Carmen Panegyricvm,* aiij[2]v-[5]v, esp. [5]r ("alterum [librum] abhinc annos XIV. beneficio tuo nanctus sum"); the dedication is dated 1 November 1662. In the introduction to the ed. of the *Carmen* in MPL, 141: 787-822, are found Valois' notes, but unfortunately not the dedication. Since his preface to the notes refers (correctly) to the MS as "Pauli Petauij V.C. nomine manuque notatum" (*Carmen Panegyricum,* 767; MPL, 141: 787), Carozzi assumed (Adalbero, *Poème,* cli, clvii) that the MS was in the library of Paul Petau's son Alexander when Valois used it; so too did Meyier, *Paul en Alexandre Petau,* 140.

Valois described the manuscript as "a small old codex, annotated with the name and in the hand of Paul Petau." Among other things ("præter cetera") it contained, he said, the *Carmen*, a cartulary of the abbey of Lyre in Normandy (doubtless the "old cartulary of a certain church" of the Clermont inventory), the *Life* of Abbot Suger, the letter of Count Etienne to his wife, the *Iudicium Varennense* (the plea of 898 that follows the *Carmen*), and finally the *ordo* for the consecration of a king and queen, whose initial rubric he quoted in full.[101] The ceremonial interested him enough for him to make excerpts from it for Etienne Baluze.[102] The "cetera" that Valois omitted from his description of Vyon's manuscript must have included the letters of Ivo of Chartres and Agostino Stenco's account of navigation on the Tiber, which were part of the codex when it was in Clermont and are still part of BN, lat. 14192, as well as the letters of the bishop of Mainz that had been in the manuscript in Clermont and that, as will be seen, were in it in 1672. Whether Valois' "cetera" also included the register of the confraternity of the church of Saint-Maur-et-Saint-Fiacre cannot be determined. The manuscript's contents were presumably unchanged when Valois published his edition and notes in 1663, and they may have been unaltered when the codex passed, sometime before 1672, to the library of Pierre Seguier, chancellor of France (1588-1672).

---

[101] "Ante aliquot annos nanctus sum veterem codicem exiguum, Pauli Petauij V.C. nomine manuque notatum, quo Adalberonis episcopi Laudunensis Carmen ad Rotbertum Regem Francorum, Chartarium Lirensis Monasterij, Vita Sugerij Abbatis, Epistola Stephani Comitis ad Adelam conjugem, Iudicium Varennense, vel, ut vulgo vocant, Placitum Ermengardis Reginæ & Principum Ludouici filii Bosonis anno DCCCXCVIII. Indictione VIII. item Percunctatio siue electio Episcoporum ac Clericorum necnon populorum ad Regem consecrandum, vna cum ordinatione Reginæ præter cetera continebantur": *Carmen Panegyricvm*, 767; MPL, 141: 787. Valois went on to note that the *Life of Suger* had been published, he thought ("ni fallor"), by François Duchesne; that "someone had recently published" ("nuper quidam vulgauit") the *Iudicium;* and that he himself had seen to the publication ("publicandum curaui") of the letter of Count Etienne in 1661, in Achery's *Spicilegium:* see n. 90 above. I have been unable to locate the published ed. of the *Iudicium*. The *Life of Suger* was first edited by Charles de Combault, baron of Auteuil, who said that his ed. (published in 1642) was based on "des Anciens Manuscrits de S. Denis," and who remarked that it was also "dans les memoires MSS. de feu André du Chesne [1584-1640]" and that a translation by "Baudouyn" (Jean Baudoin) had appeared in 1640: *Histoire des Ministres d'Estat*, 244, 276-93, followed by (ibid., 293-97) the circular letter on Suger's death and the poem on Suger copied after the *Life* in BN, lat. 14192, fols. 11r-14r. François Duchesne (1616-93) indeed edited the work "ex veteri codice MS.", and his book appeared in 1648; he presumably relied as well on the copy owned by his father, who by 1640 knew the codex that Vyon acquired and may have used it for his transcription of Guillaume's *Life:* Stein, *Bibliographie générale*, 313, no. 2286; see n. 105 below. On this ed. and Baudoin's translation, see the BN catalogue of printed books, s.v. Guillaume de Saint-Denis; and Lecoy de La Marche, ed., Suger, *Œuvres complètes*, xvi-vii, xxi.

[102] See 98-101 below.

Seguier bequeathed his manuscripts to Henri-Charles du Cambout (1664-1732), bishop of Metz and in 1710 duke of Coislin and a peer of France.[103] Shortly after Seguier's death in 1672, his holdings were inventoried and appraised, and little value was set on the codex that the chancellor had presumably acquired from Vyon d'Herouval. Valued at 2 l., it was said to include simply Guillaume's *Life of Suger*, "etc.," Count Etienne's letter to his wife, the letters of a bishop of Mainz, and Adalbero's *Carmen*.[104] Nothing was said of the coronation *ordo*—or the rest of the manuscript's contents. Thus it is impossible to know whether the cartulary of the abbey of Lyre (of which a fragment still survives) was detached from the codex before 1672 or afterwards; the manuscript evidently lost the letters of the bishop of Mainz after this date.[105] The complex history of the codex became simpler after its acquisition by Cambout de Coislin. After his death it passed, with the rest of his manuscripts, to Saint-Germain-des-Prés and then, with the abbey's holdings, to the Bibliothèque nationale.[106]

Neither the manuscript itself nor the history of its wanderings resolves the question of the circumstances of its creation or its original provenance. Its presence in Beauvais by 1404 and the veneration that it was accorded there must be explained. But before these issues can be considered, the text of the *ordo* must be examined.

2. "Franks, Burgundians, and Aquitanians" In the *Ordo* of Lat. 14192

As has been seen, the *ordo* of lat. 14192 is based on the early (A) version of the second English coronation *ordo*. This ceremonial dates from the tenth century. Its oldest extant witness is the *ordo* in the Sacramentary of Ratold, abbot of Corbie between 972 and his death in 986; curiously, the *ordo* survives in no known English

[103] Anselme, *Histoire genealogique*, 7: 807; Delisle, *Cabinet des manuscrits*, 2: 50, 78-99.

[104] Delisle, *Cabinet des manuscrits*, 2: 92. Some unimpressive manuscripts were appraised at as little as 1 l., but a large missal with many miniatures was valued at 260 l., an illustrated copy of the first ten books of Augustine's *De civitate Dei* at 50 l.: ibid., 91-93.

[105] Stein gives useful information regarding the thirteenth-century cartulary, in *Bibliographie générale*, 313, no. 2286; the surviving fragment is in BN, lat. 11053, fols. 10r-13v. In 1640 Dom Anselme Le Michel copied extracts from the booklet, which was brought to his attention by André du Chesne, probably after it had returned to Paris from Clermont; other copies were made from it in 1704, when the MS was more complete than is now the case.

[106] Delisle, *Cabinet des manuscrits*, 2: 50; Balayé, *La Bibliothèque Nationale*, 415-17.

exemplar.[107] A number of other manuscripts—including BN, lat. 14192—contain closely related versions of this *ordo*, but these recensions are not based directly on the *ordo* in Ratold's Sacramentary and may possibly derive from an ancestor of that *ordo*'s parent text. This text in turn could have been known at Saint-Vaast of Arras, whose influence on the Ratold Sacramentary is revealed by the Sacramentary's calendar and its two masses for Saint Vaast (even though the dates to which the masses are assigned are incorrect).[108] The many surviving copies of close relatives of the Ratold *ordo* testify to the popularity of the English ceremonial in northern France and the Empire in the twelfth and thirteenth centuries.[109]

The *ordo* of lat. 14192 differs in many respects from the *ordo* in the Ratold Sacramentary. Some elements of the Ratold *ordo* are lacking, most notably that *ordo*'s two odd references to "Albion" in the consecration prayer and its designation of Saint Gregory as "the Apostle of the angels" ("angelorum," replacing "anglorum," or "English") in the prayer *Extendat omnipotens deus*. Neither "Albion" nor Gregory's title appears in the *ordo* of lat. 14192 or in closely related copies, including one found in a pontifical of *ca* 1050 (Cologne, Dombibliothek 141, which contains material from other *ordines*), and one copied in northern France in the late eleventh or early twelfth century (BN, lat. 13315).[110] Again, where in the Ratold *ordo*'s consecration prayer the king is admonished—perfectly reasonably—not to abandon the scepters of the Franks ("sceptra Francorum"), these two *ordines* read *Saxonum Merciorum Nordanhimbrorumque* for *Francorum*. So too do most of the other surviving manuscript versions of the Ratold *ordo*.

---

[107] Nelson, "Second English Ordo," passim; Ward, "Early Version," 345-49; Hohler, "Some Service-Books," 64-69; Bouman, *Sacring*, 158; see p. 15 above. In her "Second English *Ordo*," 363 n. 1, Dr. Nelson kindly refers to "Appendix I" of the present study for a discussion of the MSS connected with the Ratold *ordo*; although in an early version I considered this question in some detail in an appendix, my conclusions are now incorporated into the text.

[108] Ward, "Early Version," 347-50; Hohler, "Some Service-Books," 64-69, concludes (ibid., 69) "that [the Sacramentary's] text was transmitted in successive recopyings from Saint-Denis to Dol and from Dol to Wells (with a journey to Orleans [*sic*] before or in the course of its stay in Wells) and then to Arras and thence to Corbie, gathering fresh material and sundry modifications at every move."

[109] A copy of one recension, in a late-twelfth-century pontifical of Reims (Reims, BM, MS 342, fols. 69v-80r), contains annotations dating from the early thirteenth century; this could, but does not necessarily, mean that it was used and modified in connection with actual ceremonies: Jackson, "*Ordines*," 64-65; idem, "Manuscripts, Texts," 46-48. I am grateful to Paul L. Ward for lending me his microfilm of this text.

[110] Ward, "Early Version," 347, 348: Leroquais, *Pontificaux*, 2: 180-84; Jackson, "Manuscripts, Texts," 49-50. In 1643 Marlot (*Theatre d'Honnevr*, 659-60) offered interesting comments on the presence of Albion in the Ratold *ordo*.

The *ordo* of lat. 14192 is unique among surviving manuscript copies in reading *francorum burgundiorum aquitanorum.*[111] As in the cases of the *ordines* of Cologne, Dombibliothek 141, and of BN, lat. 13315, this triplet suggests that the source of the *ordo* of lat. 14192 contained the tripartite formula "Saxons, Mercians, and Northumbrians." Neither the *ordo* of Cologne, Dombibliothek 141, nor that of BN, lat. 13315, however, can have been the parent text of the *ordo* of lat. 14192, since their additional variants (and, in the case of the *ordo* at Cologne, its additional portions) distinguish them from the *ordo* of lat. 14192,[112] which contains numerous idiosyncratic variants.[113]

The redactor of the *ordo* of lat. 14192 did not invent the formula "Franks, Burgundians, and Aquitanians." In the early twelfth century the Franks, Burgundians, and Aquitanians were regarded as the chief peoples of what was coming to be considered the kingdom of France, and their preeminence was some two centuries old.[114] Since at least the late ninth century special importance was attributed to the three regions and the people who inhabited them. Discussing the election of Eudes as king of the Franks in 888, Abbo of Saint-Germain-des-Prés declared in his poem on the Norman siege of Paris, "Francia laetatur, quamvis is Nustricus esset . . . Nec, quia dux illi Burgundia defuit; . . . Sic uno ternum congaudet ovamine regnum. Praeterea astutos petiit praeceps Aquitanos."[115] Here the "three-fold kingdom" consists of Francia, Neustria, and Burgundy: the acclamation of these three realms gave Eudes the right to claim authority over the people of Aquitaine.[116] Over time, however, the various peoples[117] whom Eudes and his successors were said to rule were narrowed to three, considered particularly important: the Franks, Burgundians, and Aquitanians. A charter of King Raoul of France dated 13 September 983 entitled him "gratia Dei, Francorum et Aquita-

---

[111] BN, lat. 14192, fol. 75v; cf. Ward, "Early Version," 352 n. 6; see n. 50 above. In the MS the phrase appears on a single line and a space for approximately eight letters remains at the end of the line. The next line begins *sceptra non deserat*. See 91 below.

[112] Ward, "Early Version," 347-49.

[113] See Ward, "Early Version," 350-61, and Jackson's forthcoming ed. (see n. 50 above).

[114] Kienast, "Französischen Stämme," in idem, *Studien*, 130-50. Schneidmüller gives useful background, in "Französisches Sonderbewußtsein," 49-91, esp. 66; and in *Die Entstehung Frankreichs*.

[115] *Le siège de Paris*, 100. In "Französischen Stämme," 130-32, Kienast considers this and other texts cited below.

[116] Guillot, "Les étapes," 218-21; Werner, "Avant les Capétiens," 18-21.

[117] A poem concerning Eudes' coronation in 888 declares, "Amen resultet Gallia, / amen cantent Burgundia, / Bigorni regni spacia, / Wasconia et Teutonia": Schramm, "Krönung," 200-201; idem, *Kaiser*, 2: 214-16. Guillot ("Les étapes," 217) persuasively argues that it should be linked with Eudes' consecration at Reims on 13 November 888, rather than with the earlier ceremony at Compiègne on 29 February 888.

norum atque Burgundionum rex pius, invictus ac semper augustus."[118] The formula found in this charter was widely adopted. The eleventh-century *Historia Francorum Senonensis* refers to the "Franci, Burgundiones et Aquitanenses proceres" in treating Eudes' election in 888.[119] Between 1082 and 1103 this passage was cited in the continuation of the history of Aimoin of Fleury written at Saint-Germain-des-Prés.[120] In the first decade of the twelfth century the three peoples appeared virtually simultaneously—again with reference to Eudes—in a number of important histories, all influenced by the *Historia Francorum Senonensis* and by Fleury:[121] first, the chronicle beginning *Antenor et alii* (generally termed the *Abbreviatio*)[122]; second, the chronicle of Saint-Pierre-le-Vif of Sens[123]; finally, the history commencing *Ex genere Priami*.[124] Ivo of Chartres cited the three peoples when treating Eudes' election in a letter discussing the coronation of Louis VI at Orléans in 1108.[125]

Although the names of these three peoples most often appeared in connection with Eudes' accession in 888, Hugues of

---

[118] *Recueil des actes de Robert Ier*, 90-96 (esp. 93, 95), no. 21.

[119] Kienast, "Französischen Stämme," 130. The earliest known MS of this history seems to be English and to date from the beginning or first half of the twelfth century: Ehlers, "Die *Historia Francorum Senonensis*," 22 n. 1.

[120] Kienast, "Französischen Stämme," 131. Lemarignier discusses the history, in "Autour de la royauté française" 31-34 ("La Continuation d'Aimoin et le ms. lat. 12711 de la Bibliothèque nationale").

[121] In "La place de l'abbaye de Fleury-sur-Loire," 32-33, Bautier treats Fleury's relation to the *Historia Francorum Senonensis* and the histories beginning *Antenor et alii* and *Ex genere Priami*. See also Bautier and Gilles, ed., *Chronique de Saint-Pierre-le-Vif*, x (connections between Saint-Pierre-le-Vif and Fleury), xxxvii (the chronicle of Sens [675-1096] and its dependence on the *Historia Francorum Senonensis*).

[122] MGH, *Scriptorum*, 9: 402. The oldest extant copy of this history originally belonged to the abbey of Bec: Delisle, "Le psautier de saint Louis," 172-77. It is also preserved in a twelfth-century MS of Jumièges (Rouen, BM, MS 1173). Popular in northern France, it was known in the late twelfth or early thirteenth century at Saint-Feuillien-du-Rœulx, Saint-Corneille of Compiègne, and Saint-Quentin: Lair, "Mémoire sur deux chroniques," at 558-61; Clark, "Art and Historiography," 37-46 (esp. n. 3). The text is also found in a mid-twelfth-century MS of the house of the Blessed Virgin in Reading (Cambridge, Caius College, MS 177/210, fols. 89v-115v). There seems no reason to connect its composition, as has often been done, with the abbey of Saint-Denis: see, e.g., Spiegel, *Chronicle Tradition of Saint-Denis*, 41-44.

[123] *Chronique de Saint-Pierre-le-Vif*, 68.

[124] In Paris, Bibliothèque Mazarine, MS 2013, a historical miscellany of Saint-Denis compiled between the early and the mid-twelfth century, this work is found on fols. 158v-175v; the formula appears on fol. 170v. This MS is discussed in Brown and Cothren, "Crusading Window," 14-15 n. 65; Brown, "Saint-Denis and the Turpin Legend," 55 n. 12; Du Pouget, "Recherches sur les chroniques latines," 5-11, summarized in *Positions des thèses de l'Ecole des Chartes*, 1978, 41-46; I am grateful to M. Du Pouget for permitting me to read his thesis. Spiegel (*Chronicle Tradition of Saint-Denis*, 40-41) presents the MS as a universal chronicle that she terms the *Gesta gentis Francorum*. The history *Ex genere Priami* should not be confused with a royal genealogy beginning with the same phrase, which is also in the Mazarine MS, fol. 222r; see Waitz, in MGH, *Scriptorum*, 9: 342.

[125] MPL, 162: 194, no. CLXXXIX; Luchaire, *Louis VI . . . Annales*, 32, no. 59.

Fleury invoked them in two quite different contexts. At the very end of his *Historia ecclesiastica* he said that Charles the Bald (843-77) "franciam burgundiam & aquitaniam obtinuit solus."[126] In his *Historia moderna* he recorded that the coronation of Philip I of France in 1059 was attended by ecclesiastics "Franciae, Burgundiae et Aquitaniæ,"[127] a statement that reflects historical reality, since the magnates of these regions played an important role at this and other coronations. In his memorandum on Philip I's coronation in 1059 Gervais, archbishop of Reims, listed the dukes of Aquitaine and Burgundy first among those singled out for special mention.[128]

In the region of Paris the formula "Franks, Burgundians, and Aquitanians" was familiar not only at Saint-Germain-des-Prés but also at Saint-Denis. There a historical miscellany, composed in large part of works from Fleury and assembled early in the twelfth century, contained both *Ex genere Priami* and the *Historia ecclesiastica* of Hugues of Fleury.[129]

Thus, by the early twelfth century the materials from which the *ordo* of lat. 14192 could have been confected were available in and near Paris. But what prompted the creation of the ceremonial? The use of the formula "Franks, Burgundians, and Aquitanians" in the prayer of consecration and the production of a *libellus* containing the *ordo* suggests that it may have been devised for a specific ceremony. The haste with which the text seems to have been prepared indicates, further, that the ceremony itself was quickly planned.

3. The Historical Moment

One occasion seems strikingly consistent with the physical characteristics and probable date of the *ordo* of lat. 14192: the marriage of Louis VII (1137-80) and Eleanor of Aquitaine in 1137 and the ceremonies accompanying their union. The formula "Franks,

---

[126] Hugues of Fleury, *Chronicon*, 181; Paris, Bibliothèque Mazarine, MS 2013, fol. 136v. On Hughes' works, see Waitz, in MGH, *Scriptorum*, 9: 342-47; and Bautier, "La place de l'abbaye de Fleury-sur-Loire," 25-33.

[127] MGH, *Scriptorum*, 9: 389.

[128] BAV, Ottobon. lat. 811, fols. 113r-14r; in *Scriptores*, ed. Duchesne, 4: 161-62; and *Recueil des historiens*, 11: 32-33; cf. *Sacrosancta Concilia*, 12: 56; see n. 88 above. An apparently independent account, which Du Chesne discovered at Saint-Thierry of Reims in a MS entitled *De ratione temporum*, lists the "legat[o]s Balduini Marchionis" before the duke of Aquitaine and the representative of the duke of Burgundy: *Scriptores*, ed. Duchesne, 4: 162-63; *Recueil des historiens*, 11: 33. See Kienast, "Französischen Stämme," 147-48 (esp. n. 77), 148-49.

[129] Paris, Bibliothèque Mazarine, MS 2013, fols. 136r, 170v. On this MS see n. 124 above.

Burgundians, and Aquitanians" had special relevance to the events that seemed destined to accomplish the incorporation of Aquitaine into the kingdom of France through the marriage of the duchy's heiress to the young Louis, who had been crowned in 1131.[130]

Before Duke William X of Aquitaine died as a pilgrim in Compostela on 9 April 1137, he entrusted his lands and his daughter and heiress Eleanor to Louis VI of France (1108-37).[131] Messengers announcing the duke's death arrived in Paris at the beginning of June,[132] and, as may have been William's express wish,[133] plans were made at once for Eleanor to be married to Louis VI's son and namesake. As the chronicler of Morigny says, "King Louis exerted every effort to see that such a great thing should speedily be accomplished."[134] The monarch had no desire to arouse the Aquitanians' apprehensions. Thus the wedding would be lavish and would be held in Bordeaux, where Eleanor would be crowned, doubtless by the archbishop of Bordeaux.[135] By absenting himself from the embassy sent to the south, the aged archbishop of Reims, Renaud II, would have safeguarded the privileges regarding coronation that he enjoyed within his province,[136] and there

[130] I am not the first to advance the hypothesis that I present here. Struck by the significance of the formula "Franks, Burgundians, and Aquitanians," the canon of Beauvais who in the late seventeenth century described the copy of the *ordo* of lat. 14192 at Saint-Lucien of Beauvais commented of the phrase, "ce qui doit s'entendre de Louis VII qui épousa vers 1137 Alienor de Guienne ou Aquitaine": Lanoë, "Quelques manuscrits." See also n. 50 above.

[131] The most complete account and chronology are found in Suger, *Vie de Louis VI*, ed. Waquet, 280-82; see Luchaire, *Louis VI . . . Annales*, 263-65, nos. 579-81. Three other contemporary sources are particularly useful. First, the chronicle of Geffroy, prior of Vigeois (fl. 1168, d. post 1184), in *Recueil des historiens*, 12: 431, 434-35; on him, see Arbellot, "Etude historique," 135-61. Second, *Chronique de Morigny*, 66-68. Third, Orderic Vitalis, *Historia Æcclesiastica*, 6: 480-82, 490. See also Richard, *Histoire des comtes de Poitou*, 2: 51, 56-61.

[132] Luchaire, *Annales . . . Louis VI*, 264-65, no. 580.

[133] *Chronique de Morigny*, 65-66, says that William bound his magnates to see that Eleanor and Louis were married and his lands given to the couple "secundum consuetudinem coniubii." See also Orderic Vitalis, *Historia Æcclesiastica*, 6: 482 ("Filiam uero suam Ludouico iuueni Francorum regi in coniugem dari precepit, ipsumque regem totius iuris sui heredem constituit"), 490 ("ut filiam Pictauensis ducis uxorem duceret, totumque ducatum sicut Guillelmus dux constituerat sibi subiugaret").

[134] " . . . pater Ludovicus itineri necessaria preparat, et, ut tanta res cito effectui mancipetur, elaborat": *Chronique de Morigny*, 66.

[135] Suger, *Vie de Louis VI*, ed. Waquet, 280-82; *Chronique de Morigny*, 67; Luchaire, *Louis VI . . . Annales*, 268, no. 589.

[136] On Renaud, *Gallia Christiana*, 9: 82-83. Urban II's privilege of 25 December 1089 for the archbishop of Reims awarded him primacy of the province of Belgica secunda, gave him the "first power" (*prima potestas*) of anointing the king and queen, and specified that when the archbishop or his successor was present at the "solemn processions at which kings were crowned" ("sollemnibus processionibus quibus eosdem reges fuerit coronari"), no other prelate should crown the king; the archbishop was also given the right to wear the pallium "in benedictione regis ac reginæ": MPL, 151: 309-11, no. XXVII. Suger refers to the claim, voiced in 1108, that the archbishop of Reims possessed "prime regis

is no evidence that he participated in the preparations or the ceremonies. Doubtless to win the favor of the southerners, Louis VI issued a sweeping charter of privilege to the churches of the province of Bordeaux, and the young Louis reissued this charter in his own name (as "Ludovicus junior, magni Ludovici filius") in Bordeaux, at or soon after his marriage.[137] According to Suger, Louis VI solemnly enjoined those who traveled to the south "not to seize anything in the whole duchy of Aquitaine and not to harm the land and its poor, lest they make enemies of friends."[138] Doubtless as an acknowledgment of the duchy's special status, after his marriage Louis VII added *dux Aquitanorum* to his title *rex Francorum*.[139]

Since Louis VI was ailing, there was good reason for speed. The king was concerned about his health, and before his delegation departed for the south he discussed with Abbot Suger the specific site at Saint-Denis where he wished to be buried.[140] He bade his son a solemn farewell.[141] The king and his councilors

---

corone primitias": *Vie de Louis VI*, ed. Waquet, 86. Special circumstances led to the coronation of Louis VI in Orléans in that year: Schramm, *König*, 1: 117-20; Hinkle, *Portal of the Saints*, 26-27. I am grateful to Uta Renate Blumenthal and Robert Somerville for their counsel regarding the privilege of 1089, whose authenticity seems beyond question. Baluze first edited it (1713) in *Miscellanorum liber sextus*, 372-75; Migne's ed. relies on the copy published in 1724 in Ruinart, *Ouvrages posthumes*, 3: 352-54; ibid., 71, for the source, "ex veteri codice ms.," very likely the *Liber Lamberti*, the record book of Lambert, bishop of Arras (1093-1115), whose contents are preserved in two seventeenth-century copies, in Arras, BM, MS 1051 (140), pp. 66-69, and MS 1062 (222), fols. 30r-31v.

[137] Luchaire, *Louis VI . . . Annales*, 265, no. 581; Richard, *Histoire*, 2: 57-58; Luchaire, *Etudes . . . Louis VII*, 83; 97-98, no. 1.

[138] " . . . ne quid in toto ducatu Aquitanie rapiant, ne terram aut terre pauperes ledant, ne amicos inimicos faciant": Suger, *Vie de Louis VI*, ed. Waquet, 282.

[139] Chaplais, "Traité de Paris," 131; Berger, "Formule," 305-13, who lists (ibid., 306-8) the charters, all dating from 1152-54, in which the double titulature appears.

[140] Moved, perhaps, by the dangers associated with travel, Suger drew up his testament on 17 June 1137; on the same day, for his soul's sake, he assigned to the abbey's treasury Norman property that he had reclaimed for Saint-Denis, and granted privileges and donations to the church of Saint-Paul at Saint-Denis, ordering the presentation of a special gift on the anniversary of his death on condition that the church's clerics celebrate it at Saint-Denis, "if God permitted him to be buried there," and otherwise at their own church: *Œuvres complètes*, 333-49, nos. VII-IX; Cartellieri, *Abt Suger*, 33-34. The acts were apparently prepared in haste, and there are discrepancies in dating: ibid., 138-39, nos. 88-90; Luchaire, *Louis VI . . . Annales*, 264-65, no. 580. Not until some time after Suger's return was his elaborate testament drawn up in final form, at the same time as he redacted his *Ordinatio* of 1140: Suger, *Œuvres complètes*, 349-60, no. X; Cartellieri, *Abt Suger*, 140-41, no. 108. The list of prelates witnessing the will is precisely the same as that found in the *Ordinatio* and includes Samson, archbishop of Reims, who did not assume office until 1139. Four of the 25 witnesses from Saint-Denis (excluding Suger) who witnessed the act concerning the Norman property are absent from the similarly ordered group of 48 Dyonisian witnesses to the testament; two of the 16 witnesses to the act for Saint-Paul do not appear in the testament, although one of these is found in the act concerning Norman property. See Benton, "Suger's Life," 7, 11 n. 59.

[141] Suger, *Vie de Louis VI*, ed. Waquet, 270-80, 284.

may well have thought that he might soon die, as in fact happened on 1 August.[142]

The elaborate preparations for the marriage of Eleanor and Louis were made in less than three weeks.[143] A host of nobles and ecclesiastics was assembled; Suger, Orderic Vitalis, and the chronicler of Morigny refer to them as an "army," which Suger says included "five hundred knights and more."[144] Thibaud IV, count of Blois, and Raoul, count of Vermandois, headed the entourage; the impressive clerical contingent included Suger, the bishop of Chartres (a papal legate), and probably Peter the Venerable, abbot of Cluny.[145] Suger, characteristically emphasizing his own importance, mentions the two counts but does not refer to any ecclesiastic except himself.[146]

An *ordo* was evidently needed for the coronation ceremony that would follow the marriage of Eleanor and Louis in Bordeaux. If the solemn installation at Poitiers, which occurred on 8 August, was planned before the entourage left Paris, thought would also have been given to that ceremony's form. The *ordo* of lat. 14192, I believe, was prepared in the first weeks of June 1137 for the coronation in Bordeaux, and perhaps for the ceremony in Poitiers as well.

---

[142] Luchaire, *Louis VI . . . Annales*, 270, no. 595.

[143] Suger, *Vie de Louis VI*, ed. Waquet, 281 n. 4; Richard, *Histoire*, 2: 61 n. 1. Waquet hypothesizes that Louis and his escort left Paris on 15 June, but Richard's date of 18 June (based on the date of Suger's testament) is more convincing.

[144] ". . . nobilissimum virorum exercitum, quingentorum et eo amplius militum de melioribus regni colligit": Suger, *Vie de Louis VI*, ed. Waquet, 280; Orderic Vitalis, *Historia Æcclesiastica*, 6: 490 ("cum exercitu Galliæ"). The chronicle of Morigny describes the group as "militum agmina non parva" and says that "ad ampliacionem regii comitatus urbes et opida suorum multitudinem habitatorum emittunt": *Chronique de Morigny*, 66.

[145] Luchaire, *Louis VI . . . Annales*, 264, no. 580. *Chronique de Morigny*, 66, mentions the two counts, and also Guillaume, count of Nevers, Rotrou, count of Perche, and Geffroy, bishop of Chartres. Geffroy of Vigeois states that the archbishop of Tours, Hugues de la Ferté, and Archbishop Alberic of Bourges were at Saint-Martial of Limoges on 29 and 30 June 1137, for the celebration of the patron's feast on 30 June. Describing the arrival of the young Louis on 1 July, he remarks that after a triumphal procession at Saint-Martial the king and princes fixed their tents near the River Vienne. He notes as present there ("aderant ibi") the two counts, Peter the Venerable, Suger, and Abbots Amlardus of Saint-Martial and Ademar of Vigeois: *Chronicon*, in *Recueil des historiens*, 12: 435. He gives no list of those who departed with Louis for Bordeaux, but Suger certainly accompanied the young king, and it seems likely that Peter the Venerable and the other two abbots did so. Geffroy gives details about Louis' marriage that he could have learned from the abbots of Saint-Martial and Vigeois on their return; had Peter the Venerable been at Saint-Martial for the saint's feast before Louis' arrival, it seems likely that Geffroy would have noted this. No additional evidence regarding Peter's whereabouts in the summer of 1137 survives; he had visited Aquitaine at least twice before, in 1125 and between 1130 and 1134: Constable, ed., *Letters of Peter the Venerable*, 2: 260, 335-39.

[146] Suger (*Vie de Louis VI*, ed. Waquet, 280) states "Nos autem familiares ejus et quoscumque sanioris consilii repperire potuit ei concopulavit."

Abbot Suger had been involved in planning Louis' coronation in 1131, and he may well have played a major part six years later in determining the form of the ceremony and the contents of the *ordo.*[147] Renowned for his knowledge of the early history of the Franks, particularly interested in Charles the Bald, he doubtless knew the histories gathered in the miscellany treasured at his abbey and would have paid special attention to the sections that concerned Charles the Bald.[148] There he would have found the phrases *francia burgundia & aquitania* and *franci. burgundiones. & aquitanenses,* in passages describing both Charles the Bald's achievements and the election of Eudes. He would have recognized the appropriateness of introducing, in an *ordo* intended for Louis and Eleanor, a formula based on these phrases. The phrase would have appealed to the Aquitanians and would have been particularly fitting for ceremonies signaling the union of Aquitaine and Poitou with the *regnum Francorum.*[149]

This argument suggests the possibility that a version of the *ordo* which was modified to include the formula "Franks, Burgundians, and Aquitanians" was already being used for the coronation of the kings of France. This is likely—although not surely—the case. The memorandum that Archbishop Gervais of Reims wrote to commemorate the coronation of Philip I in 1059 at first sight suggests that an *ordo* of the Ratold family could not have been employed on that occasion. According to Gervais, at the beginning of the ceremony Philip (then only seven years old) received, read, and subscribed a profession or pledge. This included not only the *promissio regis* to protect and defend the church's rights which is

[147] See 41 below. Suger was one of the witnesses to Louis VI's charter in favor of the churches of Bordeaux; Luchaire, *Louis VI . . . Annales,* 265, no. 581; see 36 above.

[148] Suger's biographer, Guillaume of Saint-Denis, wrote of him "Erat illi historiarum summa notitia. ut quemcumque illi nominasses francorum regem uel principem. statim eius gesta inoffensa uelocitate percurreret," and "Omni tempore uel estatis uel hiemis. quoniam sompno contentus erat breuissimo. post cenam aut legebat aut legentem diutius audiebat. aut considentes exemplis instruebat illustribus. Lectio quidem erat de libris patrum auctenticis. aliquando de ecclesiasticis aliquid legebatur historiis": BN, lat. 14192, fols. 2r, 5r-v; in Suger, *Œuvres complètes,* 382, 389. The *Historia ecclesiastica* of Hugues of Fleury was copied in the historical miscellany of Saint-Denis (Paris, Bibliothèque Mazarine, MS 2013; see n. 124 above), and William's reference to *ecclesiasticis historiis* may allude to this work. In his *Life of Louis VII,* Suger included a reference to Herbert of Vermandois and Charles the Simple that is reminiscent of—although it does not reproduce verbatim—a passage from the chronicle *Ex genere Priami,* copied in the miscellany: Suger, *Vie de Louis le Gros,* ed. Molinier, 155; Paris, Bibliothèque Mazarine, MS 2013, fol. 171r; see also Lair, "Fragment inédit," 586-87.

[149] Orderic Vitalis commented of the coronation at Poitiers, "et sic regnum Francorum et Aquitaniæ ducatum quem nullus patrum suorum habuit nactus est": *Historia Æcclesiastica,* 6: 490. He also noted (ibid., 6: 508) the presence at Louis VII's Christmas court at Bourges in 1138 "nobilium et mediocrium uirorum de omni Gallia et Aquitania aliisque circumsitis nationibus." See also Chaplais, "Traité de Paris," 131-32, and 36 above.

found at the beginning of the *ordo* of lat. 14192 and similar ceremonials, but also the pledge that he would "by his authority confirm to the people entrusted to him the guardianship of laws to which they were rightfully entitled."[150] The appearance *before the consecration* of a profession including the promise to rule the people lawfully is striking: in none of the *ordines* of the Ratold family does such a promise precede the service. Rather, they all commence with the king's simple undertaking to protect and defend the church's rights, and at the end come the three *precepta:* that church and people will always preserve true peace[151]; that the king will forbid rapacity and iniquity; that he will judge equitably and mercifully. In the second (B) version of the second English *ordo* (*ca* 960-973),[152] these pledges were transferred to the beginning of the ceremony, but the first evidence of similar modification in any French *ordo* of the Ratold family occurs in a thirteenth-century notation added to a late-twelfth-century copy in a pontifical of the cathedral of Reims.[153] The practice observed at Philip I's consecration may possibly reflect English influence or distant French precedents; it may represent a first step toward later developments in France.

---

[150] "Ego philippus deo propitiante mox futurus rex francorum in die ordinationis mee. promitto coram deo & sanctis eius quod unicuique de uobis [& ecclesiis uobis] commissis. canonicum priuilegium & debitam legem. atque. iustitiam conservabo. & defensionem quantum potuero adiuvante domino exhibebo. sicut rex in suo regno. unicuique episcopo & Ecclesie sibi commisse. per rectum exhibere debet. Populo quoque nobis credito. me dispensationem legum. in suo iure consistentem. nostra auctoritate concessurum": BAV, Ottobon. lat. 811, fol. 113r (which entitles the memorandum "Exemplar Regis Professionis"); in Du Chesne, *Scriptores*, 4: 161-62; and *Recueil des historiens*, 11: 32; cf. *Sacrosancta Concilia*, 12: 55 (the text from Beauvais, which contains the bracketed words); see n. 88 above. In his *Recueil des Roys* for Charles IX (BN, fr. 2848, fol. 165r), Du Tillet translated the text from Beauvais, rendering the oath, "Je Philippes par la grace de dieu prochain d'estre ordonné Roy de france promectz ou Jour de mon sacre deuant dieu et ses sainctz que Je conserueray le priuilege canonique loy et Justice deue a vng chacun de vous prelatz, et vous defendray tant que Je pourray (dieu aydant) comme vng Roy doit par droit defendre en son Royaume chacun euesque et leglise a luy commise, Et octroyeray au peuple a nous commis la defense des loix en leur droict consistant en nostre auctorité." See Schramm, "Krönung," 188-89; and idem, *Kaiser*, 2: 196-97. In "Les étapes," 210-11, Guillot discusses earlier pre-coronation pledges; see also Bautier, "Sacres," 14-15, 45-48.

[151] See 40, 42 below; Ward, "Early Version," 357. In "Les *Ordines*," 64-65, "Composition and Transmission," and "Manuscripts, Texts," 47-48, Jackson discusses the syntactical problems associated with the oath as it appears in the Ratold *ordo* and shows how the pledge was later modified so that, in the changed wording, all Christian people, under the king's guidance, would preserve true peace for the church of God.

[152] Nelson, "Second English *Ordo*," 369-74.

[153] Reims, BM, MS 342, fol. 70r. See n. 109 above, and Jackson, "*Ordines*," 64-65. In the *ordo* of Reims, the *ordo* of 1250, and subsequent *ordines*, the *promissio regis* and the *tria precepta*, augmented after the Lateran Council of 1215 by a fourth pledge to expel heretics, were combined into a single, five-part oath that the king swore at the beginning of the coronation ceremony: *Ceremonial*, ed. Godefroy, 1: 14, 27; 104 below (the *Ordo maior* of Croix); *Coronation Book*, ed. Dewick, 19. See David, "Serment du sacre," 236-41; cf. Schramm, "Krönung," 188-90; idem, *Kaiser*, 196-98.

But what *ordo* was employed in 1059? On this point there is no certainty. The pledge concerning the dispensation of laws to the people that Gervais records is unusual. It resembles a clause of the *professio* of Louis the Stammerer at Compiègne in 877, where he declared that he would "preserve the laws and statutes to the people committed to [him] by God's mercy to rule"; it is also striking that Louis "reread and confirmed [his promise] by his own hand,"[154] for Gervais emphasized that Philip I read and subscribed his *professio*. Philip's pledge regarding the laws has only the slightest connection with the final precept at the end of the Ratold *ordo* (and the *ordo* of lat. 14192): "that the king will render equity and mercy in all judgments so that to him and us the clement and merciful God may grant his mercy."[155] There is equally little reason to associate the pledge with the third of the royal promises in the German coronation *ordo:* that the king should "rule and defend the kingdom granted him by God according to the justice of his fathers."[156] This *ordo* includes no *promissio regis* at the commencement and hence is far less similar to the form described in Gervais' memorandum than are the French *ordines* related to the Ratold *ordo* and the *ordo* of BN, lat. 13315. Yet, as Marcel David and Richard A. Jackson point out, the archbishop's exposition of the Catholic faith and the king's endorsement of and promise to defend it (before the royal profession) and the general acclamation of the king (at the end of the service) are reminiscent of practices associated with East Frankish and German usage.[157] The *ordo* of 1059 may well have been Gervais' cre-

[154] "Polliceor etiam me servaturum leges et statuta populo, qui mihi ad regendum misericordia Dei committitur, pro communi consilio fidelium nostrorum. . . . [R]ectitudinis et iustitiae amore hanc spontaneam promissionem meam relegens manu propria firmavi": MGH, *Legum Sectio II, Capitularia,* 2^2: 364, no. 283. Then follows the king's promise to conserve and defend bishops and churches, given in response to the bishops' petition: ibid., 365. In "Manuscripts, Texts," 68, Jackson observes that Philip's pledge "differs from the older text in important ways." Bautier postulates, on the basis of a monogram found in a copy of the act, that in 888 Eudes not only made a verbal *promissio* but also subscribed a written document: *Recueil des actes d'Eudes*, 210-11, no. 54; see also Bautier, "Sacres," 44-48.

[155] "Tertium est ut in omnibus iudiciis aequitatem & misericordiam praecipiat. ut illi & nobis indulgeat suam misericordiam clemens & misericors deus": Ward, "Early Version," 357. See also 96 below, for the reading in the *ordo* of lat. 14192.

[156] "Vis regnum tibi a Deo concessum secundum justiciam patrum tuorum regere et defendere," with the response, "In quantum divino fultus adjutorio ac solatio omnium fidelium suorum valuero, ita me per omnia fideliter acturum esse promitto": Waitz, "Die Formeln," 85.

[157] " . . . exposuit ei fidem catholicam. sciscitans ab eo utrum hanc crederet. & defendere uellet. Quo annuente delata eius professio. quam accipiens ipse legit. dum adhuc septennis esset. eique subscripsit"; "laudauerunt ter proclamantes. laudamus uolumus. fiat": BAV, Ottobon. lat. 811, fols. 113, 114; in Du Chesne, *Scriptores*, 4: 161-62; and *Recueil*

ation, based on one or more available texts and *ordines*—East Frankish, as well as an *ordo* of the Ratold family, perhaps the parent text of the *ordo* of lat. 14192.[158] As Jackson emphasizes, there are no grounds for assuming that a particular *ordo* was ever considered prescriptive. It is far more likely that various ceremonials were modified, adapted, and combined to suit the needs of the moment.[159]

There is no clearer evidence about the form of the *ordo* used in 1108 for the coronation of Louis VI at Orléans by Daimbert, archbishop of Sens. In this case, the only source that describes the ceremony is the account given by Abbot Suger in his *Life of Louis VI*. Suger says that after anointing Louis and celebrating a mass of thanksgiving, the archbishop of Sens "took from Louis the sword of secular warfare and girded him with the ecclesiastical sword intended for the punishment of evil-doers, happily crowned him with the diadem of the kingdom, and most devoutly invested him with the scepter and rod (and, through these, with the defense of churches and the poor), and with various royal insignia."[160]

The performance of the mass before the anointing and the bestowal of the regalia casts no light on the identity of the *ordo* used in 1108, since the placement of the mass at coronations varied. The *ordines* of the Ratold group give no specific instructions on the point, and in 1059 the mass commenced before the king took his oath and was crowned.[161] But the terms that Suger uses to describe the royal paraphernalia are similar to those employed in the *ordines* of the Ratold family,[162] and statements that Suger made regarding the obligations which the coronation oath imposed on the king indicate that Louis' pledges included those

des historiens, 11: 32-33; cf. *Sacrosancta Concilia*, 12: 55 (which reads "quod annuente"); see also David, "Serment du sacre," 184; Jackson, "Manuscripts, Texts," 50-52, 68; Bouman, *Sacring*, 27, 30, 158 n. 17.

[158] Schramm, *König*, 1: 100; Jackson, *Vive le Roi!*, 222 (Fr. ed., 207); idem, "Manuscripts, Texts," 50-52, 68.

[159] Jackson, "Manuscripts, Texts," 52, 68. A contemporary description of preparations for the coronation of Charles VIII in 1484 records, however, that ecclesiastics and others reviewed and compared "les anciens Liures, & Ordinaires du mystere" in the expectation that the ceremony which they confected would obviate the need for similar research in the future: *Ceremonial*, ed. Godefroy, 1: 191; Jackson, *Vive le Roi!*, 40 (Fr. ed., 42-43).

[160] ". . . sacratissime unctionis liquore delibutum, missas gratiarum agens abjectoque secularis militie gladio ecclesiastico ad vindictam malefactorum accingens, diademate regni gratanter coronavit necnon et sceptrum et virgam et per hec ecclesiarum et pauperum defensionem et quecumque regni insignia, approbante clero et populo, devotissime contradidit": Suger, *Vie de Louis VI*, ed. Waquet, 86; on the ceremony, Luchaire, *Louis VI . . . Annales*, 30-31, no. 57; Bautier, "Sacres," 54.

[161] *Recueil des historiens*, 12: 30; Schramm, *König*, 1: 100.

[162] Schramm, "Krönung," 186; idem, *Kaiser*, 2: 195; idem, *König*, 1: 119-20; David, "Serment du sacre," 182-83, 186; see also Lewis, *Royal Succession*, 53-54 (Fr. ed., 84-85).

found in such *ordines*. Thus, in his *Life of Louis VI* Suger says that because of their oath of office ("offitii jure votivo") kings repress the boldness of tyrants who pillage, disturb the poor, and destroy churches.[163] In a letter to Louis VII written in 1149, he reminded the king of the profession and oath "that [he] made when [he] received the crown of the kingdom," which Suger implies bound the king to defend the kingdom from those who disturbed the realm ("perturbatores").[164] The abbot's assertions have suggestive links to the second of those *ordines'* three coronation precepts ("to forbid rapacity and all evil acts to all people") and to the more general first precept ("ut ecclesia dei & omnis populus christianus ueram pacem seruet [*sic*] in omni tempore"), provided that syntactically confused statement is interpreted to imply the king's duty to see that "true peace" is maintained.[165] Suger's declarations also recall the *promissio* that King Eudes made in 888, to defend ecclesiastics and their churches "contra depredatores et oppressores,"[166] and the oath taken by Louis VI in 1108 may have been influenced by this widely-known and venerable precedent. The oath that Louis swore could have been devised for the occasion; Louis needed the support of the ecclesiastics in attendance and was in no position to resist suggestions regarding ceremonial that they may have made.

Suger's testimony does not preclude the use of an *ordo* of the Ratold family in 1108, but it offers no sure resolution of the issue. One fact deserves emphasis. Never does Suger say that he attended the ceremony, and given his character, it is difficult to imagine that he would have failed to mention the fact if he had been present.[167] He did not write the *Life of Louis VI* until 1143 or 1144, some thirty-five years after Louis' coronation, and, as in the case of the monk of Ramsey who described the coronation of

[163] ". . . offitii jure votivo, reprimitur tirannorum audacia, quotiens eos guerris lacessiri vident, infinita gratulantur rapere, pauperes confundere, ecclesias destruere": Suger, *Vie de Louis VI*, ed. Waquet, 172-74.

[164] "Redierunt regni perturbatores; et tu, qui defendere deberes, quasi captivatus exulas. . . . Rogamus igitur celsitudinem tuam . . . ne post transitum Paschæ ibi vel modicum demoreris, ne reus professionis et juramenti quod in susceptione coronæ regno fecisti in oculis Dei appareas": Suger, *Œuvres complètes*, 259. In "Suger's Views," 51, Lewis analyzes the significance of Suger's terminology.

[165] Jackson, "Manuscripts, Texts," 47-48; n. 151 above; 96 below.

[166] *Recueil des actes d'Eudes*, 209-11, no. 54; MGH, *Legum Sectio II, Capitularia*, 2[2]: 376, no. 288; Schramm, "Krönung," 134-36; idem, *Kaiser*, 2: 153-55, 214; Bautier, "Sacres," 48.

[167] In his *Life of Louis VI*, Suger mentions a number of missions that he carried out for Saint-Denis between 1106 and 1112: *Vie de Louis VI*, ed. Waquet, vi-vii, 48, 52, 56-60, 66, and xi (the date of the *Life*); Lewis, *Royal Succession*, 53 (Fr. ed., 84).

Edgar of England in 973 thirty years after the event,[168] Suger's account of Louis' coronation may have been influenced by an *ordo* that he came to know in the years following the consecration.

No evidence survives concerning the *ordines* used at the coronations of Adelaide of Maurienne in Paris in 1115, of Adelaide's and Louis VI's twelve-year-old son Philip at Reims in 1129, and, after Philip's tragic death, of their ten-year-old son Louis (the future husband of Eleanor of Aquitaine), again at Reims, just twelve days after his brother's death, on 25 October 1131.[169] In this case, the fact that Louis was crowned by Pope Innocent II in the presence of ecclesiastics from many lands, assembled for the council over which the pope was presiding, diverted attention from the ceremony itself. Suger claims for himself and the king's other familiars credit for advising the king to have his son, "crowned with the royal diadem, elevated as king by the unction of the holy liquor."[170] He reports that at the ceremony the boy was made king "by the unction of holy oil and the wearing of the kingdom's crown."[171] He says nothing more about the service, nor does he explicitly indicate that he was present, although on 2 November 1131 he obtained from the pope two privileges for Saint-Denis.[172] The chronicle of Morigny gives a rich description of the pope's impressive reception of the royal entourage on 24 October and the route of march followed for the coronation the next day.[173] No more than Suger, however, does the chronicler give details about

[168] Ward, "Coronation Ceremony," 169 (sources for the coronation of 973).

[169] Luchaire, *Louis VI . . . Annales*, 97, no. 192; 200-201, no. 433; 221, no. 476. Prince Philip's age is discussed in Waquet, ed., Suger, *Vie de Louis VI*, 267 n. 2; *Chronique de Morigny*, 55, calls Philip "plus minus quatuordecim" at the time of his death, which occurred "a consecratione vero duos [annos] et sex menses." The chronicle (ibid., 59) refers to Louis as "puerulum decem annos plus minus habentem" when he was crowned.

[170] "Qui ergo intimi ejus et familiares eramus . . . consuluimus ei quatinus filium Ludovicum . . . regio diademate coronatum, sacri liquoris unctione regem secum . . . constitueret. Qui consiliis nostris adquiescens . . . ": Suger, *Vie de Louis VI*, ed. Waquet, 266-68. In contrast, the chronicle of Morigny emphasizes the role of the pope and the papal legates who visited the king, saying that after their arrival to console him for the death of his son Philip, "Initur consilium, ut rex quantocius ad concilium [over which Innocent was presiding at Reims] propararet et Ludovicum filium . . . subrogaret in regem": *Chronique de Morigny*, 56. Orderic Vitalis, *Historia Æcclesiastica*, 6: 422, says that the king, queen, and "tota nobilitas Franciæ" petitioned the pope for Prince Louis' coronation and calls attention to the machinations of "some people" (*quosdam*) "qui progeniem eius a regni fastigio alienare moliti sunt." See Bur, *Suger*, 155-56.

[171] " . . . sacri olei unctione et corone regni deportacione in regem sublimatum, felicem providit regno successorem": Suger, *Vie de Louis VI*, ed. Waquet, 268.

[172] Cartellieri, *Abt Suger*, 136-37, nos. 75-76; Bur, *Suger*, 156.

[173] *Chronique de Morigny*, 56-59, esp. 58-59, describes the pope's garb and his procession from the archiepiscopal palace to the church of Saint-Remi, where the king and his son were staying; the ceremonious progress of the pope and young Louis to the cathedral church; and their reception at the church by king, prelates, and nobles.

the service, although like Suger he stresses the unction, saying that Louis was anointed with the heaven-sent oil with which Saint Remi had anointed Clovis.[174]

These two witnesses provide the first unimpeachable evidence of the use of the holy oil at a coronation ceremony since 869—a legend and rite that, once proclaimed and instituted, were generally adopted.[175] In his *Philippidos libri XII*,[176] composed between 1214 and 1224/25, ninety years later, Guillaume le Breton expatiated on the antiquity and virtues of the holy oil, proclaiming that it had been sent by God, "by angelic hands," for the coronation of Clovis and all future kings of France, and had been used for all consecrations since Clovis'—including that of Philip Augustus in 1179.[177] The phrases that Guillaume employed—*liquor, sacra unctio, sanctum oleum, angelicis manibus, detulit angelus*—recall those of the chronicler of Morigny and of Suger, whose work Guillaume must have known. Suger's account of the young Louis' coronation indeed suggests that it was he and Louis VI's other councilors who advised the use of the oil to anoint the boy once he had been crowned by the royal diadem.[178] He lays more emphasis on unction than on coronation. Rather than describing Louis as "regio diademate coronatum, sacro liquore unctum," he wrote that

---

[174] "Intrant ecclesiam, puerum ad altare presentant, et oleo quo sanctus Remigius per angelicam manum sibi presentato Clodoveum regem Francorum in christianum unxerat, puerulum . . . cum ingenti tripudio dominus papa consecravit": *Chronique de Morigny*, 59; Schramm, *König*, 1: 147.

[175] Hinkle, *Portal of the Saints*, 37-40, analyzes the development of the legend of the holy oil, pointing to the long silence between 1131 and the earliest prior reference, Hincmar's allusion to it in connection with the coronation of Charles the Bald at Metz in 869. In his *Recueil des Roys*, Du Tillet stressed Hincmar's role: see n. 240 below. See Bautier, "Sacres," 38-39.

[176] Delaborde, ed., *Œuvres de Rigord et de Guillaume le Breton*, 1: lxviii-lxx; Brown, "Notion de la légitimité," 81-82 (esp. n. 20).

[177] Guillaume le Breton, *Philippidos libri XII*, in *Œuvres de Rigord et de Guillaume le Breton*, 2: 14-15, 20-21 (emphasizing the rights of Reims, 21); Delaborde, ibid., 1: lxxi-iii (the date of the work); Schramm, *König*, 1: 148, and 2: 97 nn. 2-3; Hinkle, *Portal of the Saints*, 37-39; Jackson, "Manuscripts, Texts," 65-68. Schramm and, in greater detail, Hinkle and Jackson point out that there is no other contemporary evidence regarding the use of the holy oil for Philip Augustus' coronation, but this does not mean that the testimony of Guillaume le Breton is worthless: Bournazel and Poly, "Couronne et mouvance," 227-28, 232-33. Hinkle convincingly argues that the Dyonisian historian Rigord failed to allude to the oil in 1179 because of royal antipathy to the claims of Reims, which he believes prompted Philip Augustus' coronation with his wife at Saint-Denis in 1180. The emphasis that Rigord lays on the accidental spilling of what he calls heaven-sent oil on the heads of the king and queen in 1180 suggests to me that a special oil may well have been used at Reims in 1179: *Œuvres de Rigord et de Guillaume le Breton*, 1: 20-22; see also Bournazel and Poly as cited above; and n. 191 below.

[178] Jackson ("Manuscripts, Texts," 66-67) persuasively stresses the importance of the legend in buttressing the right of Reims to serve as the site of the coronation, which Guillaume le Breton emphasizes: *Œuvres de Rigord et de Guillaume le Breton*, 2: 21, verses 347-49; Schramm, *König*, 1: 148; Bautier, "Sacres," 38 (Hincmar), and 14, 22 (coronation and unction).

"regio diademate coronatum," he was to be constituted as king "sacri liquoris unctione," thus indicating that it was *by* the unction that the young man would be made king. Yet this important aspect of the ritual would not necessarily have affected the form of the service.

The testimony regarding eleventh- and early-twelfth-century coronations is, in sum, frustratingly scanty and inconclusive—although it does not rule out the use of an *ordo* of the Ratold family, and indeed of the form of service recorded in the *ordo* of lat. 14192. If this *ordo,* complete with Franks, Burgundians, and Aquitanians, was in fact employed, the BN copy would simply be the single surviving witness to a ceremonial often observed. If this were the case, however, it would be hard to explain why so many manuscripts, earlier and later, witness the popularity of the form of the *ordo* with Saxons, Mercians, and Northumbrians, and why the *ordo* with Franks, Burgundians, and Aquitanians is so rare. Thus it seems most likely that a version of the Ratold *ordo* containing the phrase "Saxons, Mercians, and Northumbrians" was known and perhaps being utilized in France by the first decades of the twelfth century, and that it served as the source of the *ordo* of lat. 14192 precisely because it was thought authoritative and appropriate, and possibly because it was traditional for the king's coronation.

Another problem remains. The most significant difference between the *ordo* of lat. 14192 and the other *ordines* of the Ratold family occurs in the prayer for the consecration of the king—not in the queen's ceremonial. Why would an *ordo* containing a coronation ceremony for both king and queen have been prepared and copied for the consecration of a woman whose future husband had been crowned at Reims six years earlier? Note, however: only one medieval *ordo* containing simply the queen's ceremonial survives. This suggests that redactors may have had good reason for including ceremonials for the king as well as the queen in their compilations.[179] Such would not be the case, of course, if kings who had already been consecrated were simply expected to wear their crowns at the queen's ceremony "to honor the solemnity," as Gislebert of Mons wrote of the coronation of Isabelle, wife of Philip Augustus, in 1180, and as Jean du Tillet later put it.[180] Under these circumstances the ritual for

---

[179] I owe this information to Richard A. Jackson.

[180] In his *Chronicon,* written shortly after 1200, Gislebert of Mons says that at the consecration and coronation of Philip Augustus' wife Isabelle at Saint-Denis in 1180, the king "ad sue nupte noveque regine honorem, regalem cum ea gestavit coronam": MGH,

consecrating a king would have been superfluous in ceremonials fashioned for a queen's coronation. Such services may, however, have included at least some portions of the king's *ordo*, and this may have happened when Louis wedded Eleanor of Aquitaine.

There were precedents for second coronations of kings,[181] and in the twelfth century it was not unusual for a king to wear a crown at the coronation of his queen. On 29 January 1121, when Henry I of England (1100-35) married his second wife Adela, daughter of Godfrey VII of Louvain, duke of Lower Lorraine, he was enthroned and crowned for the ceremony; the fact that the archbishop of Canterbury had not placed the crown on the king's head led to discussion, and ultimately to the archbishop's removing and replacing the diadem.[182] Later, an eye-witness to the coronation in 1160 of Louis VII's third wife, Adele of Champagne, which was held at Notre-Dame of Paris, wrote that Hugues, archbishop of Sens, "anointed her and crowned the king with her."[183] What rituals were performed on these occasions is unknown; in two other cases, however, contemporaries regarded similar ceremonies as second coronations of the kings who participated in them.

The first coronation of the young Henry, son of Henry II of England (1154-89), occurred when he was fifteen. It took place at Westminster on 14 June 1170, and because of Henry II's struggles

---

Scriptorum, 21: 529. Having stated that Philip Augustus wore his crown for this occasion, Du Tillet (*Recveil des Roys*, 186) remarked that Louis VII likewise "was present, crowned," at the coronation of his third wife, "pour honnorer la solennité."

[181] Schramm, "Krönung," 120-26 (the second coronation of Louis II in 878), 138-41 (the second coronation of Eudes in 888), and ibid., 141 (these ceremonies distinguished from later festival crown-wearings); idem, *Kaiser*, 2: 143-48, 155-58, 188. Guillot persuasively suggests that the second coronation of Eudes at Reims on 13 November 888 signaled his actual accession: "Les étapes," 207-23. Brühl ("Fränkischer Krönungsbrauch," 265-326) discusses ninth-century precedents for crown-wearings and second coronations; see also Marlot, *Theatre d'Honnevr*, 403-14; idem, *Histoire de la ville, cité et université de Reims*, 3: 193-96, 285-86. Schramm considers Louis VII's different coronations as festival crown-wearings: *König*, 1: 126, 128-30; cf. 122-23; see also Orderic Vitalis, *Historia Æcclesiastica*, 6: 308 (Christmas 1138 at Bourges). In "Sacres," Bautier stresses the frequency of multiple coronations and unctions under the Carolingians.

[182] Eadmer, *Historia novorum*, 292-93; Du Cange, "Dissertation V," in idem, *Histoire de S. Lovys*, pt. 2, 163, and in idem, *Glossarium*, 7: 22 (at end). Following his coronation at London, Henry II (1154-89) was crowned at Lincoln in 1158 and at Easter of 1159 at Worcester with Eleanor of Aquitaine; in 1159 he and Eleanor deposed their crowns on the altar and vowed never to wear them again: Du Cange, ibid.; Roger of Howden, *Chronica*, 1: 213, 216.

[183] " . . . eam inunxit regemque cum ipsa coronavit": Suger, *Vie de Louis VI*, ed. Waquet, 167. The chronicle of Saint-Pierre-le-Vif of Sens states, more fully, "Rex vero Ludovicus . . . accepit in conjugem filiam . . . comitis Theobaudi, quam postmodum predictus Hugo, Senonensis archiepiscopus, Parisius in reginam unxit, ipsamque cum domino suo rege Ludovico, ipsa die, . . . in ecclesia Beate Marie coronavit et in eadem ecclesia . . . misse officium sollempniter celebravit": *Chronique de Saint-Pierre-le-Vif*, 204. Robert of Auxerre reproduced this passage in his chronicle: Auxerre, BM, MS 123, fol. 303r; in MGH, *Scriptorum*, 26: 237-38. See Bautier, "Sacres," 55.

with Archbishop Thomas Becket of Canterbury, Roger of Pont-l'Evêque, archbishop of York, officiated. For reasons that remain obscure, Marguerite, daughter of Louis VII of France and Henry's wife of ten years, was not installed as queen when the young prince was crowned—which greatly angered her father.[184] After hostile exchanges and protracted negotiation, she was consecrated, and the young king Henry and she were crowned together at Winchester on 27 August 1172, by Rotrou, archbishop of Rouen.[185] Henry II's repentance for the murder of Becket and, even more, his desire to placate Louis VII may account for the elaborateness of the ceremony in 1172; one source (generally well-informed) indicates that the archbishop crowned the young Henry before proceeding to the consecration of his wife.[186] Contemporary historians—the author of the *Gesta Regis Henrici secundi* (1171-*ca* 1192), Roger of Howden (d. post 1201), and Gervase of Canterbury (d. *ca* 1210)—all considered it young Henry's second coronation, although they made it clear that only Marguerite was consecrated.[187]

Similarly, when in 1180 Philip Augustus (crowned in 1179) was married to Isabelle of Hainaut at Saint-Denis, the Dyonisian historian Rigord reports that Philip "placed the diadem on himself for the second time, and then Elizabeth [Isabelle], his venerable queen, was anointed." The abbey church, he declared, was filled with people who wanted to see the king and queen "distinguished by diadems."[188] Rigord's assertion that Philip Augustus

[184] Barlow, *Thomas Becket*, 55, 57, 61, 67-68, 206-7. Such episodes as these, rare as they were, gave rise to idiosyncratic interpretations. Two English annalists say that Henry II "filio suo . . . diadema imposuit"; the annalist of Waverley states that the king "semetipsum deposuit": *Annales monastici*, 1: 50 (Annals of Tewkesbury, to 1263); 2: 239 (Annals of Waverley, to 1291).

[185] *Gesta Regis Henrici secundi* (1: 31) distinguishes with particular care, saying that the archbishop "Henricum regem juniorem coronavit, et eadem die unxit in reginam et consecravit et coronavit Margaretam filiam regis Franciæ."

[186] See the preceding note, and for the *Gesta*, Gransden, *Historical Writing*, 222-25.

[187] *Gesta Regis Henrici secundi*, 2: 5-6, 30-31; Roger of Howden, *Chronica*, 2: 4-6, 34-36; Gervase of Canterbury, *Chronicle*, 1: 219-20, 237. Robert of Torigny, abbot of Mont-Saint-Michel (1154-86), having said that Henry was "crowned" (*coronari*) in 1170, states that in 1172 the officiants anointed the queen "et coronaverunt regem et uxorem ejus": *Chronique*, ed. Delisle, 2: 17; *Chronicle*, ed. Howlett, 245. Ralph Diceto (d. *ca* 1201) simply states that the queen was consecrated and the "diadema regni" placed on her husband's head: *Ymagines*, 1: 352. On the English historians, Gransden, *Historical Writing*; for Robert of Torigny, Molinier and Polain, *Sources*, no. 2204. See also Barlow, *Thomas Becket*, 206-7; Heslin, "Coronation," 165-78.

[188] ". . . quarto kalendas junii, . . . in ecclesia Beati Dionysii, ad suggestionem et consilium cujusdam boni viri qui zelum dei videbatur habere, idem rex Philippus secundo imposuit sibi diadema, et tunc inuncta fuit Elisabeth uxor ejus venerabilis regina . . . et ut viderent regem et reginam diademate insignitos conflictum cum tumultu facerent": *Œuvres de Rigord et de Guillaume le Breton*, 1: 20-21 (esp. n. 7 [the possible identity of the "bonus vir"]); Cartellieri, *Philip II*, 1: 68. One of the two versions of the Annals of

crowned himself is surely not to be taken literally, but his account does show that the king was crowned at his wife's consecration.[189] Rigord, dedicated champion of Saint-Denis, emphasized the importance of the ceremony and excluded elements that detracted from its dignity. Thus his description of the service was elliptical, probably because he wished to avoid emphasizing the role played at Saint-Denis by Guido, archbishop of Sens, who roused the ire of Guillaume, archbishop of Reims, by performing the ritual. Rigord does not mention the indignation of the archbishop, Philip Augustus' maternal uncle, whose importance at Philip's coronation in 1179 he had stressed[190]; he refers to Guido simply as archbishop without mentioning Sens and restricts his role to the bestowal of "the nuptial benediction" on the king and queen. Elevating the ceremony's significance, Rigord interpreted as a miracle the accidental spilling of oil from the three lamps above the main altar onto the heads of the king and queen, viewing it as a heaven-sent sign of the plenitude of gifts of the Holy Spirit that effectively transformed the occasion into a consecration of both king and queen.[191]

The accounts of other historians, who lacked Rigord's intense dedication to Saint-Denis, are less oblique. Robert of Torigny wrote that in 1180 Philip Augustus and his wife were "coronati" when his wife was consecrated and noted the anger of the archbishop of Reims.[192] The English historian Roger of Howden, following the *Gesta Regis Henrici secundi,* stated that in 1180 Philip determined that he and his wife "should be crowned" and, prob-

---

Saint-Denis in BAV, Reg. lat. 309, notes that in 1180 the queen was consecrated and the king crowned; the other mentions simply the queen's coronation: Berger, "Annales," 279, 288. The ceremony is discussed in Cartellieri, *Philip II,* 1: 67-68; Baldwin, *Government of Philip Augustus,* 375-76; and Bournazel and Poly, "Couronne et mouvance," 232-33.

[189] Cartellieri, *Philip II,* 1: 67 n. 5. Thegan's description of Charlemagne at the coronation of Louis the Pious in 813 is strikingly similar: "ornavit se cultu regio et coronam capiti suo imposuit"; see Brühl, "Fränkischer Krönungsbrauch," 276-77, and also 278 (Frederick II's coronation of himself in 1245); Bautier, "Sacres," 25.

[190] *Œuvres de Rigord et de Guillaume le Breton,* 1: 12-13. Like Marlot (and perhaps following him), Brial convincingly suggests that the archbishop of Reims was excluded from the ceremony in 1180 because of the enmity that existed between him and Philippe of Alsace, count of Flanders and Philip's guardian, who had arranged for the bishop of Senlis to marry the young king to his niece at Bapaume: "Guillaume de Champagne," 510; Marlot, *Theatre d'Honnevr,* 170; idem, *Metropolis Remensis Historia,* 2: 412-13; see also Baldwin, *Government of Philip Augustus,* 15-16. Hinkle (*Portal of the Saints,* 27, 38) emphasizes the rivalry between Reims and Saint-Denis; see n. 177 above. Bautier provides background, in "Sacres," 38.

[191] ". . . in signum plenitudinis donorum Spiritus Sancti celitus missum, miraculose effusum . . . et ad dilatandam famam nominis ipsius gloriam in omnem terram circumquaque diffundendam": *Œuvres de Rigord et de Guillaume le Breton,* 1: 22; see n. 177 above, and Poly and Bournazel, "Couronne et mouvance," 233.

[192] *Chronique,* ed. Delisle, 2: 96; *Chronicle,* ed. Howlett, 290.

ably by analogy with the two coronations of the young Henry of England, treated the ensuing ceremony as the king's "second coronation" ("secunda coronatio"), commenting that the archbishop of Reims complained to the pope about the violation of his church's *dignitas*.[193] Likewise, forty-three years earlier Louis VII may well have determined that he should be ceremoniously crowned with Eleanor of Aquitaine in 1137—and also that prayers should be said for him as well as for her.

In the case of Louis and Eleanor, two reliable witnesses suggest that at Eleanor's coronation as queen of France, Louis' role was more than that of a royal spouse respectfully donning his crown. The chronicle of Morigny reports that following the marriage of Louis and Eleanor "each of them was distinguished by the imposition of golden diadems," after which Louis received pledges of fidelity and homage.[194] According to Suger, "Louis joined to himself in marriage the aforesaid maiden, crowned with him with the diadem of the kingdom," a term the abbot employed with special reference to the coronation crown.[195] These accounts indicate that, as concerned Louis, something more than a simple crown-wearing occurred in Bordeaux, and that Louis and Eleanor were crowned there together. A similar ritual seems to have been performed at Poitiers on 8 August, a week after the death of Louis VI. There, according to Orderic Vitalis, "the young Louis was crowned and thus obtained the kingdom of the Franks and the duchy of Aquitaine, which none of his ancestors had held."[196] As this statement makes clear, Louis was acceding to the rule of lands that for centuries had been independent[197]; further, he and

[193] *Gesta Regis Henrici secundi*, 1: 245 (the king's summons "ad coronationem ipsius et uxoris suæ"); 246 ("suæ [the king's] coronationis"; "fecit se et uxorem suam coronari"); Roger of Howden, *Chronica*, 2: 193-94, 197 ("statuit Philippus quod ipse et uxor ejus coronarentur"); cf. ibid., 2: 4-6, 34-35 (the two coronations of the young Henry of England); see *Gesta Regis Henrici secundi*, 1: 5, 30-31. Hinkle (*Portal of the Saints*, 27) states that the king "insisted that he be crowned again." Ralph Diceto, *Ymagines*, 2: 5, mentions only the anointing of the queen. For Gislebert of Mons, see n. 180 above. Richer used different phraseology in describing the coronation of Queen Adelaide in 982: Bautier, "Sacres," 51-52, esp. nn. 157-58.

[194] "Ibique uterque est inposicione aureorum diadematum insignitus. Ibi eciam Ludovicus fidelitatum et homachiorum pacta accepit et in proprio habere cepit": *Chronique de Morigny*, 67.

[195] ". . . prefatam puellam cum eo diademate regni coronatam sibi conjugio copulavit": Suger, *Vie de Louis VI*, ed. Waquet, 282. Suger refers (ibid., 86) to "diademate regni" in connection with the coronation of Louis VI in 1108, and (ibid., 268) to "regio diademate" (and also "corone regni") in describing the coronation of Louis VII in 1131.

[196] ". . . Ludouicus puer Pictauis coronatus est; et sic regnum Francorum et Aquitaniae ducatum quem nullus patrum suorum habuit nactus est": Orderic Vitalis, *Historia Æcclesiastica*, 6: 490. See n. 149 above.

[197] Chaplais, "Traité de Paris," 129-31, treats the relationship between the county of Poitou and the duchy of Aquitaine.

his councilors are unlikely to have been ignorant of his father's death a week earlier, which made him the sole ruler of the kingdom of France. Both at Bordeaux and, even more, at the subsequent coronation at Poitiers[198] prayers from the coronation *ordo* would have been eminently appropriate.

For such ceremonies a full coronation *ordo* would have been necessary. The service customarily employed at coronations—and particularly the one used for Louis VII's own coronation in 1131—would most naturally have been employed, although other *ordines* might well have been consulted. Such circumstances as these could—and, I believe, do—account for the confection of the *ordo* of lat. 14192. The parent *ordo*'s text would have been examined; "Franks, Burgundians, and Aquitanians" would have been introduced, probably in place of "Saxons, Mercians, and Northumbrians"; a copy in a small booklet, suitable for the journey to the south and for use at services, would have been prepared by a scribe proximate and accessible to the royal court, who would have worked in some haste.[199] Abbot Suger, dedicated student of France's past and councilor of Louis VI and his son, is the person most likely to have suggested the incorporation of Franks, Burgundians, and Aquitanians in an *ordo* intended for the consecration of Eleanor of Aquitaine as queen of France and her husband's accession, through her, to rulership of Aquitaine. His involvement with the planning of Prince Louis' coronation in 1131 would have paved the way for his intervention in 1137. After the embassy's return to the north, through Suger the *ordo* of lat. 14192 might have reached his abbey's library and remained there for a time.

If this is the case, how can the presence of the *ordo* in the cathedral library of Beauvais in the early fifteenth century be explained? Why would it have been accorded the luxurious binding that then adorned it? The possibility that it was confected at Beauvais itself seems highly unlikely, for the role that bishops of Beauvais later filled at royal coronations was not yet established.[200] Bishop Eudes II of Beauvais (1133-44) is not known to have played any part in the coronation of Eleanor of Aquitaine. He was, however, close to Suger and in 1140 attended the dedication of the new abbey church of Saint-Denis and witnessed the

[198] Luchaire, *Louis VI . . . Annales*, 268, no. 589. At the end of the twelfth century a special coronation ceremony was created for the duke of Aquitaine; this may have occurred in part because of the ceremony of 1137. Cf. Schramm, *König*, 1: 128-29.

[199] Rasmussen, "Le 'Pontifical,' " 415-16, cites "exemples de l'emploi d'un rituel particulier pour une fonction liturgique particulière, soit sous forme de rouleaux, soit sous forme de *libelli*."

[200] See 22 (esp. n. 75) above.

sealing of Suger's testament and *Ordinatio;* either he or his successor and homonym was present for the consecration of the church in 1144.[201] If the *ordo* of lat. 14192 was at the abbey, Eudes could have seen it there and been given it (or simply have taken it) and carried it back to Beauvais. The characteristics of the booklet that have been discussed—the haste with which it was prepared, the sort of decoration that adorns it—militate against the possibility that it is a copy of the original *ordo* specially made for Eudes in Paris or at Saint-Denis. Another possible source of transmission is Louis VII's brother Henri, who was bishop of Beauvais between 1149 and 1162. Henri's relations with Suger were strained because of his involvement in 1150 with a rebellion in Beauvais against the king's authority, but Suger died in 1151.[202] After his brother's divorce from Eleanor of Aquitaine in 1152, an *ordo* linked with their marriage and her coronation would have held little interest for the king or for Suger's successor, Eudes of Deuil (1151-62), and Henri might have taken it to Beauvais. There the ceremonial's connection with a failed project for integrating Aquitaine into the kingdom of France would have seemed unimportant. However the booklet reached Beauvais, as time passed the testimony it seemed to offer to the ties of Beauvais to earlier royal consecrations would have appealed to bishops elevated to the peerage and endowed with special offices at the coronation. This could account for the pride that the chapter evidently took in the small volume, reflected in the rich binding which it received. By adorning the *ordo* with a plaque bearing images of Bishops Hervé and Roger, the church's rulers in the tenth and eleventh centuries, the clerics of Beauvais may have hoped to suggest that the see's prerogatives were far more ancient than was the case.[203]

The *ordo* of lat. 14192 exercised virtually no influence during the remainder of the Middle Ages. Although a copy once existed in a pontifical of the church of Saint-Lucien of Beauvais, it seems most likely to have been made from the *ordo* of lat. 14192, housed in its splendid covers in the cathedral's library.[204] The paucity of exemplars of the ceremonial contrasts strikingly with the abundance of related *ordines* containing other English formulae, and particularly "Saxons, Mercians, and Northumbrians." Why might this be so?

---

[201] See 22-23 (esp. n. 76) above.
[202] Bur, *Suger,* 300, 303; Suger, *Œuvres complètes,* 277-80; *Gallia Christiana,* 9: 722.
[203] See 21 above.
[204] See 21-22 above.

If the *ordo* was redacted and used for the coronation of Eleanor of Aquitaine in 1137, the sad fate of the marriage may have turned Louis VII against it. He might well have been unenthusiastic about employing it for the coronation of his second wife, Constance of Castile, by Hugues, archbishop of Sens, at Orléans in 1154, or for that of his third wife, Adele of Champagne, crowned by Archbishop Hugues, this time at Notre-Dame of Paris, in 1160.[205] Having lost direct control over Aquitaine because of his divorce from Eleanor in March 1152, he might have been sensitive about an *ordo* that instructed him not to renounce the Aquitanians' scepter; given Eleanor's marriage to Henry, king of England and count of Anjou, two months after the divorce, and the birth of their first son in 1153,[206] he might have welcomed an allusion to rights to the scepters of the Saxons, Mercians, and Northumbrians. This, however, is speculative, for Louis could have chosen to assert his suzerainty over Aquitaine; he did not abandon the title *dux Aquitanorum* until August 1154, after his marriage to Constance.[207] Similar motivations might have prompted the use—or rejection—of the *ordo* of lat. 14192 for the coronation in 1179 of Louis' son Philip Augustus at Reims (attended by the young king Henry, son of Henry II of England and Queen Eleanor) and for Philip's marriage to and the coronation of Isabelle of Hainaut at Saint-Denis in 1180.

The provenance and origin of the *ordo* of lat. 14192 cannot, in the end, be firmly established. The physical characteristics of the manuscript, however, are consistent with its having been produced for the marriage of Eleanor of Aquitaine and Louis VII and for their subsequent coronation as rulers of Eleanor's lands. Abbot Suger's background, learning, and influence at the royal court suggest that he had a hand in crafting a ceremonial to be taken to the south by the embassy in which he prominently figured. If these hypotheses are justified, the *ordo* of lat. 14192 stands as testimony to the plasticity of ritual in medieval France, and to the readiness of those who planned ceremonies to adapt

[205] For Constance, Brown and Cothren, "Crusading Window," 28-29. She was sent to France in the fall of 1153, and the marriage occurred before she and Louis traveled to Compostela in October 1154: ibid.; Luchaire, *Etudes . . . Louis VII*, 65. Robert of Auxerre associated with Louis' marriage to Constance the response of Ivo of Chartres to the protests of envoys from Reims regarding the archbishop's right to consecrate the kings and queens of France; Ivo was in fact dealing with complaints registered after the coronation of Louis VI in 1108: Auxerre, BM, MS 123, fol. 302r; in MGH, *Scriptorum*, 26: 237; and MPL, 162: 193-96, no. CLXXXIX; cf. Suger, *Vie de Louis VI*, ed. Waquet, 86-88; and 33 above and also n. 136. See as well 46 (esp. n. 183) above (Adele of Champagne).

[206] Brown, "Eleanor of Aquitaine," 15-16.

[207] Berger, "Formule," 312-13, and 36, 38 above.

traditional services to the particular circumstances that confronted them. The ceremonial of lat. 14192 would have been strikingly fitted to serve the needs of Louis VI and Louis VII in 1137, emphasizing as it did the prestige and the antique heritage of the Aquitanians, the proud people whom Duke William X had entrusted to the French king's care.

Whether or not the service in the *ordo* of lat. 14192 was employed in later times, it was the ceremonial of the Ratold family featuring the Saxons, the Mercians, and the Northumbrians that was copied in numerous late-twelfth- and thirteenth-century northern French pontificals, including those of Reims. This ritual influenced those who drafted the *ordines* associated with later French coronations—the *ordo* of Reims of 1226-50, the *ordo* of 1250, and the last direct Capetian *ordo* of 1250-70.[208] In all likelihood some form of the Ratold ceremonial was employed or consulted for royal coronations until one of those *ordines* became the prime source used to plan the order of service. Whether those who organized the ceremonies or those who attended them had any thought that the consecration prayer expressed an implicit claim of the French king to dominance over the English remains a mystery.[209] Whatever the case, for four centuries the royal consecration prayer with Franks, Burgundians, and Aquitanians disappeared from view.

[208] For these dates and comments on each *ordo*, Jackson, *Vive le Roi!*, 26, 222-23 (Fr. ed., 31, 207-9); idem, "Manuscripts, Texts," 53-60. Jackson accepts the title (although not the date) that Schramm assigned to the last of the *ordines*, but since Louis XVI was considered a a representative of the third line of French kings and hence a Capetian, it seems more appropriate to designate the *ordo* the "last *direct* Capetian *ordo*." See Schramm, "Ordines-Studien II," 33-38, no. 17. The *ordo* associated with the consecration of Charles IV's wife Jeanne d'Evreux in 1326, whose differences from earlier *ordines* will be considered below, 139-42, has an even better claim to the title.

[209] Cf. Elze, "Ein Krönungsordo," 325. See 75-76, 84-85 below.

II. THE REAPPEARANCE OF "FRANKS, BURGUNDIANS, AND AQUITANIANS" IN EARLY MODERN FRANCE

1. Jean du Tillet

After four hundred years the Franks, Burgundians, and Aquitanians regained the importance that they had for a time been accorded in the twelfth century. The formula featuring them was given new life through an *ordo* promoted by two learned students of French history and royal ceremonial: Jean du Tillet (d. 1570) and Theodore Godefroy (1580-1649) and, secondarily, their sons and literary executors, Helie du Tillet, lord of Gouaix,[210] and Denys II Godefroy (1615-81).[211] Du Tillet could have seen the phrase in the *ordo* of lat. 14192 (or the copy at Saint-Lucien of Beauvais) when he worked at Beauvais in the 1550s. However it came to his attention, he was struck by its pertinence and inserted it in an *ordo* that he created by 1566. Through this ceremonial the formula acquired renown that it had not possessed in earlier times. In turn, Theodore and Denys Godefroy, who studied Du Tillet's writings,[212] assured his *ordo* and the formula enduring fame.

[210] The posthumous publication and edition of Du Tillet's works were overseen by his children, and, according to Hervé Pinoteau, Roman d'Amat, and the BN catalogue of printed books, primarily by his second son, Helie: Pinoteau, "Quelques réflexions," in idem, *Vingt-cinq ans*, 114-16, and also 100-14, esp. 100-101 (emendations and additions, and bibliography on the Du Tillet family); Roman d'Amat on Jean du Tillet in *Dictionnaire de biographie française;* see as well the publisher's introduction to the eds. of Du Tillet's works published between 1580 and 1618.

[211] On the Godefroy family, Godefroy-Ménilglaise, *Les savants Godefroy*, esp. 111-39 and 157-88; the articles by Trenard on Denis II Godefroy, and by Morembert on Theodore Godefroy, in *Dictionnaire de biographie française;* Ranum, *Artisans of Glory*, 55-56; *Ceremonial*, ed. Godefroy, 1: [4]r-v. Although the title of the book states that it was compiled by Theodore Godefroy and published ("mis en lumiere") by Denys, "Advocat en Parlement, & Historiographe du Roy," the royal privilege issued to Sebastien Cramoisy on 30 October 1648 refers to the book's contents as "Recueillies & mises en lumiere par Theodore, & Denys Godefroy, Historiographes du Roy"; *Ceremonial*, ed. Godefroy, 1: [3]v, and the title page. Denys Godefroy's "Aduertissement au Lecteur," written before Theodore's death in 1649, shows that Theodore did most of the work on the collection before 1643 but was then distracted by other duties, and that Denys saw it through to publication: ibid., fols. [4]r-[5]v. In *Sources*, 569-72, Franklin gives information concerning the *Ceremonial*.

[212] See 81-85 below (Du Tillet's *ordo*), and n. 9 above and 85 below (his *Recueil des Angloys*). Their extensive collection of texts included copies of various writings by Du Tillet: BIF, MS Godefroy 294, fols. 13[bis]r-16r (memorandum on French royal rights in Spain and

Both Du Tillet and the Godefroys twisted truth to their own purposes, for reasons that they doubtless believed justified alterations they made in their sources to make the *ordo* more credible and acceptable. To understand how they manipulated their texts and why they did so, some background is necessary.

From 1530 until he died in 1570 Jean du Tillet served four kings of France, Francis I (1515-47), Henry II (1547-59), Francis II (1559-60), and Charles IX (1560-74). Under them he held the important offices of prothonotary and secretary, and *greffier civil* of the Parlement of Paris.[213] Called upon to organize and inventory the monarchy's archives under Francis I, he conceived the plan of composing *recueils* of historical sources "to serve posterity."[214] By early 1555 he had completed the first installment, the *Recueil des Roys de France*. In it he treated the kings of France from Hugh Capet onwards, the royal house, the kingdom's history, and the monarchy's rights, prerogatives, ceremonies, and officers.

Du Tillet presented his *Recueil* to Henry II in two luxuriously bound exemplars, both decorated with the devices of the king and his mistress, Diane de Poitiers, and both carefully copied on parchment in studied parlementary script.[215] At the end of most chapters Du Tillet presented detailed inventories of the documents on which he based his narrative. Of great interest to historians and antiquarians, these lists appear to have been of less concern to Henry II. A particularly fine presentation copy, whose binding bears the interlaced initials of Henry and Queen Catherine de Medicis, contains only the discursive portions of the *Recueil*.[216] Whether the initiative for preparing this copy lay with the king or with Du Tillet, its confection suggests that Henry II was (or was thought to be) less interested in the sources on which Du Tillet had relied than in the substance of his work.

The first part of the *Recueil* contains chapters devoted to each king from Hugh Capet through Henry II, and to the various branches of the royal house. The second part turns to analysis,

Italy); MS Godefroy 532, fols. [35r-45v] (memorandum on apanages), and MS Godefroy 533, fols. [73r-78v] (memorandum on French royal rights to Savoy, Milan, Genoa, and Aragon); see also MS Godefroy 520, fols. 306r-8v (notes on the Du Tillet family). It may be no coincidence that in the dedication of his *Ceremonial de France* to Louis XIII, *ij[1]r-v, Theodore Godefroy twice referred to the work as a *Recueil*.

213 In *Histoire du Parlement de Paris*, 1: 230-36, Aubert discusses the importance of the position and the functions of the *greffier civil*.

214 Louis Regnier, lord of La Planche, "Histoire," ed. Buchon, 308-309, and ed. Mennechet, 1: 265.

215 SS, Fr. F. v. IV, No. 8/1; BN, fr. 2854. On these MSS, Brown, *Du Tillet and his* Recueils.

216 BN, fr. 18653. On the binding, Laffitte, "D'autres reliures," 435, 438; Hobson, *Humanists*, 209-11 (the binder, Gommar Estienne). On the different eds. of Du Tillet's works, see n. 9 above.

treating numerous themes related to the monarchy. Consecration and coronation are given pride of place. After chapters on the origins of the French, the titles and grandeur of their kings, and the prerogatives of their queens, Du Tillet treats coronation in the fourth chapter, before going on to regencies and numerous other topics.[217]

In the chapter on consecration Du Tillet presents a history of ceremonies extending back to the Germanic past. He discusses the holy ampulla, the privileged status of Reims as the site of royal consecration, the election of kings, the regalia, and the consecration of queens. He ends by remarking that since the consecration and coronation of Henry II and Catherine de Medicis have been sufficiently recorded, there is no need to lengthen the *Recueil* by discussing the event.[218] The inventory of sources that follows contains twelve items, only one of which—the last—is a coronation *ordo*. Du Tillet describes it as follows: "La forme et ceremonie des sacre et couronnement des Roy et Royne, est Registre en papier Jntitulé, double de plusieurs Lettres, extraictz & autres choses, assemblées de diuerses matieres et chambre des comptes Liure cotte + feuillet ix^{xx}. xix. Soubz tel signe .V."[219] This entry is neither entirely clear nor completely grammatical. It shows, however, that Du Tillet consulted the "form and ceremonial" for the consecration and coronation of the king and queen found on fol. 199 of a paper register in the Chambre des comptes, designated by a cross and entitled "Copy of several letters, extracts, and other things, assembled from various sources." The entry's significance has long been obscured, both by the printed version of the inventory, first published in 1607, which renders

---

[217] A table comparing the contents of the first and second recensions of the *Recueil des Roys* is found in Brown, *Du Tillet and his* Recueils, Appendix II.

[218] BN, fr. 2854, fol. 142v; SS, Fr. F. v. IV, No. 8/1, fol. 130v; see also n. 306 below (the coronation oath sworn by Henry II). Writing during the reign of Henry III (1574-89), Vincent Carloix, secretary for thirty-five years of François de Scepeaux, made a similar comment in his *Mémoires*, 1: 377-78 (in *Nouvelle collection*, ed. Michaud and Poujoulat, 1st ser., 9: 74). The coronation of Henry II resulted in various publications: Lelong, *Bibliothèque historique de la France*, 2: 709, nos. 26053-60. Some are fulsomely laudatory with, at best, brief descriptions of the ceremony: Chichon, *De adeptione Regni*; Lestrange, *Orationes duæ*. The anonymous *Le Sacre et covronnement du Roy Henry deuxieme de ce nom* gives a full description of the ceremony but includes only the titles of prayers. An account of the coronation published by Theodore Godefroy in 1619 in his *Ceremonial de France*, 309-38, was republished by Denys Godefroy in 1649 in *Ceremonial*, 1: 279-93; he there presented (ibid., 1: 298-310, 510-18) additional material on Henry's consecration and the coronation of Catherine de Medicis. I am grateful to Susanne Roberts for her help with the *Ceremonial de France*, which consists exclusively of sixteenth-century material; in *Titles of Honor*, 255-56, Selden discusses the *ordines* in the volume.

[219] BN, fr. 2854, fol. 144r; SS, Fr. F. v. IV, No. 8/1, fol. 131v.

"+" as "4",[220] and also by Du Tillet's phrase "et chambre des comptes," which should surely be "es chambre des comptes"—"in the Chambre des comptes." As the entry, thus deciphered, makes clear, Du Tillet had studied an *ordo* found in the register called *Croix*, which was housed in the Chambre des comptes and contained copies of important documents related to the monarchy's affairs.[221]

In his narrative Du Tillet does not refer directly to this source, although "the forms" used for consecration profoundly interested him. He began the chapter by recalling that in Germanic times "la forme de couronner et declairer les Roys de france" was elevation on a shield; he also proclaimed that, in bygone ages, "la forme . . . du couronnement des Roys" was the approval given by the assembled estates.[222] He said little of ceremonial, simply stating that "the old form" ("la vieille forme"), recorded in an account of the coronation of Philip I in 1059 (the memorandum of Archbishop Gervais of Reims),[223] could be found in a book owned by the chapter of Beauvais, that this ceremonial showed that the king was elected by the assembled estates (a custom whose demise Du Tillet approved), and (remarkably) that the king's coronation oath had not subsequently been changed.[224]

In this chapter Du Tillet was more concerned with Reims and its special status than with the rite of consecration. Reims' prerogative he linked with the creation of the twelve peers of France, asserting that this occurred at the same time as the city was made

---

[220] Du Tillet, *Recveil des Roys* (1607 ed.), 275. Because they relied on the ed. of 1587 (rather than 1607), Vic and Vaissete say of Du Tillet and Godefroy that "ils ne citent aucun registre de cette chambre où [l'ordre] se trouve": *Histoire generale* (1730-45 ed.), 3: 576, (1872-93 ed.), 7: 75.

[221] *Croix* and its contents are discussed in Langlois' preface to Petit et al., *Essai*, ii-iii, vi-vii, xi, xiv-xv.

[222] BN, fr. 2854, fol. 138v; SS, Fr. F. v. IV, No. 8/1, fol. 127r; BN, fr. 18653, fol. 66r.

[223] In the chapter on the consecration here, as well as in the *Recueil des Roys* for Charles IX and the *Recueil des honneurs et rangs des grands* of *ca* 1567 (the two latter of which include a translation of Archbishop Gervais' memorandum of 1059), Du Tillet dated the document correctly, but in the chapter on the peers in the *Recueil des Roys* for Henry II and Charles IX he assigned it to 1058: BN, fr. 2854, fols. 139v, 234r; SS, Fr. F. v. IV, No. 8/1, fols. 127v, 213v; BN, fr. 18653, fols. 67r, 97r; cf. Du Tillet, *Recveil des Roys*, 183-85, 255; ibid., 359-60 (*Recueil des honneurs et rangs*). See n. 88 above, for the Latin text of the memorandum. In *Le sacre et couronnement*, 9-11, Péré discusses Du Tillet's use of the text.

[224] BN, fr. 2854, fols. 141v-42r; SS, Fr. F. v. IV, No. 8/1, fols. 129v-30r; BN, fr. 18653, fol. 69r. I treat Du Tillet's views regarding election more fully below. Jackson discusses the background of the debate over hereditary and elective kingship in France, in "Elective Kingship," esp. 143-45 (Du Tillet and François de Belleforest); see also idem, *Vive le Roi!*, 115-27, esp. 123-24 (Fr. ed., 107-19, 115-16). The ideas of Boulainvilliers on the subject are set forth in a treatise ed. in Simon, *Un révolté*, 100-105. See also Leber, *Des cérémonies*, 252-90; Haueter, *Krönungen*, 290-98.

the site of royal coronation.[225] He spent some time musing about just when this might have happened, without reaching any firm conclusion. In the eleventh chapter of the second part of the *Recueil,* devoted to the peers of France, he pointed out that Gervais' account of the coronation of 1059 showed that the peerage had not yet been established. Du Tillet assumed that the peers would all have attended the ceremony had they existed, and Gervais' narrative showed that the bishop of Beauvais, the duke of Normandy, the count of Champagne, and the count of Toulouse were not present, and that those in attendance who would later be peers were not accorded any special rank and performed no special function. Later in the chapter Du Tillet said that he had reason to think that the establishment of the peerage had occurred between 1179, when the bishop of Langres received his county, and 1216, when Philip Augustus was assisted by the peers in judging a dispute over the county of Champagne. Thus, he declared, the institution of the peers was the work of either Louis VII or Philip Augustus.[226] His statements imply that one of the two granted Reims its prerogative, created the peers,[227] and assigned them their duties at the coronation.

After presenting this *Recueil* to Henry II, Du Tillet continued his investigation of the archives and history of France. For Henry II he wrote two additional *Recueils:* the *Recueil des Angloys,* finished by February 1558, which treats relations between France and England since the Norman Conquest; and the *Recueil des or-*

---

[225] BN, fr. 2854, fol. 141r; SS, Fr. F. v. IV, No. 8/1, fol. 129r; BN, fr. 18653, fol. 68v.

[226] "Ce qui a este deduict ou chapitre des sacre & couronnement des Roys, lesquelz n'estoit lors necessite faire a Reims, confirme que les pairs de france n'estoient encores Jnstituez, Joinct celluy du Roy Philippes premier, faict en leglise dudict Reims, lan mil cinquante huict, ouquel ne se trouuerent leuesque de Beauuays, les duc de Normandye, contes de champaigne et Tholose, et les autres qui y furent ne tindrent Ranc, et ne feyrent office que de prelatz et barons, desquelz grande partie est nommee en leur ordre. Depuys la creation desdictz pairs lesdictz sacre et couronnement nont peu estre faictz ailleurs que oudict Reims. . . . Depuys le Roy Hue capet ny a eu office nomme conte du palays & le parlement compose desdictz prelatz, barons et officiers domestiques, a Rendu la Justice souueraine. Encores que linstitution desdictz pairs de france ne se trouue par escript, Jay matiere penser qu'elle est depuys lan mil cent soixante dixneuf, ouquel l'Euesque de Langres eut son conte, Force est Recognoistre quelle est auparauant lan mil deux cens seize, que le Roy Philippes Auguste assiste desdictz pairs autres prelatz, et barons de france, Jugea lhommage des contes de Champaigne et Brye: Parquoy Je la vouldrois attribuer au Roy Loys le Jeune, ou audict Auguste": SS, Fr. F. v. IV, No. 8/1, fols. 213v-14r; BN, fr. 2854, fol. 234r-v; BN, fr. 18653, fols. 97r-98r. See also 10-11 above (the importance attributed to the bishop's acquisition of the county of Langres in 1179). For the dispute of 1216, *Layettes du Trésor des chartes,* 1: 431-32, no. 1182.

[227] The creation of the peers of France is discussed in many works, including Brussel, *Nouvel examen,* 1: 646-57; Pange, *Roi Très-Chrétien,* 371-74; Valon, *Les pairs de France,* esp. 68-73; Vic and Vaissete, and Molinier, *Histoire générale* (1872-93 ed.), 7: 74-83 n. 26; Lot, "Quelques mots," esp. 40; Péré, *Le sacre et couronnement,* 17. Jackson, *Vive le Roi!,* 262 n. 8 (Fr. ed., 148 n. 8) gives additional bibliography; see also idem, "Peers of France."

donnances, a compendium of royal legislation from the reign of Philip I (1060-1108) to that of John II (1350-64). He began to compile sources concerning precedence, which he eventually employed in the *Recueil des honneurs et rangs des grands,* presented to Charles IX sometime after July 1566 (and probably in 1567).[228] His research (and doubtless his ambition) prompted him to undertake a massive revision and expansion of the *Recueil des Roys,* which he presented to Charles IX in 1566.[229] In his dedication, Du Tillet stressed the labor and money that he had expended; had he received the financial support that Henry II and Catherine de Medicis had promised, he suggested, he might have accomplished even more.[230]

Du Tillet aimed to make the new and expanded *Recueil* more impressive, more interesting, and less formidably scholarly than the full version with inventories composed for Henry II. That a special deluxe presentation copy lacking the inventories should have been prepared for Henry and Catherine de Medicis suggests that the king and queen considered (or that Du Tillet believed they did) the lists of sources tedious and dispensable. Du Tillet may have reasoned that the young king Charles, just sixteen in 1566, would be even less interested in such apparatus than Henry II—and hence that he and his mother Catherine de Medicis would be more inclined to admire the work and favor him if the new *Recueil* contained simply text, without documentary justification. Thus the new *Recueil* did not include lists of sources like those found in the *Recueil* for Henry II; nor did the first printed editions of the *Recueil des Roys.* Not until 1607 were the inventories, excerpted from the *Recueil* for Henry II, appended to relevant chapters of the *Recueil des Roys* composed for Charles IX.

[228] Brown, *Du Tillet and his* Recueils; eadem, *Du Tillet and the French Wars of Religion,* (the date of the *Recueil des honneurs et rangs des grands*); eadem and Famiglietti, *The* Lit de Justice.

[229] Brown, *Du Tillet and his* Recueils, discusses BN, fr. 2848 (the presentation copy), SS, Fr. F. v. IV, No. 9 (perhaps a prototype of the presentation copy, which was seen and apparently approved by the Charles IX), and BPU, MS fr. 84 (a copy of the presentation copy, on paper, seemingly made for Du Tillet or a contemporary Parisian antiquarian); see also eadem and Famiglietti, *The* Lit de Justice.

[230] In *Portraits des rois,* 2-4, Omont eds. Du Tillet's dedication to Charles IX in BN, fr. 2848, published in the eds. of Du Tillet's works with an addition found as an apparently contemporary marginal addition (in an Italic block script, not in Du Tillet's distinctive cursive script) in SS, Fr. F. v. IV, No. 9, fol. 2r: "Pline est auteur que le Roy Alexandre le grand despendit iiii^{xx} M talens Qui sont xlviii M escuz en voiages et autres fraiz quil faillut faire pour auoir la cognoissance des proprietez des animaulx Dont Aristote aiant celle charge de luy composa Cinquante liures. La viii^{e} part eust fourny a parfaire mesdictes oeuures"; see Du Tillet, *Portraits des rois,* ed. Omont, 3 n. 1. The only other MS copy of the *Recueil* in which this passage appears is a sixteenth-century paper copy, BN, fr. 5000, fol. 2r, on which see Brown, *Du Tillet and his* Recueils.

The scope of Du Tillet's changes in and additions to the *Recueil des Roys* is nowhere clearer than in the chapter on consecration and coronation. Since Du Tillet had transferred to the beginning of the new *Recueil* the material in the chapter on the origin of the French with which the second part of the *Recueil* for Henry II had commenced, the chapter on coronation became the third chapter of the analytical section following the accounts of the kings of France (here beginning with Meroveus) and different branches of the royal house.[231]

Du Tillet proved himself a rigorous editor. He condensed the historical introduction to the chapter, made many stylistic changes, and clarified a number of sentences. He radically modified his remarks on the election of kings by the estates to emphasize that this practice was an antique custom which had long since been superseded.

In the first recension Du Tillet had declared that the description of Philip I's coronation in 1059 which he had found at Beauvais showed that before being anointed and crowned Philip had been "elected by the estates, for this purpose summoned and assembled." He went on to note that this was to be interpreted simply as "a declaration or acceptance and submission to a king who had been elected, designated, and predestined by God, who kept and made him nearest to the crown." It did not signify, he maintained, "a right of the estates to dispose of the kingdom by their voices and election, since it had always been considered hereditary, during pagan times as well as Christian," and when changes in the royal line had occurred this principle had been enforced. Election had been done away with for good reason, since it led to sedition and roused the kings' fears; thus rulers of the second and third lines (the Carolingians and the Capetians) had their sons crowned before they died or had their leading subjects swear to crown them after their deaths. The principle of election, he said, gave the people an occasion to ransom their true rulers, as had happened to Louis the Stammerer (877-79) and others, "who had been impoverished" to gain the crown, "to the great disorder and detriment of the state." It was this principle, he declared, that had caused kings' reigns to be dated from the day of their coronation, rather than from the day the throne became va-

[231] BN, fr. 2848, fols. 161v-78r; SS, Fr. F. v. IV, No. 9, fols. 160v-77r; BPU, MS fr. 84, 198v-220r.

cant. Thus John, posthumous son of Louis X, was not numbered among the kings of France.[232]

Du Tillet radically transformed this section, perhaps in part because, having studied the memorandum of 1059 more closely, he realized that the term election appeared there only with reference to Archbishop Gervais of Reims. Du Tillet had also become aware, however, that the word appeared in a prayer (*Omnipotens sempiterne Deus*) of what he termed "the new form of consecration."[233] The trials endured by the monarchy since Henry II's death in 1559 must have made him particularly anxious to emphasize that the king's subjects had no right to select their ruler.[234] Excising his earlier references to the estates, he declared that the words implying election in the memorandum of 1059 and in the prayer were to be taken as "declaration or acceptance and

---

232 " . . . l'on veoyt que le Roy estoit auant que estre sacre et couronne eleu par les estatz pour ce appellez et assemblez: qui se doyt prendre pour declaration, ou acceptation, & submission au Roy eleu, designe & predestine de dieu, qui la conserue et faict le plus proche de la couronne, non pour droict aux estatz de donner le Royaume par leurs voix & election, car Il a tousiours este tenu hereditaire, tant durant le paganisme, que cristianisme, et tel lont transfere a leur posterite ceulx qui par la force y ont faict les mutations, Agathie le confesse [Liure premier]: Neantmoins a tresJuste cause; a este ostee la susdicte election, laquelle bailloit couleur de seditions & craincte aux Roys: qui a meu les vngs de la seconde & tierce lignee faire couronner leurs enfans durans leurs vies, les autres de stipuler des principaulx subiectz le couronnement de leurs enfans, comme feyt le Roy Loys huictiesme & aux puissans & mutins subiectz donnoit matiere de ranconner leurs vrays Roys, Ainsi quil fut faict a Loys le begue & autres, apauurys pour estre sacrez & couronnez, ou grand desordre & detriment de l'estat. De la susdicte election estoit pris que lon comptoit anciennement le Regne du Jour du sacre & couronnement non du Jour du Royaume escheu, comme lon a faict depuis et est continue: qui a este cause que le Roy Jehan posthume du Roy Loys hutin n'a este nombré, entre les Roys": BN, fr. 2854, fols. 141v-42r; see also SS, Fr. F. v. IV, No. 8/1, fols. 129v-30r; BN, fr. 18653, fol. 69r. Du Tillet may have had in mind the passage in Agathias' *History*, bk. 1, ch. 3, in which the Greek historian describes hereditary succession among the Franks; Agathias commented on God's control of events in bk. 2, chs. 1, 15. Du Tillet may have known the *History* from the Latin translation published in Rome in 1516. See *Patrologiæ . . . Series græca*, 88: 1283-84, 1329-30, 1363-64; and Cameron, *Agathias*, esp. 91-94 (Agathias' ideas on divine providence).

233 The memorandum of Gervais mentions election in the statements "quomodo ad evm [Gervais] pertineat maxime electio regis," and "[Gervais] elegit eum in regem"); BAV, Ottobon. 811, fols. 113v; in Du Chesne, *Scriptores*, 4: 162; and *Recueil des historiens*, 11: 32; see also *Sacrosancta Concilia*, 12: 56. Du Tillet translated these phrases as "comment à luy appartenoit principalement l'election," and "Il eleut ledict Philippes son filx en Roy": BN, fr. 2848, fol. 165v. The consecration prayer contains the phrase "quem [the king] supplici deuotione in regnum pariter eligimus": see 91, 107, 124 below.

234 According to a contemporary Catholic history of the first three wars of religion, in 1562 "la province de Bourgogne déclara qu'elle aimerait mieux changer de roi que de foi"; the history also reports the rumor that after taking Saint-Denis in 1567 the Protestants crowned Louis, prince of Condé, in the abbey church and issued money with the inscription " 'Louis XIII, par la grâce de Dieu, roi de France, premier roi chrétien' "; Hauser, "Un récit catholique," 300, 306 (esp. Hauser's comments in the notes to these passages); Anselme discusses the rumors when treating Condé's life, in *Histoire genealogique*, 1: 332-33.

submission" to the king chosen by God. In speaking of dynastic changes, Du Tillet took care to stress that this occurred by divine providence, "which alone installs and removes kings." No longer was it election, but rather the lack of discipline tolerated by irresponsible rulers that produced the fear which had moved kings to crown their heirs before their deaths or impose oaths on their chief subjects to crown them later. Philosophizing, he commented, "Thus the inverted power of the members against their head had overthrown some kings," and he went on to recall Louis the Stammerer and others who had been held up for ransom, to what he now said was "the *very* great disorder and detriment of the state." Again, rather than attributing to election the former custom of regnal dating, he simply acknowledged the existence of the practice, commenting that it had "since been changed and altered for the better."[235] He excised the brief reference to Louis X's son John, and he modified accordingly his comments on John in his chapter on Louis' reign. There, in the first recension, he had said that John "was not counted among the kings because he was not crowned, although he was called King John in some documents and registers of the royal archives."[236] Now he added that John was "justly" termed king, "since by the death of the preceding king the crown, by law of the kingdom, passed immediately to the successor, from which day, immediately, the years of the reign are counted, and not from the day of the consecration and coronation."[237] Thus Du Tillet revealed the

[235] "Les motz delection estans en ladicte vieille forme et demourez en aucune oraison de la nouuelle des sacre & couronnement des Roys doibuent estre prins et entenduz pour declaration ou acceptation et submission au Roy eleu destiné et predestiné de dieu qui la conserue et faict le plus proche de la couronne non pour aucun droict aux subiectz de donner le Roiaume par leurs voix ou ellection / Car il a tousiours este tenu hereditaire Tant durant le Paganisme que Christianisme et tel lont transferé a leur posterite ceulx qui par la prouidence diuine (A laquelle seulle appartient mectre et oster les Roys y ont faict les mutations. Ce que Agathie [Liure 1] confesse Vray est que quant lesdicts Roys ne faisans leur office ont souffert leursdicts subiectz estre Indisciplinez et desbridez, La craincte a meu les vngs de la seconde et tierce lignee faire couronner leurs filz de leur viuant dont y a plusieurs exemples Les autres de stipuler de leurs principaux subiectz Apres leur deces le couronnement de leursdicts filz / comme fit le Roy Loys huictiesme Aussi la puissance Renuersee des membres contre leur chef auoit destitue aucuns Roys Autres (comme Loys le Begue et aucuns autres auoient este Rançonnez et appouuriz pour faire accorder estre sacrez & couronnez ou tresgrand desordre & detriment de lestat. Anciennement on comptoit le Regne du Jour du sacre et couronnement non du Jour que la couronne estoit escheue comme lon a depuis faict & change en mieulx": BN, fr. 2848, fol. 166r-v; SS, Fr. F. v. IV, No. 9, fol. 165r-v (here cited from this source); Du Tillet, *Recveil des Roys*, 185-86.

[236] " . . . n'est compte entre les Roys pource quil ne fut couronne, combien que en aucuns tiltres et Registres du tresor Il soit appellé le Roy Jehan": BN, fr. 2854, fol. 92v; SS, Fr. F. v. IV, No. 8/1, fol. 84r; BN, fr. 18653, fol. 46v.

[237] " . . . n'est compté entre les Roys pource qu'il ne fut couronne /. Combien que en aucuns tiltres et Registres du Tresor des Chartres Il soit appellé le Roy Jehan Justement Car par la mort du Roy predecesseur la couronne par la loy du Royaume eschoit Incon-

increasingly conservative political sentiments that the tumult of the 1560s had engendered in him.[238]

Because he wanted to produce a larger and more informative compendium (and perhaps because he was including no inventories of documents), Du Tillet incorporated some of his source material into his revised narrative. He inserted a summary of a letter describing Navarrese coronations, the date of Louis IX's letter to the abbot of Saint-Denis concerning the regalia, and an expanded description of Henry II's additions to and restoration of the royal paraphernalia in 1547. To illustrate "the form" of the coronation ceremony, Du Tillet added two lengthy texts, in French translations. The first is the complete memorandum that he had found in Beauvais, in which Archbishop Gervais of Reims described the coronation of Philip I in 1059.

The second text, far longer, is a full coronation *ordo,* which ends the chapter. This coronation *ordo,* Du Tillet says, was instituted by Louis VII and followed thenceforth with greatest sumptuousness. Du Tillet signals the importance that he attributes to the *ordo* in a passage dealing with the prerogative of Reims and the role of the peers at the coronation.

In the first *Recueil des Roys* Du Tillet simply linked the institution of the peers with the bestowal of Reims' prerogative, declaring that the two events occurred between 1179 and 1216 and attributing them to Louis VII or Philip Augustus. In the *Recueil* for Charles IX the events are precisely dated: in 1179 Louis VII, wishing to have his son crowned, granted the prerogative of royal consecration to Reims. In the same year the king commanded the preparation of an *ordo* to be used for the consecration of his son and all their successors, and this *ordo* gave the peers of France, whom the king then created, their offices at the ceremony.[239] This

tinant au successeur / duquel aussi tost les annees du Regne sont comptees non du Jour du sacre et couronnement": BN, fr. 2848, fols. 120v-21r; SS, Fr. F. v. IV, No. 9, fols. 119v-20r; Du Tillet, *Recueil des Roys,* 135. In *Theatre d'Honnevr,* 373, Marlot misrepresented Du Tillet, saying that he declared "expressément que les fils de Roy ne sont inserez au catalogue des Roys de France, si d'auanture ils viennent à deceder auant leur couronnement"; see also Quéant, *Etude sur le Sacre,* 312 n. 279. Lewis reviews the evidence regarding John's status in *Royal Succession,* 151-52 (Fr. ed., 198-99).

[238] Brown, *Du Tillet and the French Wars of Religion.* Writing shortly after Du Tillet, Jean Bodin quoted and analyzed the memorandum of 1059 (referring to the copy at Beauvais but citing one from Reims) in refuting the "Erreur de ceux qui pensent que le Royaume de France soit tombé en election." "Ceux qui ont soustenu que les Rois estoyent esleus par les estats," he wrote, "n'ont pas pris garde que l'Archeuesque de Rheims pretendoit ce droit luy appartenir priuatiuement à tous autres." See *Six Livres* (bk. 6, ch. 5), (1579 ed.), 982, (1583 ed.), 983 (which adds, "chose toutesfois impossible & incompatible auec la foy, & hommage que les Archeuesques de Rheims font au Roy de France").

[239] In "Les pairs de France," 321-48, Contamine discusses the functions associated with the various peers in the late fourteenth and fifteenth centuries.

ordo, Du Tillet declares, was registered in the Chambre des comptes in Paris and, like the prerogative of Reims, had ever since been observed; thereafter the royal consecration had never been celebrated without the peers or anywhere except at Reims.[240] This is the *ordo* whose text Du Tillet presents.[241] The ceremonial is far more elaborate than (and twice the length of) the *ordo* of lat. 14192, but here too "Franks, Burgundians, and Aquitanians" replace "Saxons, Mercians, and Northumbrians" in the prayer of consecration.

Du Tillet did not indicate whether he was publishing a French text that he had found or whether he himself had translated or commissioned a translation of a Latin *ordo*. The edition published in the Godefroys' *Le Ceremonial François* in 1649 casts light on the question. There the *ordo* is said to have been "Commandé par le Roy Louys le Ieune l'an 1179. & enregistré en la Chambre des Comptes à Paris. Traduit du Latin en François, & inseré dans le Recueil des Rois de France, par le Greffier du Tillet."[242] This suggests that Du Tillet was responsible not only for including in his book an *ordo* registered in the Chambre des comptes, but also for

[240] "Le Roy Loys le Jeune voulant faire sacrer et couronner son filx le Roy Philippes auguste lan .M. C. lxxix donna ladicte prerogatiue a ladicte eglise de Reins de laquelle estoit archeuesque Guillaume cardinal saincte Sabine frere de la Royne Alix sa femme / eut ce credit de faire vuyder le different quj en auoit esté pour le sacre du Roy Loys le groz et bailla matiere de l'arrester pour laduenir / feit escripre ledict Roy lordre desdictz sacre & couronnement tant pour sondict filx que successeurs Roys / Departit aux pairs de france lors créés leur office oudict sacre / Lequel ordre est enregistré en la chambre des comptes a Paris / a tousJours depuys esté gardé ensemble ladicte prerogatiue / Et n'a ledict sacre et couronnement este faict sans lesdictz pairs ne ailleurs que oudict Reins / Le Roy Charles septiesme differa longuement son sacre pource que ladicte ville de Reins estoit occuppée par les Angloys et alla en armes pour les en chasser et s'y faire sacrer ne le pouuant estre ailleurs / Auparauant que ladicte prerogatiue fust faicte certaine / quant le sacre estoit faict en autre prouince larcheuesque dicelle et ses suffragans faisoient loffice / et si celluy de Reins ses suffragans ou autres prelatz. s'y trouuoient / n'estoit que pour lassistance hormis ce quj aduint a Treues a cause de la fraternité des deux eglises ou sacre de Charles le chauue en Roy de Lorraine / ou ledict Hincmar archeuesque de Reins Recita le miracle de la saincte empoule enuoyee du ciel a Sainct Remy / et tesmoinga quil en auoit encores qui est ancienne approbation dudict miracle": BN, fr. 2848, fol. 164v; SS, Fr. F. v. IV, No. 9, fol. 163r-v; Du Tillet, *Recveil des Roys*, 183. Later, in his chapter on the peers, Du Tillet stated, "Ledict Roy Loys le Jeune oudict an .M. C. lxxix donnant a leglise de Reins la prerogatiue de sacrer et couronner les Roys auparauant debatue crea lesdictz douze pairs pour lesdictz sacre & couronnement et pour Iuger auec le Roy les grandes causes oudict parlement / Lequel pource / et quilx ont priuilege de n'estre Iugés ailleurs de leur honneur et estat / est appellé la court des pairs et eulx les pairs de la court de france par abregé les pairs de france": BN, fr. 2848, fol. 228r; SS, Fr. F. v. IV, No. 9, fol. 227r; Du Tillet, *Recveil des Roys*, 256. See also Du Tillet's preface to his *ordo*, 117-18 below.

[241] See Appendix, I D, 117-35 below (the text of the *ordo*).

[242] *Ceremonial*, ed. Godefroy, 1: 1. On the different dates assigned to the translation, n. 10 above, and n. 264 below.

translating it into French. If he did not translate the *ordo* himself, he must have supervised the work.

The *ordo* was the one to which Du Tillet referred in the inventory of sources relating to coronations in the *Recueil des Roys* for Henry II. Found on fol. 199[243] of Register "+" (or *Croix*) of the Chambre des comptes, the *ordo* is the sole ceremonial mentioned there. Familiar as Du Tillet was with the records of the Chambre des comptes, it is little wonder that he paid special attention to and later decided to use this elaborate *ordo*, long known to exist in a separate gathering at the end of *Croix*, the Chambre's most prestigious register.[244]

The *ordo* is most suitably designated the *Ordo maior* of *Croix*, to distinguish it from the French translation of the *ordo* of Reims (a directory for the coronation, written between 1226 and 1250), which was copied in this and other registers of the Chambre des comptes.[245] In the fourteenth century the longer Latin *ordo* was recognized as "better"—doubtless because fuller—than that translation.[246]

---

[243] The page of *Croix* on which the *ordo* began has generally been said to be 205, rather than 199, as Du Tillet's inventory and other sources give it: Petit et al., *Essai*, no. 372; BN, Dupuy 142, fol. 19r; AN, P 2288, p. 1290; and 102 n. 3 below. The confusion has arisen because two copies of the register, differently paginated, existed after 1585; in one of them, probably the original, the *ordo* must have commenced on fol. 199, in the other on fol. 205: Langlois' preface to Petit et al., *Essai*, xiv-xv. On 7 September 1585 Michel Louvet, clerk of the *greffe*, received 10 *écus soleil* for a copy of *Croix*, described as "premier des Registres dudict Greffe, duquel l'escriture s'efface par antiquité": BIF, MS Godefroy 184, fol. 1r; see fol. 2r (the *ordo* of Reims), and fol. 4v (the *ordo* at the end of *Croix*); distinctions between the pagination of the "old" and "new" copies are drawn in BN, n. a. f. 7232 (Brienne 263), fols. 1r, 6v, 7r; AN, KK 1442, fols. 3r, 8r, 10v, and esp. 11r. Since the original register and its copy were destroyed with most of the other documents of the Chambre des comptes in the fire of 1737, their actual pagination cannot be verified.

[244] "Ordinacio coronandi regem libro. +, folio xxv. Et in fine . . . Et a[d] longum in dicto libro . + . in quodam quaterno in e[i]us fine suto vbi circa principium Intercetera que Rex pr[est]at Iuramenta vnum est quod sequitur Item In omnibus Iudicijs equitatem et misericordiam propiciam vt michi et vobis Indulgeat suam misericordiam clemens et misericors dominus. facit ad hoc dictum constantinj Romanj dignitas Imperij de fonte nascitur pietatis": BN, lat. 5991A, fol. 23v, and also fols. 47r, 147v ("ad longum"). See Petit et al., *Essai*, 70 n. 1; and, on *Croix*, Langlois as cited in n. 243. The *ordo* is edited in Appendix, I C, 102-16 below.

[245] *Croix* (fol. 25r), *Pater* (fol. 163r), *Noster* (fol. 250r), and *Qui es* (fol. 27r) are listed at the beginning of the copy in AN, P 2288, pp. 706-15; in each of these volumes (ibid., p. 713) the king's *ordo* was followed immediately by the queen's. See Petit et al., *Essai*, nos. 64-65, 287-88, and no. 372, for *Noster*[1] (BN, lat. 12814), an original register (*Liber parvus viridus*) of the Chambre des comptes, in which the translation of the *ordo* of Reims appears on fols. 27r-30r. Langlois discusses this register in his preface to Petit et al., *Essai*, vii, xi-xiii; see also Couderc, "Note sur le manuscrit latin 12814," 645-53.

[246] Above the copy of the *ordo* of Reims in *Noster*[1] is noted, in a contemporary hand, "melius hec ordinacio ponitur & scribitur in fine libri memorialis signato +": BN, lat. 12814, fol. 27r.

The *Ordo maior* was a modified version, a new recension, of the last direct Capetian *ordo* of 1250-70. It seems to have been prepared in the 1330s,[247] after the *ordo* of Charles IV (1322-28) and his third wife Jeanne d'Evreux (crowned in 1326),[248] and to have been used by the redactors of the so-called *ordo* of Charles V (1364-80) in 1364/65.[249] This *ordo* served Du Tillet well. The fact that it had been registered in the Chambre des comptes gave it authority, and through judicious editing and emendation Du Tillet increased its attractiveness. Indeed, the *Ordo maior* was similar enough to *ordines* recently employed in France to appear their legitimate prototype; it may possibly have influenced the ceremonial used at the coronation of Charles IX on 15 May 1561, five years before Du Tillet completed his new *Recueil des Roys.*[250] Thus Du Tillet presented his *ordo* as the coronation ceremonial that he claimed had been "up to the present observed with the greatest sumptuousness."

2. Du Tillet's Version of the *Ordo Maior* of *Croix*

In assigning it to 1179 and associating it with Philip Augustus, Du Tillet imposed on the *Ordo maior* of *Croix* a role that it was not easily capable of fulfilling. However much it may have troubled Du Tillet, the *ordo*'s allusion to the Saxons, Mercians, and Northumbrians as the peoples whose scepters the king was admonished not to relinquish was consistent with other French ceremonials. If it was to be linked with the late twelfth century, however, the text of the *ordo* posed other problems with which Du

[247] The dates of the documents contained in *Croix* are given as 1223-1334 in Paris, Bibliothèque Mazarine, MS 3039 (1810), fol. 16r, and as 1223-1337 in a roughly contemporary copy of extracts from *Croix*, BIF, MS Godefroy 184, fol. 2r. The *Ordo maior*, inserted as a separate booklet at the end of the original *Croix*, may possibly postdate the other documents in the register, although it was surely composed before the *ordo* in the Coronation Book of Charles V (London, British Library, Cotton Tiberius B. viii), which is dated 1365: Jackson, *Vive le Roi!*, 26-37, 223 (Fr. ed., 31-40, 208-9); idem, "Manuscripts, Texts," 61-64; Appendix II, 139-42 below.

[248] The MS of this *ordo* is in the Rare Books and Special Collections Library of the University of Illinois at Urbana-Champaign: on it, see Bober, "Coronation Book," esp. 7; Sherman, "The Queen in Charles V's 'Coronation Book,' " 261, 263; Pinoteau, "Tenue de sacre de saint Louis," 466-67 n. 20; Hedeman, "Commemoration." The fact that the Coronation Book contains the king's ceremonial as well as the queen's does not preclude the *ordo*'s use for the coronation of Jeanne d'Evreux; as has been seen, prayers from the king's *ordo* may have been recited when he was crowned at his queen's consecration. In "Commemoration," Hedemann suggests that the volume may have been prepared for a female relative of Jeanne d'Evreux who took part in Jeanne's coronation; although it seems likely that the *ordo* was used at the service, there is no proof that this was the case.

[249] In Appendix II, 139-42 below, I discuss the relationship of these *ordines* to the *Ordo maior.*

[250] Jackson, *Vive le Roi!*, 35-36 (Fr. ed., 39-40).

Tillet had to deal. Thus he did not publish a simple, literal translation of the ceremonial. Intent on glorifying and magnifying the institutions of France, dedicated to establishing their antiquity and uniqueness, concerned with current practice and ceremonial,[251] he tailored the *ordo* so that it fit more comfortably with its alleged date and provenance and appeared worthier to serve as the prototype of future royal consecration ceremonies.[252]

What prompted Du Tillet to associate the *ordo* with Louis VII and Philip Augustus is a mystery. There is no evidence that any notation in *Croix* suggested or supported his position,[253] and when he composed the first version of his *Recueil des Roys*, he assigned no date to the *ordo* in his inventory of sources. In that *Recueil* he openly acknowledged his inability to determine precisely when the peers had been created and given their offices at the coronation, and when Reims was made the privileged site of royal consecration; he simply stated that this happened between 1179 and 1216. Before completing the new *Recueil* in 1566 Du Tillet for some reason changed his mind. Had he become convinced that, as some later maintained, the gift of the county of Langres to the bishop, which Louis VII maneuvered in 1179, was sure proof that the king was intending to create six ecclesiastical peers and wished to be able to honor the bishop of Langres along with five other favored ecclesiastics? If he did believe this, he never said so, although in his chapter on peers he mentioned the donation.[254] Another possibility, admittedly tenuous, is raised by two twelfth-century English chronicles. Both the *Gesta Regis Henrici secundi* and the chronicle of Roger of Howden report that at the coronation of 1179 the young King Henry of England carried the crown and Count Philippe of Flanders "the sword of the kingdom," and, most important, that the different nobles who preceded and followed the king "were assigned different offices as was necessary" ("diversi diversis deputati obsequiis prout res exigebat"). Also suggestive is the appearance of the phrase "regis edictum"

[251] On Du Tillet as antiquarian and activist, Brown, *Du Tillet and his* Recueils; eadem, *Du Tillet and the French Wars of Religion;* eadem and Famiglietti, *The* Lit de Justice.

[252] For far more cavalier attitudes to archival documents in the seventeenth and eighteenth centuries, see Havet, "Questions mérovingiennes," 205-71; and Soman, "The London Edition of de Thou's *History,*" 1-12. Giesey suspected Du Tillet of tampering with sources and exercising "literary inventiveness" at the expense of historical accuracy in his account of Francis I's last illness and death, but the portions that Giesey thought Du Tillet had fabricated were in fact taken from the first funeral sermon of Pierre du Chastel, bishop of Mâcon and grand almoner of France, delivered at Notre-Dame on 23 May 1547: *Royal Funeral Ceremony,* 193-95 (Fr. ed., 291-95); Brown *Du Tillet and his* Recueils; eadem and Famiglietti, *The* Lit de Justice.

[253] Cf. Buchner, "Nochmals," 343.

[254] Du Tillet, *Recueil des Roys,* 254; Brussel, *Nouvel examen,* 1: 648-49; 10-11 above.

in connection with the ceremony in the chronicle of Gislebert of Mons.[255] To be sure, the chronicles do not use the word *par* or *pares*. Nor do the English chronicles indicate that offices were given to only four lay magnates besides Henry and Philippe. As to Gislebert, far from implying that "the king's edict" was issued to regulate the service, he linked it simply with the summonses issued to leading magnates. Further, it seems unlikely that Du Tillet could have known the English texts, although his observation regarding the reason why Louis VII wore his crown at the consecration of his third wife is so close to Gislebert's comment on Philip Augustus' similar action in 1180 as to raise the possibility that he was acquainted with that chronicle.[256] If Du Tillet had encountered one of these works, their assertions might have persuaded him that the *ordo* in the Chambre des comptes should properly—or perhaps, could convincingly—be linked to the ceremony of 1179, when Philip Augustus, one of France's most revered kings, was consecrated. It seems most probable, however, that his dating of the *ordo* was arbitrary, although he himself may have believed absolutely in his position. He expected his assertions and the authoritativeness of his *ordo* to be accepted.

Du Tillet did not present a simple translation of the *Ordo maior* of *Croix*. Rather, he introduced a number of changes and modifications. Some suggest that he was consciously attempting to increase the antiquity of the *ordo* and thus mislead his audience. Others indicate the more defensible goal of clarifying obscure portions of the *ordo* and making it more suitable for actual use. These alterations must be examined to determine the likelihood of his good faith.

Du Tillet made several additions to the *ordo* that are simple glosses on the text, apparently inserted to make it more comprehensible.[257] Thus, in the account of the king's vestments,

---

[255] *Gesta Regis Henrici secundi*, 1: 240; Roger of Howden, *Chronica*, 2: 194; MGH, *Scriptorum*, 21: 528. Perhaps following Vignier (*Bibliotheqve Historiale* [1587], 3: 166) or Dupleix (*Histoire Generale de France* [1624], 2: 186), Marlot (*Theatre d'Honnevr* [1643], 673, 679) declared that Henry was performing his office as vassal and peer; like Dupleix (who also mentioned Rigord), Marlot expressed surprise that Guillaume le Breton did not mention the peers in his description of Philip Augustus' coronation. See 6-7, 9, 10-11 above.

[256] The *Gesta* was little known before modern times, although Howden's text, first published in 1596, was influential from the thirteenth century onwards: Stubbs, ed., Howden, *Chronica*, 1: lxxiii-iv. For Gislebert, see n. 180 above. The actual relevance of these and other contemporary texts to the date of the establishment of the peers is considered and (quite rightly) rejected by Brial ("Anonyme. Auteur du formulaire," 24-26), Bernardi ("Mémoire," 613-15), and Lot ("Quelques mots," 40).

[257] In "Histoire de France," 137 n. 2, Halphen notes that Du Tillet "s'est permis bien [de] changements ou gloses."

after "les chausses" Du Tillet inserted "appellées sendales ou botines," and, after "le surcot," "quj est le manteau Royal"; the royal ring is said to be placed "ou doigt medicinal de la main dextre," a phrase found in the *ordo* used for the coronation of Charles VIII in 1484.[258] Du Tillet added to the text the prescription that the abbot of Saint-Denis hand the king's silken slippers to the *grand chambellan*, the official whom Du Tillet designated as responsible for placing the slippers on the king's feet at the beginning of the service and vesting him with dalmatic and mantle after the unction.[259] Like earlier and later *ordines*, the *Ordo maior* of *Croix* refers to this official as *magnus camerarius* and *camerarius*.[260] Du Tillet knew perfectly well that the *grand chambrier* was different from the *grand chambellan* (*magnus cambellanus*), but he also knew that the office of *grand chambrier* had been suppressed in 1545.[261] Even more important, at the coronation of Francis I in 1515 it was the *grand chambellan* who was charged with the duties described in the *Ordo maior*[262]—as had been the case at the consecration of Louis XI in 1461.[263] Du Tillet seems to have been attempting, through his translation, to accommodate his source to contemporary circumstances and readers. He probably had a similar goal in translating *virga* as *main de justice*.[264] Likewise, seeking a modern-day equivalent for *senescallus francie*,[265] the dignitary charged with receiving the king's sword, Du Tillet selected the *connestable de France*, probably because (as had been true in

[258] Schreuer, "Noch einmal," 169; *Ceremonial*, ed. Godefroy, 1: 201. Gratian's *Decretum*, discussing marriage, declared that the ring was placed on the fourth finger of the left hand "ideo quod in eo uena quedam, ut fertur, sanguinis ad cor usque perueniat": pt. 2, 30.5.7, in *Corpus iuris canonici*, ed. Friedberg, 1: 1106. Jackson (*Vive le Roi!*, 89; Fr. ed., 85) discusses the significance of the placement of the ring.

[259] See 121, 126 below.

[260] See 105, 109, below; *Ceremonial*, ed. Godefroy, 1: 17 (the *ordo* of 1250); *De antiquis ritibus*, ed. Martène, 2: 225; Urbana-Champaign *Ordo*, fol. 10v; *Coronation Book*, ed. Dewick, 21.

[261] *Recveil des Roys*, 295-99 (on the *grand chambrier*), 300-303 (on the *grand chambellan*), and esp. 296 (the tendency to confuse the two titles). In October 1545 Francis I suppressed the office of *grand chambrier* and reunited the prerogatives of the office to the crown. Du Tillet listed this edict in the inventory of documents appended to the chapter on the office in the *Recueil des Roys* for Henry II (*Recveil des Roys* [1607 ed.], 415); he mentioned the suppression in the *Recueil des honneurs et rangs* (in *Recveil des Roys*, 351).

[262] *Ceremonial*, ed. Godefroy, 1: 248-49. The dukes of Guise and Longueville disputed the right to act as *grand chambellan* at the coronation of Charles IX: ibid., 1: 316-19.

[263] *Archives administratives de la ville de Reims*, 2^1: 570 ("le grand et premier chambellan de France"), 572 ("le grand chambellan de France"), both passages in n. 1 continued from 559.

[264] Pinoteau argues that this term suggests that Du Tillet's translation was prepared in the fourteenth or fifteenth century, but the expression was current in Du Tillet's own time: "Tenue de sacre de saint Louis," 467 n. 20.

[265] In *Recveil des Roys*, 286, 288, Du Tillet equates the Capetians' seneschal of France with the *grand maître* and corrects the notion that the office of constable was equivalent.

1461)[266] at the coronation of Francis I in 1515 the constable performed this office,[267] and also, perhaps, because of the great authority wielded by Du Tillet's erstwhile patron, Anne de Montmorency, constable of France from 1538 until his death in 1567.[268]

A similar desire to make the *ordo* easier to understand doubtless led Du Tillet to expand the terse connectives that bridged the passages from prayer to prayer and from prayers to explanation, prescriptions, and commentary. Thus he excised a clumsy statement that the *Ordo maior* introduced into the text of the last direct Capetian *ordo* before the bestowal of the ring.[269] He also arranged a bit more logically the prayers and benedictions of the mass and offertory. Like the *ordo* of Charles IV and Jeanne d'Evreux (and, later, the *ordo* of Charles V), the *Ordo maior* of *Croix* includes, following the description of the beginning of the mass in the last direct Capetian *ordo*, a special prayer for the king (*Quesumus omnipotens Deus*), the *Secreta* (*Munera quesumus domine*), and the *Postcommunio* (*Hec domine oratio salutaris*).[270] Du Tillet's translation separates the prayer for the king, on the one hand, from the *Secreta* and the *Postcommunio*, on the other. Between them his *ordo* has the description of the reading of the Gospel and the king's offering (which, in the other three *ordines*, follow the three prayers).[271] Du Tillet may have made this change because of the sense of the passages: the *Secreta* do in fact refer to offerings already made, although the *Postcommunio* should appear later, following rather than preceding the benedictions before the *Pax domini*. An *ordo* presumably prepared for Louis XI's coronation in 1461 (which is preserved in a treatise composed at Reims in 1478) presents the prayers at the places in the service where they must

[266] *Archives administratives de la ville de Reims*, 2[1]: 571 ("au sénéchal, ou connestable de France"), 574 ("ledict sénéchal, ou connestable de France"), both passages in n. 1 continued from 559. At the coronation of Charles VIII in 1484, the marshal received the sword: *Ceremonial*, ed. Godefroy, 1: 198.

[267] See 105, 121-22 below. For earlier *ordines*, *De antiquis ritibus*, ed. Martène, 2: 224; AN, P 2288, p. 1296; Urbana-Champaign *Ordo*, fol. 1r; *Coronation Book*, ed. Dewick, 23. For the coronation of Francis I, *Ceremonial*, ed. Godefroy, 1: 249. In his *Recueil des Roys*, 276-78, Du Tillet expressed great admiration for the constable and quoted a "registre ancien" of the Chambre des comptes that ranked him above all others except the king in the army: cf. Bryant, *King and City*, 112. In *Vive le Roi!*, 19, 21, 46 (Fr. ed., 24, 26, 48), Jackson discusses the role played by the constable at later French coronations.

[268] Bryant, *King and City*, 111-12; Rezak, *Anne de Montmorency*. Montmorency and Du Tillet were close until 1547, when Du Tillet turned to the duke and cardinal of Guise for favor and protection: Brown, *Du Tillet and his* Recueils. Du Tillet often referred to Montmorency in his *Recueil des Roys*: see, e.g., *Recveil des Roys*, 276, 280, 287.

[269] See 109, 126 below.

[270] See 113-14 below; Urbana-Champaign *Ordo*, fols. 17v-18r; *Coronation Book*, ed. Dewick, 42; cf. *De antiquis ritibus*, ed. Martène, 2: 226-27.

[271] See 129-31 below.

have been intoned: the prayer for the king following (rather than preceding) the beginning of the mass and preceding the reading of the Epistle, the *Secreta* after the royal offering, and the *Postcommunio* following the kissing of the *pax*.[272] If Du Tillet knew this or a similar late *ordo*, it would be difficult to understand why he did not place the *Postcommunio* after the kissing of the *pax*; this would not be the case if he was simply revising the *Ordo maior* himself, striving to make it easier to follow. In themselves all these alterations have little importance, but they have misled some, who have taken them to be part of Du Tillet's original source.[273]

Du Tillet introduced more extensive but similarly innocuous comments. They appear in three passages inserted at the end of the *ordo*. The first notes that when "Jehan de France," son of John II, was freed from captivity by the English on 1 February 1365, he pledged to abide by the terms of his release "on the faith of a true son of a consecrated king" ("en foy de vray filx de Roy sacré"); thus, Du Tillet declared, the consecration of the king of France honored his sons and witnessed their faith and loyalty, greater than those of the sons of unconsecrated kings.[274] The second passage points out that after the consecration at Reims the king customarily visits the shrine of Saint Marcoul (at Corbeny) to venerate the saint associated with the royal power to heal, and only thereafter begins to touch for scrofula; it mentions the deathbed instructions that Philip the Fair gave his eldest son Louis regarding this special royal power.[275] The third addition cites the

[272] *Archives administratives de la ville de Reims*, 2[1]: 574, in n. 1 continued from 559; Jackson, *Vive le Roy!*, 36-40 (Fr. ed., 40-43). The *ordo* for the coronation of Charles VIII in 1484 is ambiguous; the three prayers are grouped together, but they appear, curiously, after the benedictions preceding the *Pax domini* and before the kissing of the *pax*; the *ordo* indicates ("est à noter") that the prayer for the king was to precede the reading of the Epistle (as in Foulquart's *ordo* and in Du Tillet's translation) but does not say precisely when the other two prayers were to be said: *Ceremonial*, ed. Godefroy, 1: 204-5.

[273] See n. 264 above (*main de justice*). Buchner ("Zur Datierung," 385-87) maintains that the reference to Saint Marcoul in Du Tillet's *ordo*, to be discussed below, would have been appropriate in the twelfth century. Cf., however, Bloch, *Les rois thaumaturges*, 281; but note as well the hypotheses regarding the early cult of Marcoul presented by Poly, in "Gloire des rois," 167-88.

[274] See 132 below. The irony of Du Tillet's assertions would not have been lost on contemporaries who were aware that John II's son Louis, duke of Anjou, had broken a similar oath in 1363, thus necessitating his father's return to captivity in England in 1364: Lehoux, *Jean de France*, 1: 171-72, 192 (the oath of 1 February).

[275] See 82, 132 below, and n. 273 above; on the royal thaumaturgic power and Corbeny, see also Barlow, "The King's Evil"; Brown, "Kings Like Semi-Gods." In recounting Philip the Fair's death, Yves, monk of Saint-Denis, reports, " . . . primogenitum . . . instruxit de modo tangendi infirmos, dicens ei sancta et devota verba quæ in tangendo infirmos dicere fuerat assuetus. Similiter docuit eum quod cum magna reverentia, sanctitate et puritate deberet illum contactum infirmorum et mundis a peccato manibus exercere": *Recueil des historiens*, 21: 206-8, esp. 207.

tenth-century historian Widukind's description of the blessing of the sword, mantle, and scepter and *"main de justice"* at the consecration of Otto I in 936.[276] Finally, at the end of the *ordo* and before alluding to the coronation of Henry II and Catherine de Medicis, Du Tillet added the comment, "Et lordre susdict est gardé quant [la Royne] est sacree et couronnee ailleurs que audict Reims."[277]

Three major alterations are far more important, since they suggest that Du Tillet was intentionally striving to make his *ordo* seem more ancient and venerable than it actually was. First, he rearranged the ecclesiastical peers listed at the beginning of the *ordo.* Second, he changed the names of the saints enumerated in the prayer *Extendat omnipotens Deus.* Third and most important, in the consecration prayer he replaced the Saxons, the Mercians, and the Northumbrians with the Franks, the Burgundians, and the Aquitanians. These alterations were not prompted by a version of the last direct Capetian *ordo* known to Du Tillet but no longer extant. They are, rather, changes that he devised himself.

In the last direct Capetian *ordo* and the *Ordo maior* the peers appear, following the archbishop of Reims, in the following order: Laon, Beauvais, Langres, Châlons, and, finally, Noyon.[278] Du Tillet's *ordo,* in contrast, accords Langres precedence over Beau-

[276] See 132-33 below; Widukind, *Rerum gestarum Saxonicarum,* 55-57 (idem, *Annales,* 16-17). On him and his work, Nelson, "Ritual and Reality," 330; Schramm, *Kaiser,* 3: 33-58 at 39-42; his history was first published in Basle in 1532. This passage does not appear in BN, fr. 2847, fr. 2859, and fr. 6491, three sixteenth-century copies of the *Recueil.* BN, fr. 6491 is a hybrid copy beginning with the dedication to Henry II and including a brief account of the reign of Henry III; its contents are compared with those of the *Recueils des Roys* for Henry II and Charles IX, in Brown, *Du Tillet and his* Recueils, Appendix II. Nor is the passage found in the two 1578 eds. of Du Tillet's *Recueil des Roys,* both published as *Les Memoires et Recerches,* on which, see ibid.

[277] There are additional minor differences in phraseology between Du Tillet's translation and the *Ordo maior.* Du Tillet's *ordo* omits the phrase "qua rex debet inungi" (modifying the unction) from the description of the loosing of the king's vestments: cf. 106, 122 below; *De antiquis ritibus,* ed. Martène, 2: 224; Urbana-Champaign *Ordo,* fol. 2r; *Coronation Book,* ed. Dewick, 25. In addition, the phrase "tuamque benedictionem" does not appear in Du Tillet's translation of the prayer *Deus electorum fortitudo:* see 109, 126 below. Here Du Tillet may have been influenced by the *ordo* of lat. 14192, which lacks the phrase, or by a similar ceremonial: see 92 below. Du Tillet perhaps omitted "per diuturna tempora" from the benediction *Clerum ac populum* by oversight; this phrase appears in all *ordines* known to me that depend on the last direct Capetian *ordo;* see 114, 131 below.

[278] *De antiquis ritibus,* ed. Martène, 2: 223. See Lot, "Quelques mots," 43 and 51-52 (the ecclesiastical peers). In the thirteenth-century *ordo* of Reims the clerics are listed as follows: Reims, Langres, Laon, all *duces;* Noyon, Beauvais, and Châlons, all *comites:* see BAV, Reg. lat. 574, fol. 18r (the Latin version of the text in a MS owned by Paul Petau, on which see n. 313 below). The list of ecclesiastical peers does not appear in the French translation in Register *Croix:* BN, fr. 4596, fols. 124v-30r; BN, fr. 16600, fols. 316r-21r; BN, lat. 12814, fols. 27r-30r; AN, P 2288, pp. 706-25; *Ceremonial,* ed. Godefroy, 1: 26-29; see Petit et al., *Essai,* nos. 372-74.

vais.[279] This is the sequence in which they are found in the record of the trial of Robert of Artois in 1332, a text which Du Tillet knew well. It was to this record that he turned to answer the request that Henry II sent to the Parlement of Paris on 3 July 1547, three weeks before his coronation. The king asked the Parlement to provide him with a listing of the order and ranks of the peers of France (which, he said, must be preserved in the Parlement's registers), and in response Du Tillet presented the list in the register of the Artois trial to the king's *Conseil privé* as the first piece of evidence which he offered.[280] Shortly afterwards, Du Tillet copied the list in a memorandum on precedence that he prepared for Henry II in 1548-49.[281] He also included it in the *Recueil des honneurs et rangs des grands,* presented to Charles IX in 1567 or thereabouts, where he said that it represented the order of the peers "in ancient times."[282] This was apparently the earliest authoritative full record of precedence for the peers of France that Du Tillet knew.[283] Nor was that ranking quickly or decisively displaced. It reappeared in the proceedings of the trial in 1378 of Jean V, duke of Brittany and count of Montfort, which Du Tillet included in his *Recueil des honneurs et rangs;*[284] it is found in the treatise on the consecration that Jean Golein (d. 1403) inserted in his translation of Guillaume Durand's *Rationale divinorum officiorum*[285]; it appears in a late-fourteenth-century list of the peers

[279] See 103, 118, below. The *Ordo maior* does not contain the phrase, "eo ordine quo dictum est superius de sedendo," in describing the summoning of the peers after the bestowal of the rod. Du Tillet's translation, however, reads "ledict archeuesque, appelle par leurs noms et selon leur ordre les pairs de france," which suggests that he was familiar with another version of the service that included the fuller description. See *De antiquis ritibus,* ed. Martène, 2: 226; and cf. Urbana-Champaign *Ordo,* fol. 13r; and also 111, 127 below.

[280] *Ceremonial,* ed. Godefroy, 1: 294-95; Brown and Famiglietti, *The* Lit de Justice.

[281] The memorandum of 1548/49 (BN, fr. 17294, fols. 25r-31r, at 28r) is ed. in Brown, *Du Tillet and his* Recueils, Appendix III.

[282] Du Tillet, *Recveil des Roys,* 377 (*Recueil des honneurs et rangs*). The same list (with the notation "ou temps ancien ne auoit que .xij. pers en France") precedes the *ordo* of Charles V of 1365: *Coronation Book,* ed. Dewick, 13-14; *Ceremonial,* ed. Godefroy, 1: 30 (where the list is dated *ca* 1370); BN, fr. 18513, fol. 110r (Godefroy's own copy of the list). Foulquart included the list (with the notation "anciennement y avoit douze pairs en France") in his treatise of 1478: *Archives administratives de la ville de Reims,* 2[1]: 575, n. 1 continued from 559. Vic and Vaissete published the list in *Histoire generale* (1730-45), 3: 577; (1872-93 ed.), 7: 78; Molinier re-edited it, ibid., 7: 79 n. 2 continued from 78, from BN, fr. 18437, fol. 1r.

[283] The judgment of 1216 that Du Tillet cites in the *Recueil des Roys* for Henry II as the terminus ante quem for the creation of the peers lists the ecclesiastical peers as Reims, Langres, Châlons, Beauvais, and Noyon; the bishopric of Laon was vacant. See Brussel, *Nouvel examen,* 1: 651 n. a; Brial, "Anonyme. Auteur du formulaire," 24-25; Lot, "Quelques mots," 43; 58 above.

[284] *Recveil des Roys,* 390-91.

[285] *"Traité du sacre,"* 312, and 318 (the bishops of Langres and Beauvais seek the king "en sa chambre"). Jackson provides a useful introduction to the treatise, ibid., 305-8.

and their offices.[286] Further, at the coronation of Henry II in 1547 the bishop of Langres took precedence over the bishop of Beauvais, which would have served to confirm the antique usage.[287] It seems clear, in short, that Du Tillet altered the ranking of peers in his *ordo* because he believed in and wanted to convince others of the antiquity of the ceremonial and because he was convinced that the precedence established in the list of 1332 was more venerable than that found in the *Ordo maior.* The discordant ranking of the peers was a blemish easily remedied, and Du Tillet might well have rationalized his move by deciding that the copyist of the *Ordo maior* had simply erred.

Why did he alter the catalogue of saints? The benediction *Extendat omnipotens Deus,* which traditionally followed the bestowal of the regalia, is a prayer designating the saints, in addition to the Virgin Mary and Saint Peter, whose intervention is particularly requested for the king who is being crowned. Thus, in the *ordines* drawn up in tenth-century England, the name of Saint Gregory, "the Apostle of the English," appears; the *ordo* used for the coronation of Emperor Henry VII in Milan in 1311 includes Saint Ambrose.[288] The *Ordo maior* of *Croix* cites Saint Denis, whereas the last direct Capetian *ordo* and the *ordo* of Charles IV and Jeanne d'Evreux add Saint Remi as well.[289] Du Tillet, curiously, included simply Saint Gregory, the same saint featured in the English ceremonials and the *ordo* of lat. 14192 and most related members of the Ratold family.[290] Likewise, in the prayer *Sta et retine,* Du Tillet replaced "paterna successione" (found in the *Ordo maior* as well as the *ordo* of Charles IV and Jeanne d'Evreux and the *ordo* of Charles V) with "la suggestion de ton pere," a reading consonant with the *ordo* of lat. 14192 (and the last direct Capetian

---

[286] BAV, Ottobon. lat. 811, fol. 115r, supplies two crucial lines that are missing from the copy in the chancery formulary of the reign of Francis I ed. in Contamine, "Les pairs de France," 323, following n. 5: "Leuesque et duc de langres le sceptre / Le duc de Guienne lautre banniere" (between references to the duke of Normandy and the bishop of Beauvais).

[287] *Ceremonial,* ed. Godefroy, 1: 284-85. The *Universal Chronicle* of Guillaume de Nangis records a heated dispute over precedence between the bishops of Beauvais and Langres in 1317, from which the bishop of Beauvais emerged victorious: *Chronique latine,* 1: 432. For the coronation of Louis XVI, Valensise, "Sacre du roi," 555.

[288] See n. 5 above.

[289] *De antiquis ritibus,* ed. Martène, 2: 226; Urbana-Champaign *Ordo,* fol. 14r. Lelong noted the existence of an *ordo* of the Ratold family at Saint-Remi of Reims, in which "on [ne] voit point ce qui regarde l'Angleterre," and in which Saint Remi appeared in place of "saint Georges" (a slip for Saint Gregory): *Bibliothèque historique,* 2: 704, no. 25948. The MS in which Lelong found this *ordo* has apparently vanished, since no known ceremonial of the Ratold family features Saint Remi instead of Saint Gregory.

[290] See 31 above, and 95, 111, 128 below.

ordo).[291] These changes were evidently consciously made. Even more compellingly than the alteration in the ordering of the peers of France, they suggest that Du Tillet was attempting to make his *ordo* seem older than it was. They also support the likelihood that Du Tillet knew the *ordo* of lat. 14192 or a copy of it, which he could have easily consulted on one of his trips to Beauvais.[292] So too does Du Tillet's third major alteration.

Like the *ordo* of lat. 14192, Du Tillet's *ordo* substitutes the Franks, the Burgundians, and the Aquitanians for the Saxons, the Mercians, and the Northumbrians in the prayer of consecration. The alien peoples designated in virtually all versions of the Ratold *ordo*, the *ordo* of 1250, the last direct Capetian *ordo*, and the *Ordo maior* of *Croix* were thus displaced in favor of peoples suitable for the kingdom of France.

Du Tillet's reasons for making this particular change seem indisputable.[293] He was evidently troubled, as most of those who studied the French coronation *ordines* were not, by the inappropriateness of the formula "Saxons, Mercians and Northumbrians"—whatever the nature of former or current ambitions regarding England, which the Anglo-French conflicts and rivalry of the 1550s and 1560s encouraged. Had he chosen, Du Tillet could have accounted for the presence of the curious formula in the coronation ceremonial. Since he associated his *ordo* with Louis VII, the proffer of the English crown to Philip Augustus' son Louis in 1215[294] would not have been relevant, but he was as capable as later scholars of invoking Louis IV d'Outremer, who had a claim, however slight, to the English throne.[295] It seems most likely, however, that Du Tillet simply objected to the

[291] The two eds. of 1578 read "succession" rather than "suggestion," as do two sixteenth-century copies of the *Recueil des Roys* for Charles IX (BN, fr. 6491, fol. 303r; BN, fr. 2859, fol. 194r, corrected from *suggestion*). "Suggestion" is found in the presentation copy of the *Recueil* for Charles IX (BN, fr. 2848, fol. 174v), and in SS, Fr. F. v. IV, No. 9, fol. 173v: see 112, 129 below. It also appears in one sixteenth-century MS copy (BN, fr. 2847, fol. 102v), and in the eds. of 1580 through 1618. See also 96 below (the *ordo* of lat. 14192); *De antiquis ritibus*, ed. Martène, 2: 226 ("suggessione"); Urbana-Champaign *Ordo*, fol. 15v; *Coronation Book*, ed. Dewick, 40. For Godefroy's treatment of the phrase, see 82 below.

[292] See 24-26 above.

[293] Halphen, following Schreuer, suggests that the alteration was "peut-être une correction archaïsante de Du Tillet": "Histoire de France," 137 n. 2; Schreuer, "Noch einmal," 171, 175-76.

[294] Warren, *King John*, 246-48 (rebel negotiations with Louis and the arrival of a French contingent in the fall of 1215), 251-52 (Louis' invasion in May 1216); Poole, *From Domesday Book to Magna Carta*, 479-86. Louis did not come to terms with the English until 12 September 1217: Powicke, *The Thirteenth Century*, 1, 3-4, 8-15.

[295] Freeman, *History of the Norman Conquest*, 3: 624; Millon, ed., *Cérémonial*, 67 n. 1; Alletz, *Cérémonial*, 107-8 n. 1; Ménin, *Cérémonies*, 58 n. (a); and also 5 (Ménin's endorsement of Du Tillet's view of 1179). Both Alletz and Ménin confuse Louis IV d'Outremer with Philip Augustus' son Louis.

presence of three English peoples in a French coronation *ordo*. The names could have been omitted, but a more attractive alternative presented itself in the formula "Franks, Burgundians, and Aquitanians." By substituting the phrase Du Tillet created an *ordo* suitable, retrospectively, for the coronation of Philip Augustus and, prospectively, for all subsequent kings of France. Why he inserted Saint Gregory in place of Saint Denis is unclear, but Gregory's association with the English may have appeared to him less important than the saint's inclusion in an early *ordo;* his presence, unidentified, in a French *ordo* was hardly as jarring as was that of the Saxons, Mercians, and Northumbrians.

Du Tillet had probably found the formula "Franks, Burgundians, and Aquitanians" in the *ordo* of lat. 14192 itself. The medieval ceremonial's evident age and the veneration in which it was held at Beauvais would have appealed to him, as would its invocation of the Franks, Burgundians, and Aquitanians. On the other hand, the *ordo* would have seemed far less suitable for Du Tillet's purposes than would the elaborate and impressive *Ordo maior* of *Croix*.

Aware as he was that no blessing of the *vexillum* actually occurred at the coronation,[296] Du Tillet did not include in his *ordo* the *Benedictio vexilli* that terminates the ceremonial in many French coronation *ordines*, including the *ordo* of lat. 14192, the last direct Capetian *ordo*, the *Ordo maior* of *Croix*, and the *ordines* of Charles IV and Jeanne d'Evreux and of Charles V. However, in his chapter on Saint-Denis and the *oriflamme* (the ninth chapter of the second part of the *Recueil des Roys*) Du Tillet did reproduce the benediction, adding it and another passage to the text that he composed for the *Recueil des Roys* for Henry II.[297] There he introduced the topic by citing the quite different descriptions of the banner found in the *Philippidos libri XII* of Guillaume le Breton and in the *Grandes Chroniques de France;* the divergences, he said, cast doubt on the common opinion that it had been sent from heaven to Clovis after his baptism. Du Tillet then called attention to two documents that he believed gave information about the ensign. The first was a donation of King Robert to Saint-Denis dated 25 January 997, in which, according to Du Tillet, the king expressed the hope that "by the intercession of the holy martyrs, he would have victory over his enemies and afterwards be able to

296 Cf. Valensise, "Sacre du roi," 555 (Louis XVI's coronation).

297 The section from the first recension of the *Recueil*, together with the additions made in the second recension, are ed. in Appendix I, E, 135-38 below, where Du Tillet's sources are identified and quoted.

return to the church the *oriflamme*, the banner of the subjection of the martyrs, [which was] invincible by the aid of God." Du Tillet's interpretation of the actual charter is fanciful and erroneous,[298] but he accurately parsed his second source. This was the charter of Louis VI of 1124 in which the king recognized that the Vexin was held in homage of the holy martyrs and that the counts of the Vexin carried their banner; thus Louis received from Abbot Suger the ensign of Saint-Denis, bestowed on kings setting forth for war.

When Du Tillet revised the chapter for his new *Recueil*, he inserted after his description of Robert's charter a reference to Joinville's designation of the *vexillum* as the banner of Saint-Denis and he remarked that Louis IX took it with him on his first crusade. Du Tillet's summary of Louis VI's act then served as a convenient bridge to the *Benedictio vexilli*, which he quoted in full.[299] The context in which Du Tillet presented the blessing thus linked it to Abbot Suger and Louis VII's father, and, whether it was Du Tillet's intention or not, implicitly reinforced the ties that he maintained existed between his *ordo* and Louis VII.

The form of the blessing cited by Du Tillet suggests, yet again, that he was using two sources: the first, such a version as is found in the *ordo* of lat. 14192, the other the benediction in the *Ordo maior*.[300] Following the blessing of the *vexillum*, the *Ordo maior* gives these instructions: "ad tradendum autem vexillum domino Regi dicas ita. Diex par sa grace et par les prieres nostre glorieux patron Monseigneur Saint Denis vous doient [*sic*] avoir noble victoire de tous vos ennemis. Amen."[301] This addition Du Tillet reproduced, paraphrasing the introductory remark, rendering *Amen* as "Ainsi soit Il," and making Saint Denis "your"

---

[298] Cf. the text of the charter, ed. "sur l'original" in Felibien, *Histoire de l'Abbaye Royale, pièces justificatives*, lxxxij-iij, no. CIX; see also 136 n. 3 below.

[299] See 137-138 below. Contamine ("L'oriflamme," 209) published the benediction as it appears in the 1580 ed. of Du Tillet's works. The final phrase, replacing Du Tillet's "et cetera," is there supplied from Doublet, *Histoire de l'Abbaye de S. Denys*, 301, who reproduces Du Tillet's translation in a marginal note to the Latin version, which he took from "vn liure manuscrit fort ancien . . . appelé le liure du Sacre," kept in the abbey's treasury with the royal consecration paraphernalia. This was a copy of the *ordo* of Charles V, as the benediction's reference to Denis and his companions and all the saints of God (which Du Tillet's translation omits) reveals: see n. 303 below.

[300] See 97, 116, 137 below.

[301] See 116 below. In "L'oriflamme," 210, Contamine gives the Latin (as published by Texera, from a text with the form of the benediction in the *ordo* of Charles V): "Deus, per suam gratiam ac precibus vestri gloriosi patroni domini sancti Dionysii sociorumque ejus Rustici et Eleutherii, vobis concedat præclaram ab omnibus vestris inimicis obtinere victoriam." See Texera, *Rervm*, 223-37, esp. 229-30; and also Liebman, "Sermon de Philippe de Villette," 469-70.

(rather than "our") glorious patron.[302] Thus the saint's connection with the king and the *oriflamme* was duly (if somewhat distortedly) emphasized. But Du Tillet excised the reference to the saint that appears in the benediction itself. As in the *ordo* of lat. 14192 (as well as the last direct Capetian *ordo* and the *ordo* of Charles IV and Jeanne d'Evreux), Du Tillet's benediction simply invokes "Saint Michael, your archangel, and all celestial virtues," without mentioning the abbey's patron saint.[303]

Du Tillet's chief aim in presenting his *ordo* was hardly strict fidelity to the sources he knew. Rather, he wanted to include in his *Recueil des Roys* an impressive, comprehensive, impeccably pedigreed, and fully fitting French *ordo.* He thus devised his own version of the *ordo* deposited in the Chambre des comptes, perhaps hoping that it would be used to guide the planners of future coronations, but surely trusting that those who consulted his *Recueil des Roys* would be persuaded of the ceremonial's venerableness.

Du Tillet must have expected the authoritativeness of his *ordo* to be accepted without question. The changes that he made in the ranking of peers, the list of saints, and the formula in the prayer of consecration certainly suggest that he was aware that the *Ordo maior* of *Croix* postdated 1179, and that he intended to make it seem older than it was. His inventiveness had its limits, however. For reasons known only to himself he did not excise the clause of the coronation oath containing the pledge to expel heretics from the kingdom that was added to the oath after the Fourth Lateran Council of 1215.[304] He may have been unaware of the clause's

---

[302] Doublet (*Histoire de l'Abbaye de S. Denys,* 301) restores *nostre.* His account of the *oriflamme* (ibid., 301-5) is heavily dependent on Du Tillet's discussion, much of which (including Du Tillet's characterization of Robert's diploma of 997) he quotes or paraphrases.

[303] Ward, "Early Version," 349, 361; 97 below (*ordo* of lat. 14192); Urbana-Champaign *Ordo,* fol. 22v; and 137-138 below. The *ordo* of Charles V further expands this, appending "sed et beatorum martyrum dyonisij. rustici et eleutherij. omniumque sanctorum tuorum" to "omniumque celestium uirtutum": *Coronation Book,* ed. Dewick, 50. This *ordo* also adds "the defense of the kingdom" to that "of holy church" ("ob deffensionem regni et sancte ecclesie"). Contamine, "L'oriflamme," 208-9, prints the three versions of the *Benedictio vexilli* published without attribution by Texera: ibid., 180; see also nn. 299, 301 above. The first of Texera's versions is similar to, but differs in significant respects from, that found in early *ordines;* the second is the blessing in the *Ordo maior* of *Croix;* the third is that of the *ordo* of Charles V. Texera's account of the history of the *oriflamme* (*Rervm,* 229-30) is dependent on Du Tillet's and, like his, cites Robert's charter of 997.

[304] See 120 below. Innocent III's decree commanded that "saeculares potestates, quibuscunque fungantur officiis, ut, sicut reputari cupiunt et haberi fideles, ita pro defensione fidei praestent publice iuramentum, quod de terris suae iurisdictioni subiectis universis haereticos, ab ecclesia denotatos, bona fide pro viribus exterminare studebunt, ita, quod amodo, quandocunque quis fuerit in potestatem sive perpetuam sive temporalem assumptus, hoc teneatur capitulum iuramento firmare": *Corpus iuris canonici,* ed. Friedberg, 2: 788 (*Excommunicamus itaque et anathematizamus;* Extra V.7.13.3). Buchner hypothesized

date, for although it is clearly associated with "la nouvelle constitucion du Concile de Latran" in the *ordo* of Reims (which was also copied in *Croix*), that *ordo* specifies neither the date nor the number of the Council.[305] Perhaps, opposed as he was to the Huguenots, he permitted his animosities to overcome his better judgment.[306] The prayer accompanying the bestowal of the ring in the *ordo* he presented, after all, admonished the king "to exterminate heresies" ("exterminer les heresies"), as he rendered the phrase "hereses destruere"; Du Tillet may have known that this formula had long been part of the coronation ceremonial.[307]

Du Tillet also let stand his *ordo*'s equally anachronistic reference to the obligation of the abbot of Saint-Denis to bring the regalia to the ceremony. As he himself pointed out in his chapter on the coronation, they were not deposited at the abbey until 1260, and hence the abbot could hardly have been expected to act as their guardian in 1179.[308] Du Tillet's failure to rid the *ordo* of these two anachronistic elements could be interpreted as suggesting that his attribution of his *ordo* to 1179 was an innocent error. Excessive enthusiasm for his hypotheses concerning Reims and the peers of France might have led him to criticize his source with insufficient rigor. But the modifications that he did make in the end overbalance the anachronisms that he did not excise and seem persuasive evidence that he was consciously misleading his readers. His aims are, however, understandable, his deceit

that Du Tillet himself added the clause: "Zur Datierung," 376; idem, "Nochmals," 343. The omission of this part of the coronation oath from the *ordo* of 1250 led Schreuer to believe the ceremonial no later than the reign of Louis VIII: "Noch einmal," 153-54, 166, 177-83.

305 See n. 320 below.

306 Brown, *Du Tillet and the French Wars of Religion.* In a tract written during the second religious war of 1567-68, Du Tillet reminded Charles IX that like his predecessors he had sworn a solemn oath at his coronation "de garder lunyon de ladicte eglise et extirper de vostredict Royaume toute heresye": BN, Dupuy 240, fols. 57r-74r, at 59r; ed. in Brown, *Du Tillet and the French Wars of Religion*. Note, however, that the clause regarding heresy does not seem to have been included in the oath that Henry II swore in 1547: Jackson, *Vive le Roi!*, 57-58, 117, 210-11, 250 n. 10 (Fr. ed., 57-58, 109-10, 194-95). Jean Golein omitted the clause in his treatise on the consecration: *"Traité du sacre,"* 313 (esp. n. 56). A remonstrance regarding unjust royal letters prepared by the Parlement of Paris in the 1560s for presentation to the king (which Du Tillet corrected and expanded and may have composed) insisted, citing the example of Philip I in 1059, that "Lesdictz Roys treschretiens anciennement auant que estre sacrés et couronnés faisoient leur profession de foy," and, the remonstrance added, "Le font encores, faisant serment solennel dextirper les heresyes": BN, fr. 17294, fol. 147v. For background, Sutherland, "Was There an Inquisition?," 24; on the profession of faith, n. 157 above.

307 See 93, 110, 126 below. In *Etude sur le Sacre*, 119-20, Quéant cites the benediction from "le Formulaire de Louis VII."

308 *Recveil des Roys*, 186, and 84 below (the Godefroys' retention of this statement). The pirated eds. of Du Tillet's work, published in 1578, misdated the act 1270: see *Les Memoires et Recerches* (Troyes ed.), 154v.

well-meaning. These judgments do not apply to Theodore and Denys Godefroy, who used Du Tillet's *ordo* for purposes that Du Tillet did not intend and in all likelihood would have decried.

3. Theodore Godefroy and Du Tillet's *Ordo*

Du Tillet's *ordo* does not appear to have exercised any influence on coronation ceremonial in the years immediately following the presentation of the *Recueil des Roys* to Charles IX.[309] However, the printed editions of this *Recueil* that appeared between 1578 and 1618 publicized his *ordo*, and, as has been seen, some readers then and later were convinced that it had indeed been confected in 1179.[310] Du Tillet's pious fraud was endorsed and the case for the *ordo*'s authenticity strengthened when Theodore Godefroy chose to include it in the compilation of French coronation *ordines* that his son Denys presented in *Le Ceremonial François*.

The changes which the Godefroys made in Du Tillet's *ordo*, soon to be discussed, reveal their awareness that the *ordo* could not possibly have been created for Philip Augustus' consecration. Nonetheless they confidently (and shamelessly) identified it as "L'ordre qvi se doit observer au Sacre & Couronnement des Roys de France. Commandé par le Roy Louys le Ieune l'an 1179. & enregistré en la Chambre des Comptes à Paris." To support the date, the *ordo* was doctored to remove inconsistencies and problems that Du Tillet had ignored or disregarded. In this case the dispassionate dedication to truth that Denys Godefroy lauded in his father[311] was overbalanced by other considerations. Interested in preserving French traditions, Theodore Godefroy seems to have had fewer qualms than Du Tillet about shaping the legacy of the past when its contours displeased him. As concerns Du Tillet's *ordo*, Godefroy proved to be his predecessor's nemesis, since the later *ordines* published in the *Le Ceremonial François* refuted Du Tillet's claim that his *ordo* had been used for all subsequent coronations since that of Philip Augustus.

---

[309] Precisely what *ordo* was used for the coronation of Henry III on 13 February 1575 is unknown, but the length of the service indicates the possible use of the *ordo* of Charles V: Jackson, *Vive le Roi!*, 233 n. 33, and also 35-36 (Fr. ed., 39-40, esp. n. 33).

[310] See 5-12 above.

[311] In his introduction to *Le Ceremonial François*, Denys Godefroy assured readers that his father, who had worked on the collection for more than thirty years, had diligently compared the texts "sur les originaux en toute fidelité sans suiure aucun party ny passion que celuy de la verité, & de la bonne foy": *Ceremonial*, ed. Godefroy, 1: [4]r. In 1910 and 1912 Buchner insisted that Godefroy had controlled Du Tillet's *ordo* against at least one independent MS of the ceremonial: "Zur Datierung," 369, 375-76; "Nochmals," 344.

When he gathered materials for *Le Ceremonial François*, Theodore Godefroy should surely have rejected Du Tillet's *ordo*. He succumbed, however, to the ceremonial's attractions. The early date that Du Tillet had assigned it made it too appealing for Godefroy to disregard. If this date was accepted as accurate (and could be made to seem so), the *ordo* could take its place as the earliest of the full coronation ceremonials that he assembled, preceding the *ordo* of 1250 (which Godefroy termed the *ordo* of Louis VIII),[312] a translation of the *ordo* of Reims of 1226-50 (which he assigned to Saint Louis), the *ordo* of Charles V (1365), that of Louis XIII (1610), and miscellaneous records of other coronations.[313]

For his own edition of Du Tillet's *ordo*, Godefroy seems to have relied on a corrected manuscript copy that survives among his papers, which is exceedingly faithful to the version in Du Tillet's *Recueil*.[314] Although most of Du Tillet's extended editorial comments are omitted from the copy, it ends with the reference to the coronation of Henry II and Catherine de Medicis that terminates Du Tillet's translation. Naturally enough, Godefroy excluded this from his edition, although he inserted his own condensed version of Du Tillet's comments on Saint Marcoul, omitted from the copy. Thus, Godefroy declared, after leaving Reims the king customarily went to visit Saint Marcoul, six leagues from Reims, to make his novena, and then he touched those suffering from scrofula; Godefroy did not, however, include

[312] Jackson, *Vive le Roi!*, 222-23 (Fr. ed., 208); *Ceremonial*, ed. Godefroy, 1: 13-25. A copy of this *ordo* is preserved among Godefroy's papers: BIF, MS Godefroy 380, pp. 179-227.

[313] *Ceremonial*, ed. Godefroy, 1: 1-12 (Du Tillet's *ordo*); ibid., 1: 13-25 (the *ordo* of 1250); ibid., 1: 26-29 (the *ordo* of Reims, in French); ibid., 1: 31-51 (the *ordo* of Charles V); ibid., 1: 52-76 (the *ordo* of Louis XIII). The *ordo* of Reims survives in both Latin and French copies; see n. 278 above. According to Godefroy, his French ed. (ibid., 1: 26-29) was based on a MS in which it preceded the *Life of Saint Louis* by Guillaume de Nangis; he remarked (ibid., 1: 26) that the source, in Latin and in French, was to be found in the libraries of Dupuy and of Petau ("Ce manuscrit se trouve, tant en Latin qu'en François, és Bibliotheques de Messieurs du Puy, & Petau"). Among his notes is a copy of the French translation of the *ordo* of Reims, of which he notes "Le Memoire qui suit est en Latin[.] Monsieur du Chesne en a Coppie. Il est en la Biblioteque de Monsieur Petau, deuant la vie du Roy Sainct Louy [*sic*], escripte par Nangis": BIF, MS Godefroy 380, pp. 335-50. Godefroy must be referring to the Latin copy of the *ordo* of Reims in BAV, Reg. lat. 574, fols. 17r-19v (a single leaf and bifolium, with fol. 19r-v blank). This MS belonged to Paul Petau, notes in whose hand appear on fols. 1r, 17r, and 20r. Preceding the *ordo* it contains the abbreviated chronicle of Guillaume de Nangis (fols. 1r-16v) and, following it, Guillaume's *Life of Saint Louis* (fols. 20r-90v) and his *Life of Philip III* (fols. 91r-126r); the MS is copied and decorated in one early-fourteenth-century hand. Presumably Pierre Dupuy's library contained a copy of the *ordo* in French (or perhaps in both French and Latin). Godefroy published the *ordo* of Charles V from the version in the 2nd ed. (1631) of Selden's *Titles of Honor* (taken from London, British Library, MS Cotton Tiberius B. viii), 222-55: *Ceremonial*, ed. Godefroy, 1: 31-51; see n. 3 above.

[314] BIF, MS Godefroy 380, pp. 351-84, entitled, in Theodore Godefroy's hand, "L'Ordre qui se doibt observer au Sacre & couronnement des Rois de France, Par le Greffier du Tillet."

Du Tillet's description of Philip the Fair's deathbed instructions to his son.[315] The passage on Saint Marcoul, like other differences between Godefroy's edition and the copy,[316] show that Godefroy must have used not only his own manuscript copy but also a fuller version of Du Tillet's *ordo,* either in manuscript or in published form. Godefroy's alteration of the manuscript copy's "la suiestion de ton pere" to "la succesion de ton pere" in the admonition *Sta et retine* indicates that he may have consulted one of the two 1578 editions of Du Tillet's *Recueil des Roys* or a manuscript copy of the work containing this variant, although the modification may possibly reflect the influence of the *ordo* of Charles V.[317] Godefroy also changed the list of saints in the post-coronation blessing, *Extendat omnipotens Deus.* Whereas his manuscript copy of Du Tillet's *ordo* ends with "Sainct Gregoire et tous les Saincts," the published version, like the last direct Capetian *ordo,* the *ordo* of Charles IV and Jeanne d'Evreux, and, most important, the *ordo* used for the consecration of Louis XIII, features "sainct Denys, sainct Remy, & tous les Saints."[318] Affected by one of these *or-*

---

[315] "Au partir de Rheims le Roy à accoustumé d'aller à sainct Marcol qui en est distant de six lieues, & y faire sa neufuaine, aprés il touche les malades des escrouelles"; *Ceremonial,* ed. Godefroy, 1: 11; cf. 132 below (Du Tillet's comment, which omits the distance from Reims and includes "et non plus tost" after *Apres*).

[316] There are numerous minor differences of orthography and punctuation between Godefroy's ed. and his MS copy of Du Tillet's *ordo.* The most important are the following: MS, p. 353, "ils conduiront et reconduiront" (ed., p. 2, "ils reconduiront"); MS, p. 354, "Semblablement" (ed., p. 2, "Cependant"); MS, p. 355, includes the oath against heretics, omitted from ed.; MS, p. 362, "die ledict Archeuesque" (ed., p. 5 "l'Archeuesque dira"); MS, p. 363, "la mansuetude de Moyse, garny de la fortitude de Iosue" and "en toute chose" (ed., p. 5, "la mansuetude de Iosué" and "en toute sorte"); MS, p. 366, "uicteur est monte" (ed., p. 6, "vainqueur est monté"); MS, p. 369, "signcle [*sic*] de la saincte foy" (ed., p. 7, "signal de la sainte Foy"); MS, p. 373, "le dict Archeuesque die les oraison et benediction suiuantes" (ed., p. 8, "ledit Archeuesque die les Oraisons suiuantes"); MS, p. 373, ends the list of saints invoked with "Sainct Gregoire et tous les Saincts" (ed., p. 8, "sainct Denys, sainct Remy, & tous les Saints" [with the last direct Capetian *ordo* and the *ordo* of Charles IV and Jeanne d'Evreux]); in *Sta et retine* (*Sois stable*) MS, p. 375, "suiestion" (ed., p. 9, "succession"); ibid., following "afin que," MS, p. 376, is defective, omitting "le mediateur de Dieu et des hommes te confirme mediateur du clergé et," and including only the final portion of this phrase, "du peuple en ce throsne du Royaume" (ed., p. 9, omits both this phrase and the preceding portion cited here); in the following sentence, MS, p. 376, has "Archeuesque" (ed., p. 9, "Euesque"); ed., p. 10, corrects an omission (signaled in MS by a stroke of Godefroy's pen) and reads "le plus grand des Archeuesques, & Euesques" (MS, p. 378, omits "& Euesques"); both MS, p. 360, and ed., p. 4, omit the phrase "Nous tinuoquons seigneur sainct pere tout puissant," before the prayer beginning "Dieu eternel, qu'il te plaise"; in the same prayer both omit the phrase following *ennemis,* "Il puisse eureusement gouuerner le peuple a luy commis" (see 122 below).

[317] See the preceding n. and n. 291 above.

[318] See 74 above, and *Ceremonial,* ed. Godefroy, 1: 70 (the *ordo* of Louis XIII). Saint Remi does not appear in the *Ordo maior* of *Croix* or in the *ordo* of Charles V: 111 below; *Coronation Book,* ed. Dewick, 37.

dines, most probably the last,[319] Godefroy doubtless decided that Gregory, the apostle of the English, was as inappropriate as the Saxons, the Mercians, and the Northumbrians in an *ordo* destined for a king of France.

The most telling and significant of Godefroy's changes was his deletion from Du Tillet's *ordo* of the portion of the coronation oath referring to the expulsion of heretics from the realm. He thus revealed his knowledge that as it stood the *ordo* could not conceivably have been composed in 1179.

Godefroy fully realized that the clause regarding heretics was added to the oath after the Fourth Lateran Council of 1215. A note to his own copy of the French translation of the *ordo* of Reims remarks (beside "Et le Serment de la nouuelle Constitution du Consille de Latran") "Le Serment de mectre les heretiques hors le Royaume de France est depuis le Concile de Latran en l'an 1216 [*sic*]." Beside the same statement in *Le Ceremonial François* is the comment "Il [le Concile] fut tenu en l'an 1215. sous le Pape Innocent III. regnant Philippe Auguste."[320] Further, a long note that follows the *ordines* in *Le Ceremonial François* states that the oath against heretics was not taken by Louis VIII, and that a register of the Chambre des comptes (doubtless one containing the translated *ordo* of Reims), as well as a book on royal consecrations (which Godefroy dated *ca* 1378) owned by Jacques-Auguste de Thou (1553-1617), showed that this oath was not sworn until after the Council of 1215.[321] Thus Godefroy omitted the pledge from his edition of Du Tillet's *ordo,* inserting in its place a phrase adapted from the *ordo* of 1250, "Que toute

---

319 See 85 below.

320 BIF, MS Godefroy 380, p. 339; *Ceremonial,* ed. Godefroy, 1: 27; BAV, Reg. lat. 574, fol. 17v (see n. 313 above) ("preter iuramentum lateranensis concilij. videlicet de hereticis / de regno suo exstirpandis"). In copies in or taken from the registers of the Chambre des comptes, the phrase is translated "hors le serement de la nouele constitucion du Concile du Latran. Cest assauoir de mectre hors de son Royaume les hereges": BN, lat. 12814 (*Noster*[1]), fol. 28r; BN, fr. 4596, fol. 126r (omitting "nouele"); BN, fr. 16600, fol. 318r (omitting "nouele"); AN, P 2288, p. 708. Although the Latin version of the *ordo* states that the king is to offer thirteen gold coins at his coronation, the translations all replace "tresdecim" with ".xj." or "unze": BAV, Reg. lat. 574, fol. 18r ("tredecim aureos"); BN, lat. 12814, fol. 29v; BN, fr. 4596, fol. 129r; BN, fr. 16600, fol. 320r; AN, P 2288, pp. 714, 724. Godefroy apparently knew, perhaps from later practice, perhaps from consulting the Latin version of the ceremonial in the Vatican MS, that the king was supposed to make an offering of thirteen rather than eleven gold coins. In *Ceremonial,* 1: 29, Godefroy printed the text as he found it in his source, but in a marginal note commented, confusingly, "La Reyne n'offre que onze deniers d'or, & le Roy offre treize escus." In "De l'influence du cérémonial byzantin," Jackson discusses this custom; in "Anzeichen der Vergötterung," 99, he comments on its significance.

321 *Ceremonial,* ed. Godefroy, 1: 79-80 (revision of a note found in BIF, MS Godefroy 384, fol. 4r, where he includes his estimation of the date of de Thou's MS).

l'assistance responde aux promesses qu'aura fait le Roy, tant aux Eglises qu'au peuple, Ainsi soit-il."[322] He then appended a phrase ("puis le Roy derechef adioustera") to bridge his return to Du Tillet's *ordo* and continued, following his manuscript copy of this text, "Toutes les choses susdites ie confirme par serment."[323] Godefroy evidently deleted the pledge against heretics from Du Tillet's *ordo* in order to banish any suspicion that the *ordo* had been redacted after 1215, although, curiously, he did not excise the anachronistic reference to the abbot of Saint-Denis as guardian of the regalia.

Because he believed it consistent with the date that Du Tillet assigned to his *ordo* Godefroy retained Du Tillet's designation of the peoples whose scepters the king was not to abandon. The phrase "les Sceptres des François, Bourguignons & Aquitainiens" was particularly useful, since "Saxonum, Merciorum, Nordanchimbrorum sceptra" replaced it in the later *ordines* that Godefroy presented, and he attributed considerable significance to the change. His marginal notations to the references to Saxons, Mercians, and Northumbrians in his manuscript copies of the *ordo* of 1250 and the *ordo* of Charles V draw attention to "Le Royaume d'Angleterre,"[324] references that he expanded in his editions of these *ordines* and that of Louis XIII. Explaining the change from the Frankish to the English peoples, Godefroy repeatedly informed his readers that the formula "Saxons, Mercians, and Northumbrians" was introduced into the coronation ceremony because Philip Augustus' son Louis was elected king of England in 1216.[325] Thus, at the appropriate places in the *ordo* that he assigned to Louis VIII, in the *ordo* of Charles V, and in the *ordo* of Louis XIII, marginal notations declare, "Ces mots signifient le Royaume *d'Angleterre,* & ont esté mis depuis le Regne du Roy

[322] Cf., from the *ordo* of 1250, "Si sanctas Dei ecclesias ac rectores ecclesiarum nec non & cunctum populum sibi subjectum juste ac religiose regali providentia juxta morem patrum suorum defendere ac regere velit. . . . Tunc ergo a circumstante clero & populo unanimiter dicatur, fiat, fiat. Amen": *De antiquis ritibus,* ed. Martène, 2: 219; *Ceremonial,* ed. Godefroy, 1: 16-17.

[323] *Ceremonial,* ed. Godefroy, 1: 3.

[324] BIF, MS Godefroy 380, pp. 206, 291.

[325] See 75 above (the offer of the crown to Louis in the fall of 1215). In Godefroy's edition the following marginal notation appears beside the reference in Du Tillet's *ordo* to "François, Bourguignons & Aquitainiens": "Ces trois mots de cette Priere furent depuis changez sous le Roy Louys VIII. en ceux de *Saxons, Merciens, & Nordan-Cimbriens,* qui signifient & comprennent le Royaume d'Angleterre, ainsi qu'il se verra cy-après": *Ceremonial,* ed. Godefroy, l: 5. In 1643 Marlot (*Theatre d'Honnevr,* 660-61) attributed to Favyn the association between the phrase and the coronation of Louis as king of England in London in 1216.

Louys VIII. qui fut esleu Roy d'Angleterre en l'an 1216."[326] Following the *ordines* Godefroy included a lengthy note on the claims to England that the French kings derived from Louis VIII, in which he cited supporting passages from Jean Juvenal des Ursins and Du Tillet's *Recueil des Angloys*.[327]

Godefroy's version of Du Tillet's *ordo* thus took its place as the first text in the sequence of coronation ceremonials in *Le Ceremonial François*. Under the circumstances it is understandable that Godefroy included in his collection neither the last direct Capetian *ordo*[328] nor the *Ordo maior* of *Croix*. Godefroy may conceivably have been unfamiliar with the former, but it is hard to imagine that neither he nor his son knew the *Ordo maior* of *Croix*. Both had access to the Chambre des comptes, and they possessed a copy of extracts from *Croix* that referred to the two *ordines* in the register[329]; the longer *ordo* was listed in inventories of the registers of the Chambre and was mentioned in *Noster*[1] and in the 1607 edition of Du Tillet's *Recueil des Roys*, which included the inventories of the *Recueil des Roys* for Henry II. Had Godefroy included in his collection the *Ordo maior* of *Croix*, however, the marked similarities between it and the alleged *ordo* of 1179 would have led any thoughtful reader to question the authenticity of his first *ordo* and the date assigned to it.

The weight of the Godefroys' authority, reinforcing that of Du Tillet, was sufficient to mislead the public and later scholars, many of whom have been persuaded that Du Tillet's *ordo* in fact dates from the reign of Louis VII and that his French translation is medieval. But no more than the Godefroys has any subsequent scholar been tempted to conclude that, as Du Tillet maintained, his *ordo* was used for all royal coronations from 1179 through his own day.

Conclusion

Pursuit of the presence of the Franks, the Burgundians, and the Aquitanians in the French coronation ceremony has led from

[326] *Ceremonial*, ed. Godefroy, 1: 39 (the notation to the *ordo* of Charles V, which continues "Auparauant il se disoit: Vt Regale solium, videlicet Francorum, Burgundiorum, Aquitanorum sceptra non deserat"). See also ibid., 1: 20 (the *ordo* of 1250, attributed to Louis VIII), 1: 65 (the *ordo* of Louis XIII).

[327] *Ceremonial*, ed. Godefroy, 1: 80-82. In *Dictionnaire historique*, 1120, Chéruel writes, "Un auteur anonyme dit, que par les Cimbres on entend le royaume d'Angleterre, sur lequel nos rois se réservent expressément leurs droits incontestables depuis Louis VIII, auquel il fut déféré par la libre élection du peuple, qui avait chassé Jean sans Terre."

[328] Schramm, "Ordines-Studien II," 33-38, no. 17; Jackson, *Vive le Roi!*, 223 (Fr. ed., 208).

[329] BIF, MS Godefroy 184, fols. 2r, 4v.

the twelfth through the seventeenth century and beyond. Introduced in the twelfth century to adapt an alien *ordo* to the realities of French kingship, the phrase was quickly and abruptly rejected in favor of the exotic formula "Saxons, Mercians, and Northumbrians," which from time to time cohered with the aspirations of the French but never with political reality. If my hypotheses are correct, the *ordo* composed in the twelfth century stands as testimony to the acumen, historical sensitivity, and veneration for tradition of one of Louis VI's councilors—in all probability Abbot Suger of Saint-Denis. The revival of the formula in the sixteenth century was the work of a less centrally involved but no less politically-minded servant of the French crown, Jean du Tillet. By incorporating the antique triad into a later, venerable, and authoritative *ordo,* he presented Charles IX with a ceremonial more congruent with France's history than the *ordines* which proclaimed the French kings possessors of the scepters of the Saxons, Mercians, and Northumbrians. His efforts in part succeeded. In *Le Ceremonial François* the Godefroys published Du Tillet's *ordo* as the first in their collection of French coronation *ordines.* Through their efforts the case that Du Tillet had made for assigning the *ordo* to 1179 was strengthened, and the *ordo* given publicity. On the other hand, in their collection Du Tillet's masterpiece appeared as an object of antiquarian interest rather than as a document that might have persuaded those who planned royal coronations to banish forever the Saxons, the Mercians, and the Northumbrians from the consecrations of future kings of France and to substitute for those alien peoples the Franks, the Burgundians, and the Aquitanians.

The story of the formula "Franks, Burgundians, and Aquitanians" is one of failure: a promising idea, promoted for excellent reasons, never gained acceptance. Its prospects for success were frustrated by circumstances and by the weight of custom and tradition, whose ineluctable force its fate demonstrates. Long usage is comforting, and accepted ritual, however inappropriate, difficult to displace. The remarkable vitality of the Saxons, Mercians, and Northumbrians in a land they had never inhabited probably resulted more from French veneration for tradition than from the inattention that John Selden suspected. Their strange presence in the coronation ceremonial afforded French apologists a welcome occasion for invoking their kings' antique claims to England, and their arguments reflect French frustration at the rights the English asserted over and for a time exercised in their own nation. It is not surprising that these contrived explanations were first advanced in the seventeenth century, when national rivalries flourished. In contrast, the presence of the alien peoples in the French coronation ceremonial demonstrates the closeness of the ties that bound the ecclesiastics of western Christendom in an age when geographical obstacles posed fewer obstacles to free communication than did the national, political, and religious barriers of the seventeenth century.

The introduction of the Franks, Burgundians, and Aquitanians into the ritual of French coronation shows that tradition, however powerful, was not immutable, and that ceremonial could be altered to suit the needs of the moment. Royal inaugurations, like royal funerals, invited creativity and inventiveness, however much past rituals were studied and imitated. The incorporation of the three peoples into the French ceremonial when Louis VII married Eleanor of Aquitaine would have been consistent with the efforts of Louis VI, his son, and their dedicated adviser Suger to create a union of French lands extending royal power far beyond the Ile-de-France. These plans were aborted by the divorce of Louis and Eleanor, which made it necessary for the French kings to accomplish through conquest and negotiation what could have been won through marriage. Philip Augustus opened the new route, and there is a certain poetic justice in Du Tillet's linking with his coronation the use of the French triplet in the prayer of royal consecration.

If the addition of the French, Burgundians, and Aquitanians to the coronation ritual in the twelfth century witnesses the occasional plasticity of tradition, Jean du Tillet's revival of the phrase in the sixteenth century demonstrates both the respect with which he and his contemporaries regarded the past and their willingness to shape it to serve what they considered present needs. Du Tillet aimed to present a coronation *ordo* appropriate for the future, but rather than delineate an ideal ceremonial, he chose to link the elaborate *ordo* that he found in the Chambre des comptes with the coronation of Philip Augustus. Its association with such a prestigious monarch would, he must have reasoned, gain for it admiration it would not otherwise have commanded. His was pious deception, but the Godefroys' exploitation of his work is far less excusable. They were not creating a new ceremonial, nor were they interested in establishing an *ordo* for the future. Rather, they knowingly altered Du Tillet's *ordo* to make it appear what it was not, in order to complete the series of *ordines* that they presented as authentic records of the past. For the sum of their accomplishments, all students of the history of French ceremonial stand in their debt, as they do in Du Tillet's, but their treatment of his *ordo,* like his treatment of the *Ordo maior* of *Croix,* offers fair warning that, like tradition, standards of truth and accuracy are mutable, and that attitudes to the legacy of the past vary as widely from individual to individual as they do from age to age.

APPENDIX

I.

A.
Ordo of BN, Lat. 14192, Fols. 73r-83r

In this edition the capitalization and the punctuation of the manuscript are retained, although divisions into sections are introduced. Abbreviations are expanded. No attempt has been made to collate the text with the defective seventeenth-century copy in Chantilly, Institut de France, Musée Condé, Cabinet des livres, MS 1149 (XIX D 17), fols. 4r-9r (in which the leaf from the early pontifical is transcribed as if it were part of the *ordo*); on this manuscript, see also 15 n. 50 above.

• • • • •

Incipit per cunctatio siue electio episcoporum ac clericorum nec non populorum ad regem consecrandum. ammonitio episcoporum ad regem dicendo ita. Legatur ab uno episcopo coram omnibus.[a]

A uobis per donari petimus. ut unicuique de nobis & ęcclesiis nobis commissis canonicum priuilegium ac debitam legem atque iusticiam conseruetis. & defensionem exhibeatis. sicut rex in suo regno debet unicuique episcopo & ecclesię sibi commisse .per.

Responsio regis. ad episcopos[b]

Pro mitto uobis & per dono quia unicuique de uobis. & ęcclesiis uobis commissis canonicum priuilegium. & debitam legem atque iusticiam seruabo. & defensionem quantum potuero ad iuuante domino exhibebo sicut rex in suo regno unicuique episcopo & ęcclesie sibi commisse perrectę exhibere debet.

Deinde alloquantur duo episcopi populum in ęcclesia inquirentes eorum uoluntatem & si concordes fuerint agant deo gratias

[a] In four lines, alternatively red and blue.
[b] Rubric.

dicentes Te deum laudamus. & duo episcopi accipient[c] eum per manus. & deducant ante altare & prosternet se usque in finem te deum laudamus.

Inuocatio super regem.[d]

Te inuocamus domine sanctę pater omnipotens ęterne deus. ut hunc famulum tuum .N. quem tuę diuinę dispensationis prouidentia inprimordio plasmatum. usque inhunc presentem diem iuuenili flore letantem crescere concessisti. eum tuę pietatis dono ditatum. plenumque gratia ueritatis dedie indiem coram deo & hominibus ad meliora semper proficere facias. ut summi regiminis solium gratię supernę largitate gaudens suscipiat. & misericordię tuę muro abhostium aduersitate undique munitus plebem sibi commissam cum pace propiciationis & uirtute uictorię feliciter regere mereatur .per.

Alia.[e]

Deus qui populis tuis uirtute consulis. & amore dominaris. da huic famulo tuo spiritum sapientię cum regimine disciplinę ut tibi toto corde deuotus. in regni regimine maneat semper idoneus. tuoque munere ipsius temporibus securitas ecclesię dirigatur. & intranquillitate deuotio christiana permaneat. ut in bonis operibus perseuerans. ad ęternum regnum te duce ualeat. peruenire .per.

Alia

Indiebus eius oriatur omnibus ęquitas & iusticia. amicis ad iutorium. inimicis obstaculum. humilibus solatium. elatis correctio. diuitibus doctrina. pauperibus pietas. peregrinis pacificatio. propriis in patria pax & securitas. unicuique secundum suam mensuram. moderatę gubernans. se ipsum sedulus discat. ut tua irrigatus compunctione toto populo tibi placita prebere uitæ possit exempla. & per uiam ueritatis cum grege gradiens sibi subdito. opes frugales habundanter adquirat. simulque ad salutem non solum corporum sed etiam cordium ate concessam cuncta accipiat. Sicque inte cogitatum animi consiliumque omne componens. plebis gubernacula cum pace simul & sapientia semper inuenire uideatur. teque auxiliante presentis uitę prolixitatem percipiat. & per tempora bona usque ad summam senectutem perueniat. huiusque fragilitatis finem perfectum abomnibus uiciorum uinculis tuę pietatis largitate liberatus. & infinitę prosperitatis premia perpetua. angelorumque ęterna commercia consequatur .per.

---

[c] Corrected from *accipiunt* or *accipiant*.

[d] These lines alternate between red and blue, except that the first *Te deum laudamus* is in black.

[e] This and the next *Alia* are rubricated.

Consecratio Regis.[f]

Omnipotens sempiterne deus. creator ac gubernator cęli & terrę. conditor & dispositor angelorum & hominum. rex regum & dominus dominorum. qui abraham fidelem famulum tuum de hostibus triumphare fecisti. moysi & iosue populo tuo prelatis multiplicem uictoriam tribuisti. humilem quoque puerum tuum dauid regni fastigio sublimasti. eumque de ore leonis & demanu bestię atque golię. sed & de gladio maligno saul & omnium inimicorum eius liberasti. & salomonem sapientię pacisque in effabili munere ditasti. respice propitius ad preces nostrę humilitatis. & super hunc famulum tuum .N. quem supplici deuotione in regnum pariter elegimus. benedictionum tuarum dona multiplica. eumque dextera tuę potentię semper ubique circunda. quatinus predicti abrahę fidelitate firmatus. moysi mansuetudine fretus. iosue fortitudine munitus. dauid humilitate exaltatus. salomonis sapientia decoratus. tibi in omnibus complaceat. & pertramitem iusticię inoffenso gressu semper incedat. & tocius regni ęcclesiam deinceps cum plebibus sibi annexis ita enutriat. ac doceat. muniat. & instruat. contraque omnes uisibiles & inuisibiles hostes idem potenter regaliterque tuę uirtutis regimen amministret. ut regale solium uidelicet francorum burgundiorum aquitanorum sceptra non deserat. sed ad pristinę fidei pacisque concordiam eorum animos te opitulante reformet. ut utrorumque horum populorum debita subiectione fultus. condigno amore glorificatus. per longum uitę spatium paternę apicem glorię tua miseratione unatim stabilire & gubernare mereatur. tuę quoque protectionis galea munitus. & scuto insuperabili iugiter protectus. armisque cęlestibus circundatus. optabilis uictorię triumphum de hostibus feliciter capiat. terroremque suę potentię infidelibus inferat. & pacem tibi militantibus lętanter reportet. Virtutibus[g] nec non quibus prefatos fideles tuos decorasti. multiplici honoris benedictione con decora. & inregimine regni sublimiter colloca. & oleo gratię spiritus sancti perunge.

Ant. Vnxerunt[h] salomonem sadoc sacerdos & nathan propheta regem ingion & accedentes leti dixerunt uiuat rex inęternum

Hic ungatur oleo.[i]

Vnde unxisti sacerdotes. reges. & prophetas. ac martires. qui perfidem uicerunt regna operati sunt iusticiam atque ad epti sunt promissiones. Cuius sacratissima unctio super caput eius defluat atque ad interiora descendat. & cordis illius intima penetret. &

---

[f] Rubric.
[g] The first letter is touched with red.
[h] The first letter is touched with red.
[i] Rubric.

promissionibus quas ad epti sunt uictoriosissimi reges gratia tua dignus efficiatur. quatinus & in presenti seculo feliciter regnet. & ad eorum consorcium incęlesti regno perueniat. per dominum nostrum ihesum christum filium tuum. qui unctus est. oleo leticię pre consortibus suis. & uirtute crucis potestates aereas debellauit. tartara destruxit. regnumque diaboli superauit. & ad cęlos uictor ascendit. in cuius manu uictoria omnis gloria & potestas consistunt. & tecum uiuit & regnat deus inunitate eiusdem spiritus sancti .per.

Item[j]

Deus electorum fortitudo. & humilium celsitudo. qui inprimordio per effusionem diluuii crimina mundi castigare uoluisti. & per columbam ramum oliuę portantem pacem terris redditam de monstrasti. iterumque aaron famulum tuum per unctionem olei sacerdoctem sanxisti. & postea per huius ungenti infusionem ad regendum populum israheliticum sacerdotes reges ac prophetas perfecisti. uultumque ecclesię in oleo exhilarandum per propheticam famuli tui uocem dauid esse. predixisti. ita quesumus[k] omnipotens pater. ut per huius creaturę pinguedinem hunc seruum tuum sanctificare tua benedictione digneris. eumque in similitudine columbę pacem simplicitatis populo sibi commisso prestare. & exempla aaron in dei seruitio diligenter imitari. regnique fastigia inconsiliis scientię & equitate iudicii semper assequi. uultumque hilaritatis per hanc olei unctionem te ad iuuante tocius plebis paratum habere facias .per.

Alia ORATIO[l]

Deus dei filius ihesus christus dominus noster qui apatre oleo exultationis unctus est. preparticipibus suis. ipse per presentem sacri unguinis infusionem spiritus paracliti super caput tuum infundat benedictionem. eandemque usque ad interiora cordis tui penetrare faciat. quatinus hoc uisibili & tractabili dono inuisibilia percipere. & temporali regno iustis moderaminibus ex secuto. ęternaliter cum eo regnare[m] merearis .per.

Hic detur anulus.[n]

Accipe anulum signaculum uidelicet sanctę fidei. soliditatem regni. augmentum potentię. per que scias triumphali potentia

---

[j] Rubric.

[k] MS *qs'*, here and below.

[l] Rubric.

[m] Following this word, seven or eight letters have been abraded at the end of the line; a red line is drawn through the abraded letters; *merearis* follows at the beginning of the next line.

[n] Rubric.

hostes repellere. hereses destruere. subditos coadunare. & catholicę fidei perseuerabilitati conecti .per.

Oratio post anulum datum.[o]

Deus cuius est omnis potestas & dignitas. da famulo tuo pro spiritu suę dignitatis effectum. inqua te remunerante permaneat. semperque timeat. tibique iugiter placere contendat .per.

Hic cingatur ei gladius ab archiepiscopo.[p]

Accipe hunc gladium cum dei benedictione tibi collatum inquo per uirtutem spiritus sancti resistere & eicere omnes inimicos tuos ualeas. & cunctos sanctę dei ecclesię aduersarios. regnumque tibi commissum tueri.[q] atque protegere castra dei. per auxilium inuictissimi triumphatoris domini nostri ihesu christi qui cum patre.

ORATIO Post gladium.[r]

Deus qui prouidentia tua cęlestia simul & terrena moderaris. propiciare christianissimo regi nostro. ut omnis hostium suorum fortitudo uirtute gladii spiritualis frangatur. ac te pro illo pugnante pęnitus conteratur .per.

Hic coronetur.[s]

Coronet te deus corona glorię atque iusticię. honore & opere fortitudinis. ut per officium nostrę benedictionis cum fide recta. & multiplici bonorum operum fructu ad coronam peruenias regni perpetui. ipso largiente cuius regnum & imperium permanet insecula seculorum.

Post coronam.[t]

Deus perpetuitatis. dux uirtutum. cunctorum hostium uictor. benedic hunc famulum tuum tibi caput suum inclinantem. & prolixa sanitate. & prospera felicitate eum conserua. & ubicumque proquibus auxilium tuum inuocauerit cito adsis. & protegas ac defendas. Tribue ei quesumus domine diuicias gratię tuę. comple[u] in bonis desiderium eius corona sit ei in miseratione & misericordia. tibique domino pia deuotione iugiter famuletur .per.

Hic detur sceptrum.[v]

Accipe sceptrum regię potestatis insigne. uirgam scilicet rectam regni. uirgam uirtutis qua te ipsum bene regas. sanctam

[o] Rubric.
[p] Rubric.
[q] Over *taturi*.
[r] Rubric.
[s] Rubric.
[t] Rubric.
[u] *o* corrected from *u*.
[v] Rubric.

ęcclesiam populumque uidelicet christianum tibi adeo commissum regia uirtute ab inprobis defendas prauos corrigas. rectos pacificas. ut uiam rectam tenere possint tuo iuuamine dirigas. quatinus de temporali regno ad ęternum regnum peruenias. ipso adiuuante
cuius regnum & imperium sine fine permanet insecula seculorum.

ORATIO Post sceptrum.[w]

Omnium domine fons bonorum. cunctorumque deus institutor profectuum. tribue quesumus famulo tuo. illi. ad eptam bene regere dignitatem. & ate sibi[x] prestitum honorem dignare corroborare. honorifica eum precunctis regibus terrę. uberi[y] eum benedictione locupleta. & in solio regni firma stabilitate consolida. Visita eum insobole. presta ei prolixitatem uitę. indiebus eius semper oriatur iusticia. ut cum iocunditate & lęticia ęterno glorietur[z] in regno .per.

Hic datur[a] ei uirga.[b]

Accipe uirgam uirtutis atque ęquitatis qua intelligas mulcere pios. & terrere reprobos. errantes uiam doce. lapsisque manum porrige. disperdasque superbos. & reueles[c] humiles. ut aperiat tibi ostium ihesus christus dominus noster. qui de seipso ait. ego sum ostium. per me si quis introierit saluabitur. & ipse qui est. clauis dauid & sceptrum domus israel. qui aperit & nemo claudit. claudit & nemo aperit. Sit[d] tibi adiutor qui educit uinctum de domo carceris. sedentem intenebris & umbra mortis. ut in omnibus sequi merearis eum dequo propheta dauid cecinit. Sedes tua deus in seculum seculi. uirga ęquitatis uirga regni tui. Et imiteris eum qui dicit. diligas iusticiam. & odio habeas iniquitatem. propterea unxit te deus deus tuus oleo leticię ad exemplum illius quem ante secula unxerat preparticipibus suis ihesum christum dominum nostrum

Tunc dicatur benedictio.[e]

Extendat omnipotens deus dexteram suę benedictionis. & effundat superte donum suę protectionis. & circundet te muro fe-

---

[w] Rubric.

[x] An erasure of three letters follows, at the end of the line.

[y] *Sic;* in Ward, "Early Version," 355, *uber.*

[z] Two letters following this word have been abraded.

[a] *Sic,* for *detur.*

[b] Rubric.

[c] *Sic,* for *releues.*

[d] The initial *S* is touched with green, as are the two following capital letters, in *Sedes* and *Et.*

[e] Rubric.

licitatis ac custodia suę propitiationis sanctę MARIE[f] ac beati PETRI apostolorum principis. sanctique gregorii atque omnium sanctorum intercedentibus meritis. AMEN.

Indulgeat tibi dominus omnia mala quę gessisti. & tribuat tibi gratiam & misericordiam quam humiliter ab eo deposcis. & liberet te ab aduersitatibus cunctis. & ab omnibus inimicorum uisibilium & inuisibilium insidiis. AMEN.

Angelos suos bonos semper & ubique qui te precedant. comitentur. & subsequantur. ad custodiam tui ponat. & a peccato seu[g] gladio & abomnium periculorum discrimine sua potentia liberet. AMEN.

Inimicos tuos ad pacis caritatisque benignitatem conuertat. & bonis omnibus te gratiosum & amabilem faciat. pertinaces[h] quoque intui insectatione & odio confusione salutari induat. superte autem sanctificatio sempiterna floreat. AMEN.

Victoriosum te atque triumphatorem de inuisibilibus atque uisibilibus hostibus semper efficiat. & sancti nominis sui timorem pariter & amorem continuo cordi tuo infundat. & infide recta ac bonis operibus perseuerabilem reddat. & pacem diebus[i] tuis concessa. cum palma uictorię te ad perpetuum regnum perducat. AMEN.

Et[j] qui te uoluit super populum suum constituere regem. & in presenti seculo felicem. ęterne felicitatis tribuat esse. consortem. Quod ipse prestare.

Alia[k]

Benedic domine hunc presulem principem. qui regna omnium regum aseculo moderaris. AMEN.

Et tali eum benedictione glorifica. ut dauitica teneat sublimitate sceptrum salutis. & sanctifice propiciationis munere reperiatur locupletatus. AMEN.

Da ei atuo spirimine regere populum. sicut salomonem fecisti regnum optinere pacificum. Quod ipse prestare dignetur.

Regis status designatur.[l]

Sta & retine amodo statum. quem huc usque paterna suggestione tenuisti. hereditario iure tibi delegatum. per auctoritatem

---

[f] This word and *Petri* are touched in green, as are the the initial letters of *Indulgeat*, *Angelos*, *Inimicos*, *Victoriosum*, and each *Amen* following *Indulgeat* to the end of this page, fol. 80r (which ends *cum palma*).

[g] Corrected from *sui*.

[h] Corrected from *pertinates*.

[i] *Sic*, for *pace in diebus*.

[j] The initial letter is touched with red.

[k] Rubric.

[l] Rubric.

dei omnipotentis. & per presentem traditionem nostram. omnium scilicet episcoporum. cęterorumque dei seruorum. Et quanto clerum sacris altaribus propinquiorem prospicis. tanto ei potiorem in locis congruis honorem inpendere memineris. quatinus mediator dei & hominum te mediatorem cleri & plebis in hoc regni solio confirmet. & in regnum ęternum secum regnare faciat ihesus christus dominus noster. rex regum & dominus dominantium. qui cum deo.

Rectitudo regis est. nouiter ordinati. & in solium sublimati. hęc tria precepta populo christiano sibi subdito precipere. In primis ut ęcclesia dei & omnis populus christianus ueram pacem seruet in omni tempore. Aliud est. ut rapacitates & omnes iniquitates omnibus gradibus interdicat. Tercium est. ut in omnibus iudiciis ęquitatem & misericordiam precipiat. atilli[m] & nobis indulgeat suam misericordiam & clemens & misericors deus. qui cum patre & spiritu sancto uiuit & regnat deus. per omnia.

&[n] tunc de osculetur omnes[o] clerum populumque et dicat unusquisque uiuat rex feliciter in sempiternum tribus uicibus uiuat rex. & post[p] euangelium offerat rex ad manus archiepiscopi oblationem & uinum & super agatur[q] missa suo nomine & ordine suo. deinde communicetur ab archiepiscopo corpore & sanguine christi & sic referant deo gratias. post pergant ad mensam.[1]

Ad benedicendam reginam.

Debet enim adduci in ecclesiam & prosterni ante altare. eleuata ab oracione ab episcopis. & inclinato capite. dicat archiepiscopus hanc orationem.[r]

Ad esto domine supplicationibus nostris. & quod humilitatis nostrę gerendum est ministerio. tuę uirtutis impleatur effectu per.

---

[m] *Sic*, for *ut illi*.

[n] This section, through *ad mensam.*, is rubricated. Since the ink of this passage was effaced by the time Pithou used the MS, he copied interlinearly the text of the faded words.

[o] MS *oms'*, perhaps for *omnibus*; see Ward, "Early Version," 358.

[p] Two letters, perhaps *ss*, appear to have been abraded following this word.

[q] *Sic*, for *sic peragatur.*

[1] On the next page, fol. 81v, is the commencement of an *ordo* for consecrating a church:

Ordo Consecrationis ecclesiae. Primum ueniat episcopus indutus uestimentis sacris & clerus similiter ante ostium ecclesiae. & ab episcopo consecretur sal & aqua in consecrationem ecclesiae: Et dicat tribus uicibus. Deus in adiutorium meum intende cum gloria patri Absque alleluia

Deinde benedicens salem & aquam cum uitea cinere mixta dicens Exorzizo te creatura salis in nomine domini nostri IHESV CHRISTI. qui apostolis suis ait. Uos estis sal terrae & per apostolum dicit Cor uestrum sale sit conditum ut sanctificeris ad consecrationem istius ecclesiae ad expellendas

In the margin, at the last line is written *Lege oratorii* (for *ecclesie*).

[r] These three lines, on fol. 82r, are rubricated.

Tunc debet caput eius in ungui oleo.[s]

Innomine patris & filii & spiritus sancti. prosit tibi hęc unctio olei in honorem & confirmationem ęternam.

Sequitur ORATIO. post unctionem.[t]

Omnipotens sempiterne deus. affluentem spiritum tuę benedictionis super famulam tuam nobis orantibus propiciatus infunde. ut quę per manus nostrę in positionem hodie regina instituitur. sanctificatione tua digna & electa permaneat. ut numquam post modum de tua gratia separetur indigna .per.

Tunc debet anulus inmitti digito.[u]

Accipe anulum fidei signaculum sanctę trinitatis quo possis omnes hereticas prauitates deuitare. & barbaras gentes uirtute tibi prestita ad agnitionem ueritatis ad uocare.

Sequitur ORATIO[v]

Deus cuius est. omnis potestas & dignitas. da famulę tuę .illi. signo tuę fidei prosperum suę dignitatis effectum. inqua tibi semper firma maneat. tibique iugiter placere contendat .per.

Tunc debet imponi corona suo capiti.[w]

Accipe coronam glorię. honorem iocunditatis. ut splendida fulgeas. & ęterna exultatione coroneris.

Item Alia. ORATIO.[x]

Omnium domine fons bonorum. & cunctorum dator prouectuum tribuę[y] famulę tuę .illi. ad eptam bene regere dignitatem & ate sibi prestitam in ea bonis operibus corrobora gloriam .per.

benedictio vexilli.[z]

Inclina domine aurem tuam ad preces nostrę humilitatis. & per interuentum beati Michaelis archangeli tui. omniumque cęlestium uirtutum. presta nobis auxilium dexterę tuę. ut sicut benedixisti abraham aduersus quinque reges triumphantem. atque dauid regem intui nominis laude triumphales congressus exercentem. ita benedicere & sanctificare digneris uexillum hoc. quod ob defensionem sanctę ecclesię contra hostilem rabiem defertur. quatinus innomine tuo fideles & defensores populi dei illud consequentes. per uirtutem sanctę crucis triumphum & uictoriam se ex hostibus ad quisisse lętentur. qui cum patre

---

[s] Rubric.
[t] Rubric.
[u] Rubric.
[v] Rubric.
[w] Rubric.
[x] Rubric.
[y] *Sic.*
[z] Rubric.

B.
Excerpts Copied by Adrien de Valois (1607-92) from the Coronation *Ordo* in the Library of Paul Petau (1568-1614), BN, Baluze 379, Fols. 84v-85r

These excerpts are transcribed as they are found in BN, Baluze 379, a volume consisting largely of copies in the hand of Etienne Baluze, antiquarian and bishop of Tulle (1630-1718).[1] This edition omits the accents that Valois inserted and completes his abbreviations.

These excerpts follow Valois' transcription of long extracts from the so-called Erdmann *ordo*[2] and five investiture formulas from a pontifical of Sens that Valois judged to be 600 years old (and thus to date from the eleventh century) (fol. 84r-v); he remarked that he had copied the first *ordo* thirty years earlier ("ante annos XXX. descripsi Sequentia"); he may well have found the manuscript in the library of Vyon d'Herouval.[3] After the excerpts from the coronation *ordo* that are edited here, Valois transcribed (fol. 85r) a *Professio Regis coram deo et populo* from a manuscript of the church of Laon, for which he gave no date. Fol. 85v is blank. Valois said that the excerpts edited here were copied from an "old codex of Paul Petau," which must be the *ordo* of lat. 14192, known to Valois by at least 1648, when he saw it in Vyon's collection of manuscripts.[4] Valois' excerpts contain some variants from the text of the *ordo* of lat. 14192, but they do not seem serious enough to suggest that he was copying from another *ordo* once in Petau's library. In the following edition the variants are italicized, and omissions noted by bracketed ellipses.

In his supplement to Sirmond's edition of conciliar materials, published in 1666, Pierre Delalande presented extracts from a ceremonial containing the formula "Franks, Burgundians, and Aquitanians," which seems to have been the *ordo* of lat. 14192. Delalande gave no information about his source, remarking simply "In altero MS. codice habetur sic," and, twice, "In eodem codice MS. legitur." However, preceding the extracts he pub-

---

[1] On the Baluze manuscript, Schramm, "Krönung," 201-2, 208; idem, *Kaiser*, 2: 216, 221-22; idem, "Ordines-Studien II," 17, nos. 8-9.

[2] Schramm, "Ordines-Studien II," 17, no. 8; Jackson, "Manuscripts, Texts," 43-44.

[3] As will shortly be seen, by 1666 Pierre Delalande had edited both the *ordo* and the formulas "from a very old codex of the church of Sens" which he obtained from Vyon d'Herouval ("ex codice pervetusto Ecclesiæ Senonensis, quem nacti sumus beneficio Clariss. D. de Vion d'Herouval"): *Conciliorvm . . . Svpplementa*, ed. Delalande, 355-57, esp. 57. This phraseology recalls Valois' similar acknowledgment of Vyon's help in the dedication to his edition of Adalbero's *Carmen:* see 28 n. 100 above.

[4] See 28-29 above.

lished the text of the Erdmann *ordo* and the five investiture formulas from a pontifical of Sens, the same texts that Valois copied from a pontifical of Sens before his excerpts from the *ordo* of lat. 14192, and Delalande said that his were taken from a manuscript which Vyon had communicated to him. Thus it seems probable that he also consulted Vyon's *ordo* of lat. 14192—and, conversely, that the pontifical of Sens that Valois used was the one in Vyon's library.[5]

Delalande's extracts from the ceremonial with "Franks, Burgundians, and Aquitanians" include the full introductory rubric; excerpts from the *admonitio;* from the prayers *Omnium domine fons bonorum, Sta et retine,* and *Omnipotens sempiterne Deus,* given in this inverted order, and from the *Benedictio vexilli.* Delalande's rubrics are distinctive and apparently his own creation; he adds two comments of his own.[6] The most notable differences between his excerpts and the *ordo* of lat. 14192 are the following: he reads "paterna successione" rather than "paterna suggestione" in *Sta et retine;* he omits "tocius" before "regni ecclesiam" in *Omnipotens sempiterne deus;* in the same prayer he corrects "utrorum horum populorum" (a phrase which also troubled Valois) to read "ut trium horum populorum." The queen's *ordo* contains numerous inversions of word order, some elaborations, and some idiosyncratic variants: "sempiternæ virtutis tuæ," for example, replaces "tuę uirtutis" in *Adesto domine;* in *Omnipotens sempiterne Deus* "divinum" is substituted for "affluentem" and "nostra oratione" for "nobis orantibus," and the final phrase ("ut numquam post modum de tua gratia separetur indigna") becomes "& ineffabilis gratiæ tuæ præsidio, hoc, & in æternum munita consistat"; the commencement of the prayer *Omnium domine fons bonorum* is transformed into "Omnipotens sempiternæ [*sic*] Deus fons & origo omnium bonorum." In essence, however, Delalande's excerpts are close to the readings in the *ordo* of lat. 14192. Were he not known to have had access to Vyon d'Herouval's library, he might be thought to have drawn on another manuscript remarkably similar to that *ordo;* as it is, it seems more likely that he used Vyon's ceremonial and indulged in occasional flights of fancy in readying his excerpts for publication.

---

[5] See 98 n. 3 above, and Schramm, "Krönung," 201-2, 208, 236-37 (esp. n. 1).

[6] Delalande introduces *Sta et retine* with "Regi [*sic,* rather than *Regis*] Status designatur (id est stare jubetur Rex, ut placet viro cuidam doctissimo) & tunc dicitur ei"; he inserts after "Benedictio vexilli" "(sancti Dionysii vel similis)": *Conciliorvm . . . Svpplementa,* 357.

• • • • •

Ex ueteri codice Pauli Petauij Viri Clarissimi in superna Paris. Curia Consiliarij hæc ego excerpsi atque transcripsi.

Incipit percunctatio [. . .] Episcoporum [. . .] ad Regem consecrandum.[7]

Admonitio Episcoporum ad Regem, dicendo ita: legatur ab uno Episcopo coram omnibus.

A vobis perdonari petimus, ut unicuique de nobis et Ecclesijs nobis commissis canonicum priuilegium ac debitam legem atque iustitiam conseruetis, et defensionem *quantum potueritis adiuuante domino*[8] exhibeatis: sicut Rex in suo Regno unicuique Episcopo et Ecclesiæ sibi commissæ per *rectum exhibere debet.*[9]

Responsio Regis ad Episcopos

Promitto vobis et perdono, quia unicuique de vobis et Ecclesijs uobis commissis canonicum priuilegium ac debitam legem atque iustitiam *conseruabo,*[10] et defensionem quantumpotuero adiuuante Domino exhibebo: sicut Rex in suo Regno *per rectum*[11] exhibere debet. [. . .]

Inuocatio super Regem. Te inuocamus (etcetera que i'ay omis comme inutile) [. . .]

Consecratio Regis

Omnipotens sempiterne deus, [. . .] super hunc famulum tuum, [. . .] quem supplici[12] deuotione in Regnum pariter eligimus, benedictionum tuarum dona multiplica.— [..] quatinus [. . .] per tramitem iustitiæ inoffenso gradu semper incedat, et totius Regni Ecclesiam deinceps cum plebibus sibi annexis ita enutriat ac doceat, muniat et instruat, contraque omnes uisibiles et inuisibiles hostes idem potenter regaliterque[13] tuæ[14] uirtutis *regimine*[15] administret, ut Regale solium, uidelicet francorum, Burgundiorum, Aquitanorum sceptra non deserat, sed ad pris-

---

[7] When listing the contents of Petau's MS in 1662, Valois gave the complete introductory rubric: see 29 n. 101 above.

[8] Valois added this phrase, perhaps because his eye slipped from "defensionem" in the bishops' admonition to the same word in the king's promise, which is followed by "quantum potuero adiuuante Domino."

[9] Valois added this phrase, correcting the omission in the MS.

[10] For *conseruabo*.

[11] This phrase is rendered *perrectę* in the MS.

[12] Marginal note, *Lit. simplici*.

[13] Preceded by *idem g*, canceled.

[14] Over *suæ*, canceled.

[15] Valois incorrectly expanded the MS's *regim'*.

tinæ fidei pacisque concordiam eorum animos te opitulante reformet: ut horum[16] populorum debita subiectione fultus, condigno amore glorificatus, per longum vitæ spatium paternæ apicem gloriæ tua miseratione unatim stabilire et gubernare mereatur.— [. . .] *Eum*[17] in regimine Regni sublimiter colloca, et oleo gratiæ Spiritus Sancti perunge.

A.[18] Vnxerunt Salomonem Sadoc Sacerdos, et Nathan Propheta Regem in *Sion:*[19] Et accedentes læti dixerunt: Viuat Rex in æternum.

Vnde unxisti Sacerdotes, Reges, et Prophetas, (Hic ungatur oleo) *et*[20] Martyres. [. . .] Cuius sacratissima unctio super caput eius defluat, atque ad interiora descendat. [. . .]

Hic detur anulus. Accipe anulum, signaculum uidelicet Sanctæ fidei, soliditatem Regni, augmentum potentiæ: per quæ scias triumphali potentia hostes repellere, hæreses destruere, subditos coadunare, et Catholicæ fidei perseuerabilitati *connecti*[21] per — — [. . .]

Accipe hunc gladium, cum dei benedictione tibi collatum. (Hic cingatur ei gladius ab Archiepiscopo.) [. . .]

Hic coronetur. [. . .]

Accipe sceptrum, Regiæ potestatis insigne, uirgam scilicet rectam Regni, uirgam uirtutis: qua teipsum bene regas; (Hic detur sceptrum) sanctam Ecclesiam *et populum Christianum tibi commissum*[22] ab *improbis*[23] defendas, prauos corrigas, rectos *pacifices.*[24] [. . .]

Oratio post sceptrum. Omnium domine fons bonorum et cetera. (comme cy dessus page v. ligne 30.) [. . .]

Hic datur ei virga. Accipe uirgam uirtutis atque æquitatis, qua intelligas mulcere pios et terrere reprobos. [. . .] Tunc dicatur Benedictio. [. . .]

---

[16] Valois omitted *utrorum,* preceding *horum,* doubtless because he realized the word made no sense.

[17] Valois added this pronoun.

[18] Marginal note, *id est Antiphona.*

[19] Valois corrected the MS's correct reading *in gion.*

[20] The MS reads *ac.*

[21] Valois reasonably emended the MS's *conecti.*

[22] The MS reads "populumque uidelicet christianum tibi a deo commissum regia uirtute."

[23] Valois corrects the MS's *inprobis.*

[24] Valois corrects the MS's *pacificas.*

C.
The *Ordo Maior* of *Croix*

Because the *Ordo maior* of *Croix* is central to this study, and because no published text exists, it seems appropriate to present a provisional edition, based on the three surviving copies known to me: (1) BN, n. a. f. 7232 ("Cérémonies observées au sacre et couronnement des rois et reines de France" [1059-1610]) (Brienne 263) (seventeenth century), fols. 7v-21v[1]; (2) AN, KK 1442 (Godefroy collection of material relating to *Le Ceremonial François;* "Sacres et couronnements des rois et reines de France, 1059-1610. Couronnements de souverains etrangers, 1495-1618") (Godefroy collection; seventeenth century), fols. 11v-30r[2]; (3) AN, P 2288 ("Memoriaux / Livre Rouge. p 1. / Registre St Just p 498 / Registre +. p 1676") (eighteenth century; collated by Lourdet, *conseiller-maître*), pp. 1290-1317. Section breaks have been introduced, and capitalization, punctuation, and orthography have been simplified; the scribes' *æ*'s and *œ*'s are not reproduced, although their *j*'s have been retained. There are numerous differences among the three copies, but only the most significant variants are noted here. The copy in AN, P 2288, generally offers what appear to be the most reliable readings.

• • • • •

Ordo ad inungendum et coronandum Regem.[3]

---

[1] This copy was made in the seventeenth century for Antoine de Loménie, lord of Villeaux-Clercs and *secrétaire d'Etat* under Henry IV (1589-1610) and Louis XIII (1610-43). On his collections, see Delisle, *Cabinet des Manuscrits*, 1: 214-16. On fol. [A]r the volume is said to have been "Paraphé par nous conseillers du Roy en sa cour de Parlement commissaires en cette partie suiuant nostre proces verbal du quinziesme Januier mil Six cens cinquante deux, A. Petau [Alexandre Petau, d. 1672], Pithou [Pierre Pithou, d. 1687]"; see ibid., 1: 216, 287; 2: 8 n. 3. The paper on which the volume is copied has a number of watermarks. The initial B's on, e.g., 5-9, 13-15, 20-22, and 26 suggest that at least those folios were made by Jacques Lebe; see Briquet, *Filigranes*, nos. 8078-83, for the manufacture of such paper in the seventeenth century. The elaborate watermark, with the shields of France and Navarre, is found on paper made in the seventeenth century: ibid., no. 1854. This MS is copied in Paris, Bibliothèque de l'Assemblée nationale (Chambre des Députés), MS 195, fols. 17r-27r.

[2] This MS may also have been copied from the Brienne volume; as will be seen, the readings often agree with it, as against AN, P 2288. Although the copyists of this and the Brienne volume were not skilled, some of their readings are, to judge from the last Capetian ordo and the *ordo* of Charles V, preferable to those of AN, P 2288.

[3] Preceding the *ordo* in BN, n. a. f. 7232, fol. 7v, the scribe commented, "Ce que dessus est de mot a mot aussi au liure cotté Qui es fol. ii^{c}. viii. Du mesme liure + fol. ix^{xx}. xix. et ij^{c}. xiiij." The same notation is found in AN, KK 1442, fol. 11v. In AN, P 2288, p. 1290, the copyist noted in the left margin, "Registre Croix, fol. (*199*, canceled) 205"; above the title is found, in a slightly later hand, "Sacre et Couronnement des Rois et Reines."

Primo paratur solium in modum eschafaudi aliquantulum eminens contiguum exterius choro ecclesie inter vtrumque positum in medio in quo per gradus ascenditur et in quo possunt pares regni et aliqui, si necesse fuerit cum eis consistere. Rex autem die quo ad coronandum venerit, debet processionaliter recipi tam a canonicis quam a ceteris ecclesiis conuentualibus et sabbatho precedente diem dominicam in qua rex est consecrandus et coronandus post completorium committitur ecclesie custodia custodibus a rege deputatis cum propriis custodibus ecclesie. Debet rex intempeste noctis silentio venire in ecclesiam orationem facturus, et ibidem in oratione aliquantulum si voluerit, vigilaturus. Cum pulsatur autem ad matutinas debent esse parati custodes regis, introitum ecclesie obseruantes, qui aliis hostiis ecclesie firmius obseruatis[a] et munitis canonicos et clericos ecclesie debent honorifice intromittere ac diligenter quotiescumque opus fuerit eis. Matutine more solito decantantur, quibus expletis pulsatur ad primam que cantari debet in aurora diei. Post primam cantatam debet rex cum archiepiscopis et episcopis et baronibus et aliis quos intromittere voluerit in ecclesiam venire, antequam fiat aqua benedicta et debent esse sedes disposite circa altare hinc et inde ubi archiepiscopi et episcopi honorifice sedeant, episcopis paribus, videlicet primo, Laudunensi, postea Beluacensi, deinde Lingonensi, postea Cathalanensi, vltimum vero Nouiomensi, cum aliis episcopis archiepiscopatus Remensis sedentibus seorsum ante altare et regem ab oppositis altaris non longe a rege, nec multis indecenter interpositis.

Quomodo sacra ampulla debet venire. Sciendum est quod rex debet accipere de baronibus suis nobilioribus et fortioribus et eos in aurora diei mittere apud sanctum Remigium pro sancta ampulla, et isti debent iurare abbati et ecclesie quod dictam sanctam ampullam bona fide ducent et reducent ad ipsam ecclesiam beati Remigii. Quo facto inter primam et tertiam debent venire monachi beati Remigii processionaliter cum crucibus et cereis cum sacrosancta ampulla quam debet abbas reuerentissime deferre sub cortina serica quatuor partitis a quatuor monachis albis indutis subleuata. Et cum venerint ad ecclesiam beati Dyonisii vel vsque ad maiorem ianuam ecclesie propter turbam comprimentem debet archiepiscopus cum ceteris archiepiscopis, episcopis, et baronibus necnon et canonicis, si fieri potest occurrere sancte ampulle, et eam de manu abbatis recipere cum pollicitatione de reddendo bona fide, et sic ad altare cum magna populi reuerentia

[a] *Sic*, for *obseratis*.

deferre abbate et aliquibus de monachis pariter concomitantibus. Ceteri vero monachi debent expectare in ecclesia beati Dyonisii, vel in capella beati Nicolai donec omnia peracta fuerint, et quoad usque sancta ampulla fuerit reportata.

Quid suscepta ampulla agendum sit.

Archiepiscopus ad missam se preparat cum diaconibus et subdiaconibus vestimentis insignioribus, et pallio induendus, et in hunc modum indutus venit processionaliter ad altare more solito, cui venienti rex debet assurgere reuerenter. Cum autem venerit archiepiscopus ad altare, debet pro omnibus ecclesiis sibi subditis a rege hec petere.

Admonitio ad regem dicenda ita.[b]

A vobis perdonari petimus, vt vnicuique de nobis et ecclesiis nobis commissis canonicum priuilegium ac debitam legem atque iustitiam conseruetis, et defensionem exhibeatis sicut rex in suo regno debet vnicuique episcopo et[c] ecclesie sibi commisse.

Responsio regis ad episcopos.

Promitto vobis et perdono, quia vnicuique de vobis et ecclesiis vobis commissis canonicum priuilegium et debitam legem atque iustitiam seruabo et defensionem quantum potuero exhibebo, Domino adiuuante, sicut rex in suo regno vnicuique episcopo et ecclesie sibi commisse per rectum exhibere debet.

Item hec dicit rex et promittit et firmat iuramento.

Hec populo christiano et mihi subdito in Christi nomine promitto, vt ecclesie dei omnis populus christianus veram pacem nostro arbitrio in omni tempore seruet. Item vt omnes rapacitates et omnes iniquitates omnibus gradibus interdicam. Item vt in omnibus iudiciis equitatem et misericordiam precipiam, vt mihi et vobis indulgeat suam misericordiam clemens et misericors dominus. Item de terra mea ac iurisdictione mihi subdita vniuersos hereticos ab ecclesia denotatos pro viribus bona fide exterminare studebo.

Hec omnia supradicta firmat iuramento, tunc manum apponat libro. His factis promissionibus, statim incipiatur Te deum laudamus. Et duo archiepiscopi vel episcopi ducunt regem per manus ante altare qui prosternit se ante altare vsque ad finem Te deum. Postmodum surgit iam antea preparatis et positis super altare Corona regia, gladio in vagina incluso, calcaribus aureis, sceptro deaurato, et virga ad mensuram vnius cubiti vel amplius habente desuper manum eburneam. Item caligis sericis et iacintinis per

[b] *dicenda ita*, only in AN, P 2288, p. 1293.
[c] Only in AN, P 2288, p. 1294.

totum intextis liliis aureis et tunica eiusdem coloris et operis in modum tunicalis quo induuntur subdiaconi ad missam, necnon et socco prorsus eiusdem coloris et operis qui est factus fere in modum cappe cerice absque capparone. Que omnia abbas sancti Dyonisii in Francia de monasterio suo debet Remis[d] afferre, et stans ad altare custodire. Tunc primo rex stans ante altare deponit vestes suas preter tunicam sericam et camisiam apertas profundius ante et retro in pectore, videlicet et inter scapulas aperturis tunice sibi inuicem connexis ansulis argenteis, et tunc imprimis ibi a magno camerario Francie regi dicte calige calciantur, et postmodum a duce Burgundie calcaria eius pedibus astringantur et statim tollantur. Postmodum rex a solo archiepiscopo gladio accingitur, quo accincto statim idem gladius distringitur ab archiepiscopo et e vagina extrahitur, vagina super altare reposita, et datur ei ab archiepiscopo in manibus cum ista oratione.

Oratio in datione gladii.

Accipe hunc gladium cum dei benedictione tibi collatum in quo per virtutem sancti spiritus resistere, et eiicere omnes inimicos tuos valeas, et cunctos sancte dei ecclesie aduersarios regnumque tibi commissum tutari atque protegere castra dei per auxilium inuictissimi triumphatoris domini nostri Ihesu Christi qui cum patre, &c.

Hic cantatur ista antiphona.

Confortare et esto vir, et custodias obserua domini dei tui vt ambules in viis eius et custodias ceremonias eius, et precepta eius, et testimonia et iudicia, et quocumque te verteris, confirmet te deus.

Dum cantatur ista antiphona, dicitur ista oratio post dationem gladii.

Deus qui prouidentia tua celestia simul et terrena moderaris propitiare christianissimo regi nostro, vt omnis hostium suorum fortitudo virtute gladii spiritualis frangatur, ac te pro illo pugnante, penitus conteratur. Per.

Gladium debet rex humiliter recipere de manu archiepiscopi et offerre ad altare, et statim resumere de manu archiepiscopi, et incontinenti dare senescallo Francie si senescallum habuerit, sin autem cui voluerit de baronibus ad portandum ante se, et in ecclesia vsque ad finem misse, et post missam vsque ad palatium.

Post hec vero prepari debet vnctio in hunc modum.

Crisma in altari ponitur super patenam consecratam, et archiepiscopus sacrosanctam ampullam quam abbas beati Remigii

[d] Only in AN, P 2288, p. 1294.

attulit super altare, debet aperire, et inde cum aurea virgula aliquantulum de oleo celitus misso attrahere, et crismati parati[e] in patena diligentius cum digito immiscere ad inungendum regem qui solus inter vniuersos reges terre hoc glorioso prefulget priuilegio, vt oleo celitus misso singulariter inungatur. Parata vnctione qua rex debet inungi ab archiepiscopo, debent dissolui ansule aperturarum vestimentorum regis ante et retro, et genibus regis in terram positis, duo archiepiscopi vel episcopi incipiunt litaniam, qua finita archiepiscopus debet super eum dicere has orationes antequam eum inungat. Debet autem sedere sicut sedet cum consecrat episcopos.

Oratio.

Te inuocamus, domine sancte pater omnipotens eterne deus, vt hunc famulum tuum N. quem tue defensionis[f] prouidentia in primordio plasmatum usque in hunc presentem diem iuuenili flore letantem crescere concessisti cum tue pietatis dono dicatum[g] plenumque gratia veritatis de die in diem coram deo et hominibus ad meliora semper proficere facias, vt summi regiminis solium gratie superne largitate gaudens suscipiat et misericordie tue muro ab hostium aduersitate undique munitus, plebem sibi commissam cum pace propitiationis et virtute victorie feliciter regere mereatur, Per dominum nostrum, &c.

Alia oratio.

Deus qui populis tuis virtute consulis et amore dominaris, da huic famulo tuo spiritum sapientie tue cum regimine discipline vt tibi toto corde deuotus in regni regimine semper maneat idoneus, tuoque munere ipsius temporibus securitas ecclesie dirigatur, et in tranquilitate deuotio ecclesiastica permaneat, vt in bonis operibus perseuerans ad eternum regnum, Te duce, valeat peruenire, Per dominum nostrum, &c.

Alia oratio.

In diebus eius oriatur omnibus equitas et iustitia, amicis adiutorium, inimicis obstaculum, humilibus solatium, elatis correctio, diuitibus doctrina, pauperibus pietas, peregrinis pacificatio, propriis in patria pax et securitas, vnumquemque secundum suam mensuram moderate gubernans, seipsum sedulus regere discat, vt tua irrigatus compunctione toti populo tibi placita prebere vite possit exemplo et per viam veritatis cum grege gradiens sibi sub-

---

[e] *Sic,* for *parato.*

[f] In AN, P 2288, p. 1297, *divine dispensationis; defensionis,* in BN, n. a. f. 7232, fol. 11r; *defentionis,* in AN, KK 1442, fol. 16r.

[g] *Sic,* for *ditatum.*

dito opes frugales abundanter acquirat, simulque ad salutem non solum corporum sed etiam cordium a te concessa[h] cuncta accipiat, sicque in te[i] cogitatum animi consiliumque omne componens, plebis gubernacula cum pace simul et sapientia semper inuenire videatur, teque auxiliante presentis vite prosperitatem et prolixitatem percipiat, et per tempora bona vsque ad summam senectutem perueniat huiusque fragilitatis finem perfectum ab omnibus vitiorum vinculis tue pietatis largitate liberatus, et infinite prosperitatis perpetua premia angelorumque eterna commercia consequatur, Per dominum, &c.

Consecratio regis.

Omnipotens sempiterne deus, creator ac gubernator celi et terre, conditor et dispositor angelorum et hominum, rex regum et dominus dominorum qui Abraham fidelem famulum tuum de hostibus triumphare fecisti. Moysi et Iosue populo tuo prelatis multiplicem victoriam tribuisti, humilem quoque puerum tuum Dauid regni fastigio sublimasti, eumque de ore leonis et de manu bestie atque Golie, sed et de gladio maligno Saul et omnium inimicorum eius liberasti, et Salomonem sapientie pacisque ineffabili munere ditasti, respice propitius ad preces nostre humilitatis et super hunc famulum tuum N. quem supplici deuotione in regnum pariter eligimus benedictionum tuarum dona multiplica, eumque dextera potentie tue semper et vbique circumda, quatenus predicti Abrahe fidelitate firmatus, Moysi mansuetudine fretus, Iosue fortitudine munitus, Dauid humilitate exaltatus, Salomonis sapientia decoratus tibi in omnibus complaceat, et per tramitem iustitie inoffenso gressu semper incedat, et totius regni ecclesiam deinceps cum plebibus sibi annexis ita enutriat ac doceat, muniat et instruat, contraque omnes visibiles et inuisibiles hostes idem potenter regaliterque tue virtutis regimen administret, vt regale solium videlicet Saxonum, Merciorum, Nordanchimbrorumque sceptra[j] non deserat, sed ad pristine fidei pacisque concordiam eorum animos te opitulante reformet, vt vtrorumque horum populorum debita subiectione fultus et cum digno amore glorificatus per longum vite spatium paterne apicem glorie tua miseratione unatin[k] stabilire et gubernare mereatur, tue quoque protectionis galea munitus et scuto insuperabili

---

[h] *Sic,* for *concessam,* in AN, P 2288, p. 1298, and BN, n. a. f. 7232, fol. 12r; omitted in AN, KK 1442, fol. 17r.

[i] *Sitque iuste,* in BN, n. a. f. 7232, fol. 12r, and AN, KK 1442, fol. 17r.

[j] *dextra,* in BN, n. a. f. 7232, fol. 13r, and AN, KK 1442, fol. 18r.

[k] *Sic,* for *unatim* in AN, P 2288, p. 1300; omitted, in the other two copies.

iugiter protectus armisque[l] celestibus circumdatus optabilis victorie triumphum de hostibus feliciter capiat, terroremque sue potentie infidelibus inferat, et pacem militantibus letanter reportet, virtutibus[m] necnon quibus prefatos fideles tuos decorasti multiplici honoris benedictione condecora, et in regimine regni sublimiter colloca, et oleo gratie spiritus sancti perunge.

Hic inungatur inunctione crismatis et olei de celo missi primo ab archiepiscopo confecti in patena sicut superius dictum est. Inungat autem archiepiscopus eum primo in summitate capitis de dicta vnctione, secundo in pectore, tertio inter scapulas, quarto in ipsis scapulis, quinto in compage[n] brachiorum, et dicat cuilibet inunctioni,

Vngo te in regem de oleo sanctificato, In nomine patris et filii et spiritus sancti.

Dicant omnes, Amen.

Dum hec vnctio agitur, cantant assistantes hanc antiphonam,

Vncti sunt[o] Salomonem Sadoch sacerdos et Nathan propheta regem in Gyon,[p] et accendentes leti dixerunt, Viuat rex in eternum.

Facta vnctione et cantata antiphona dicat Archiepiscopus hanc orationem.

Oratio.

Christe perunge hunc regem in regimen[q] vnde vnxisti sacerdotes, reges, ac prophetas, et martyres qui per fidem vicerunt[r] regna operati[s] sunt iustitiam atque adepti sunt promissiones. Tua sacratissima[t] vnctio super caput eius defluat, atque ad interiora descendat, et cordis illius intima penetret, et promissionibus quas adepti sunt victoriossimi reges gratia tua dignus efficiatur, quatenus in presenti seculo feliciter regnet, et ad eorum consortium in celesti regno perueniat per dominum nostrum Ihesum Christum filium tuum qui vnctus est de oleo letitie pre consortibus suis, et virtute crucis potestates aereas[u] debellauit, tartara destruxit regimenque diaboli superauit, et ad celos victor ascendit, in cuius victoria et manu eius[v] gloria et potestas consistunt, et

---

[l] *animisque*, in BN, n. a. f. 7232, fol. 13r, and AN, KK 1442, fol. 18v.
[m] Only in AN, P 2288, p. 1300.
[n] *Sic*, for *compagine*.
[o] *vnctionem*, in AN, P 2288, p. 1301; for *Vnxerunt*.
[p] Only in AN, P 2288, p. 1301; *Gyin* in the two other copies.
[q] In AN, P 2288, p. 1301; *Regem* in the two other copies.
[r] Only in AN, P 2288, p. 1301; *vixerunt* in the two other copies.
[s] Only in AN, P 2288, p. 1301; *optati*, in the other two copies.
[t] Only in AN, P 2288, p. 1301; *sanctissima*, in the other two copies.
[u] Only in AN, P 2288, p. 1301; *potentialiter areas*, in the other two copies.
[v] *Sic*, for *in cuius victoria manu omnis*.

tecum viuit et regnat in vnitate spiritus sancti, deus per omnia secula seculorum. Amen.

Alia oratio.

Deus electorum fortitudo et humilium celsitudo, qui in primordio per effusionem diluuii mundi crimina castigare voluisti, et per columbam ramum oliue portantem pacem terris redditam demonstrasti, iterum sacerdotem[w] sanxisti, et postea per huius vnguenti infusionem ad regendum populum Israeliticum sacerdotes, reges, et prophetas perfecisti vultumque[x] ecclesie in oleo exhilarandum per propheticam famuli tui vocem Dauid esse predixisti, ita quesumus omnipotens deus pater vt per huius[y] creature pinguedinem hunc seruum tuum sanctificare tua benedictione digneris, eumque in similitudine columbe pacem simplicitatis populo suo[z] commisso prestare, et exempla Aaron in dei seruitio diligenter imitari, regnique fastigia in consiliis scientie et equitate iudicii semper assequi vultumque hilaritatis per hanc olei vnctionem tuamque benedictionem, te adiuuante, toti plebi paratum habere facias. Per dominum nostrum.

Alia oratio.

Deus dei filius dominus noster Ihesus Christus qui a patre oleo exultationis vnctus est pre participibus suis, ipse per presentem sacre vnctionis infusionem[a] spiritus paracliti super corpus[b] tuum infundat benedictionem, eandemque vsque ad interiora cordis tui penetrare faciat, quatenus hoc visibili et tractabili dono inuisibilia percipere et temporali regno iustis moderationibus[c] executo eternaliter cum eo regnare merearis. Per &c.

His dictis orationibus, connectuntur ansule aperturarum vestimenti regis ab archiepiscopo vel sacerdotibus vel diaconibus propter inunctionem, et tunc a camerario francie induitur tunica iacintina, et desuper socco, ita quod dexteram manum habeat liberam in apertura socci et super sinistram soccum eleuatum sicut eleuatur casula sacerdoti. Deinde datur ei ab archiepiscopo sceptrum in manu dextera et virga in sinistra. Et in datione sceptri et virge dicuntur hec orationes. Sed notandum quod antequam dentur sceptrum et virga, datur anulus. Et in datione anuli dicitur hec oratio.

---

[w] "Aaron famulum tuum per unctionem olei," found in the last direct Capetian *ordo* and the *ordo* of Charles V, is omitted from all copies.

[x] Only in AN, P 2280, p. 1302; *introitumque*, in the other two copies.

[y] *eius*, in AN, P 2288, p. 1302.

[z] *Sic*, for *sibi*.

[a] Only in AN, P 2280, p. 1303; *effusionem*, in the other two copies.

[b] *Sic*, for *caput*.

[c] *Sic*, for *moderaminibus*.

Hic detur anulus et dicatur,

Accipe anulum, signaculum videlicet fidei sancte soliditatem regni, augmentum potentie per que[d] scias triumphali potentia hostes repellere, hereses destruere, subditos coadiunare et catholice fidei perseuerare veritate[e] connecti.

Oratio post anulum.

Deus cuius est omnis potestas et dignitas da famulo tuo prosperum sue dignitatis effectum, in qua, te remunerante, permaneat, semperque timeat, tibique iugiter placere contendat, Per dominum.

Dato anulo, statim post detur sceptrum in manu dextera, et dicatur hec oratio.

Accipe sceptrum regie potestatis insigne, virgam scilicet regni rectam, virgam virtutis qua te ipsum bene regis, sanctam ecclesiam, populumque videlicet christianum tibi a deo commissum regia virtute ab improbis deffendas, prauos corrigas, rectos pacifices, et vt viam rectam tenere possint tuo iuuamine dirigas, quatenus de temporali regno ad eternum regnum peruenias ipso adiuuante cuius regnum et Imperium sine fine permanet in secula seculorum.

Oratio post sceptrum datum.

Omnium domine fons bonorum cunctorum deus institutor profectuum tribue, quesumus, famulo tuo N. adeptam bene regere dignitatem, et a te sibi prestitum honorem dignare corroborare honorifica eum pre cunctis regibus terre uberi eum[f] benedictione locupleta, et in solio regni firma stabilitate consolida, visita eum in sobole, presta ei prolixitatem vite, in diebus eius semper oriatur iustitia, vt cum Iocunditate et letitia eterne glorietur in regno, Per dominum.

Post statim datur ei virga in manu sinistra, et dicitur,

Accipe virgam virtutis atque equitatis qua intelligas mulcere pios, et terrere reprobos, errantibus[g] viam doce, lapsis manum porrige, disperdasque superbos et releues humiles, vt aperiat tibi ostium Ihesus Christus dominus noster, qui de seipso ait, Ego sum ostium, per me si quis introierit, saluabitur. Et ipse qui est clauis Dauid et sceptrum domųs Israel qui aperit et nemo claudit et claudit et nemo aperit, sit tibi adiutor qui eduxit vinctum de

---

[d] *Sic*, for *quem*.

[e] In AN, P 2280, p. 1304; *perseuerare vtilitate*, in the other two copies; for *perseuerabilitati*.

[f] Only in AN, P 2288, p. 1305; *terram vberem benedictione*, in BN, n. a. f. 7322, fol. 15v, and AN, KK 1442, fol. 21r.

[g] In AN, P 2280, p. 1305; *orantes*, in the two other copies.

domo carceris sedentem in tenebris et vmbra mortis, vt in omnibus si qui[h] merearis eum de quo propheta Dauid cecinit, sedes tua deus in seculum seculi virga equitatis, virga regni tui, et imiteris eum qui dicit, diligas iustitiam et odio habeas iniquitatem, propterea vnxit te deus deus[i] oleo letitie ad exemplum illius quem ante secula vnxerat[j] pre participibus suis Ihesum Christum dominum nostrum.

Post istam orationem, conuocantur pares nomine suo a Cancellario suo si presens est, sin autem ab archiepiscopo primo laici, secundo[k] clerici, quibus vocatis et circumstantibus archiepiscopus accipit de altari coronam regiam et solus imponit eam capiti regis, qua imposita, omnes pares tam clerici quam laici manum apponunt corone et eam vndique sustentant et soli pares. Tunc archiepiscopus dicit istam orationem.

Coronet te deus corona glorie atque iustitie honore et opere fortitudinis, vt per officium nostre benedictionis cum fide recta et multiplici bonorum operum fructu ad coronam peruenias regni perpetui, ipso largiente cuius regnum et imperium permanet in secula seculorum.

Oratio post coronam.

Deus perpetuitatis dux virtutum cunctorum hostium victor benedic hunc famulum tuum, tibi caput suum inclinantem, et prolixa sanitate et prospera felicitate eum conserua, et vbicumque pro quibus auxilium tuum inuocauerit, cito adsis et protegas ac defendas. Tribue ei, quesumus domine diuitias glorie tue, comple in bonis desiderium eius, corona eum miseratione et misericordia, tibique deo pia deuotione iugiter famuletur, Per dominum nostrum.

Statim post istam orationem dicatur ista benedictio.

Extendat omnipotens deus dexteram sue benedictionis, et circumdet te muro felicitatis ac custodia sue protectionis sancte Marie ac beati Petri Apostolorum principis sanctique Dyonisii atque omnium sanctorum intercedentibus meritis. Amen.

Indulgeat tibi dominus omnia peccata que gessisti et tribuat tibi gratiam et misericordiam quam humiliter[l] ab eo deposcis, et liberet te ab aduersitatibus cunctis, et ab omnibus Inimicorum omnium visibilium et inuisibilium insidiis. Amen.

---

[h] Only in AN, P 2288, p. 1305; *si quidem*, in the two other copies.
[i] *Deus*, repeated in AN, P 2288, p. 1305; all copies omit *tuus*, following.
[j] Only in AN, P 2288, p. 1306; *miserat*, in the other two copies.
[k] Only in AN, P 2288, p. 1306; *postea*, in the other two copies.
[l] Only in AN, P 2288, p. 1307; *similiter*, in the other two copies.

Angelos suos bonos qui te semper et vbique precedunt, comitentur et subsequantur ad custodiam tui ponat, et a peccato siue gladio et ab omnium periculorum discrimine sua potentia liberet. Amen.

Inimicos tuos ad pacis caritatisque benignitatem conuertat, et bonis omnibus te gratiosum et amabilem faciat, pertinaces quoque in tui miseratione[m] et odio confusione salutari induat super te autem participatio et sanctificatio sempiterna floreat. Amen.

Victoriosum te atque triumphatorem[n] de inuisibilibus atque visilibus hostibus semper efficiat, et sancti nominis sui timorem pariter et amorem continuum cordi tuo infundat, et in fide recta ac bonis operibus perseuerabilem reddat, et pace in diebus tuis concessa cum palma victorie, te ad perpetuum regnum perducat. Amen.

Et qui te voluit super populum suum constituere regem, et in presenti seculo felicem eterne felicitatis tribuat esse consortem. Amen. Quod ipse prestare.

Alia benedictio statim dicenda super eum.

Benedic domine hunc preelectum principem, qui regna omnium regum a seculo moderaris. Amen.

Et tali eum benedictione glorifica[o] vt dauidica teneat sublimitate sceptrum salutis et sanctifice propitiationis munere reperiatur locupletatus. Amen.

Da ei tuo spiramine regere populum, sicut Salomonem fecisti regnum obtinere pacificum. Amen. Quod ipse prestare digneris.

Regis status designatur.

Sta et retine amodo statum quem hucusque paterna successione tenuisti hereditario iure tibi delegatum per auctoritatem dei omnipotentis, et per presentem traditionem nostram omnium scilicet episcoporum ceterorumque seruorum dei, et quanto clerum propinquiorem sacris altaribus prospicis, tanto et[p] potiorem in locis congruentibus honorem impendere memineris, quatenus mediator dei et hominum te mediatorem cleri et plebis in hoc regni solio confirmet, et in regno eterno secum regnare faciat Ihesus Christus dominus noster rex regum et dominus dominantium qui cum deo. &c.

Alia oratio.

Omnipotens deus det tibi de rore celi et de pinguedine terre abundantiam frumenti vini et olei, et seruiant tibi populi et

---

[m] *Sic*, for *insectatione*.

[n] *traimphatorem*, in AN, P 2280, p. 1308; *triumphantem*, in the other two copies.

[o] In AN, P 2288, p. 1308; *locupleta*, in the other two copies.

[p] *Sic*, for *ei*.

adorent te tribus. Esto dominus fratrum tuorum et incuruentur ante te genua[q] Matris tue, et qui benedixerit tibi benedictionibus repleatur, et deus erit adiutor tuus.

Alia oratio.

Omnipotens deus benedicat tibi benedictionibus celi desuper in montibus et in collibus benedictionibus abissi iacentibus deorsum benedictionibus uberum et vuarum[r] pomorumque. Benedictiones patrum antiquorum Abraham, Isaac et Iacob confortate sint super te per dominum nostrum Ihesum Christum.

Alia oratio.

Benedic domine fortitudinem principis et opera manuum illius suscipe, et benedictione tua terra eius de pomis repleatur, de fructu celi et rore atque abissi subiacentis de fructu solis et lune, et de vertice antiquorum montium, de pomis eternorum collium, et de frugibus terre et de plenitudine eius, benedictio illius qui apparuit in rubo, veniat super caput eius et plena sit benedictio domini in filiis eius, et tingat in oleo pedem suum, cornua rinocerotis cornua illius in ipsis ventilabit gentes vsque ad terminos terre, quia ascensor celi auxiliator suus in sempiternum fiat. Per dominum nostrum Ihesum Christum. &c.

His expletis, archiepiscopus cum paribus coronam sustentantibus regem taliter insignitum deducit in solium sibi preparatum, sericis stratum et ornatum, vbi collocat eum in sede eminenti, vnde ab omnibus possit videri. Quem in sua sede taliter residentem mox archiepiscopus mitra deposita osculatur, dicens Viuat rex in eternum. Et post eum episcopi et laici pares qui eius coronam sustentant, hoc idem dicentes. His expletis missa a cantore primo et succentore[s] chorum seruantibus inchoetur et suo ordine decantetur.

Oratio pro rege.

Quesumus omnipotens deus vt famulus tuus rex noster N. qui tua miseratione regni suscepit gubernacula virtutum etiam omnium percipiat Incrementa, quibus decenter ornatus et vitiorum monstra euitare et hostes superare, et ad te, qui via, veritas, et vita es, gratiosus valeat peruenire, Per.

Secreta.

Munera quesumus domine oblata sanctifica vt et nobis vnigeniti tui corpus et sanguis fiant et huic regi nostro ad obtinendam anime corporisque salutem et ad peragendum iniunctum officium, te largiente, vsquequaque proficiant. Per dominum.

---

[q] Omitted in AN, P 2288, p. 1309; all copies omit *filii*, following.

[r] *Sic*, for *uuarum*.

[s] For *succantore; succintore*, in AN, P 2288, p. 1311.

Postmodum

Hec domine oratio salutaris famulum tuum N. regem nostrum ab omnibus tueatur aduersis, quatenus et ecclesiastice pacis obtineat tranquilitatem, et post istius temporis decursum ad eternam perueniat hereditatem. Per dominum.

Quando legitur euangelium rex et regina debent deponere coronas suas. Notandum quod lecto euangelio maior inter archiepiscopos et episcopos accipit librum euangelii et defert domino regi ad deosculandum[t] et postea domino archiepiscopo missam celebranti. Post offertorium pares deducunt regem ad altare coronam eius sustinentes. Rex autem debet offere panem vnum vinum in vrceo argenteo et tresdecim bisantos aureos et regina similiter. In eundo autem et redeundo gladius nudus defertur coram eo. Notandum quod antequam archiepiscopus dicat Pax domini sit semper vobiscum, debet dicere hanc benedictionem super regem et super populum. Sic.

Benedicat tibi dominus custodiatque te sicut voluit te super populum suum constituere regem, ita quod in presenti seculo felicem et eterne felicitati[u] tribuat esse consortem. Amen.

Clerum ac populum quem sua voluit opitulatione tua sanctione congregari sua dispensatione et tua administratione per diuturna tempora faciat feliciter gubernari. Amen.

Quatinus diuinis monitis parentes, aduersitatibus omnibus carentes, bonis omnibus exuberantes tuo ministerio fideli amore obsequentes, et in presenti seculo pacis tranquilitate fruantur et tecum eternorum ciuium consortio potiri mereantur. Amen. Quod ipse prestare.

Finita missa iterum pares adducunt regem coram altari, et ibi communicat corpus et sanguinem domini de manu domini archiepiscopi missam celebrantis. Sed notandum est quod ille qui dedit ei euangelium ad deosculandum debet post Pax domini accipere pacem ab archiepiscopo missam celebrante, et deferre regi cum oris osculo et regine in libro. Et post eum omnes archiepiscopi et episcopi regi dant osculum pacis, vnus post alium in suo solio residenti. Missa finita deponit archiepiscopus coronam de capite regis, et expoliato rege de insignioribus vestimentis et aliis indutis, iterum imponit capiti suo archiepiscopus aliam coronam minorem, et sic vadit ad palatium, nudo gladio precedente. Et sciendum est quod eius camisia propter sanctam vnctionem debet comburi.

[t] *et post eo regine*, omitted.

[u] *Sic*, for *felicitatis*.

De ampulle reductione.

Finita consecratione et missa debent iterum idem barones reducere sanctam ampullam vsque ad sanctum Remigium honorifice et secure, et eam restituere loco suo.

Ordo ad reginam benedicendam que debet consecrari statim post factam consecrationem regis.

Debet ei parari solium in modum solii regis, debet tamen aliquantulum minus esse. Debet autem regina adduci in ecclesiam et rex in suo solio parari[v] in omnibus ornamentis suis regiis sicut in solio residebat post inunctionem et coronationem suam superius annotatam. Regina autem adducta in ecclesiam debet prosterni ante altare, et prostrata debet orare, qua eleuata ab oratione ab episcopis, debet iterum caput inclinare, et archiepiscopus hanc orationem dicere. Sic.

Oratio.

Adesto domine supplicationibus nostris, et quod humilitatis nostre gerendum est misterio tue virtutis impleatur effectu. Per dominum.

Notandum quod tunica regine et camisia debent esse aperte vsque ad corrigiam, et dominus archiepiscopus debet inungere eam oleo sancto in capite et in pectore, et dicere dum inungit, In nomine patris, et filii et spiritus sancti, prosit tibi hec vnctio olei in honorem et confirmationem eternam.

Sequitur post inunctionem hec oratio.

Omnipotens sempiterne deus affluentem spiritum tue benedictionis super famulam tuam nobis orantibus propitiatus infunde, vt que per manus nostre impositionem hodie regina instuitur sanctificatione tua digna et electa permaneat, vt nunquam postmodum de tua gratia separetur indigna. Per dominum.

Post istam orationem datur ab archiepiscopo sceptrum modicum alterius modi quam sceptrum regium et virga consimilis virge regie absque orationibus. Tunc debet anulus iungi[w] digito, et dici[x] sic.

Accipe annulum fidei signaculum sancte Trinitatis que possit[y] omnes hereticas prauitates deuitare, et barbaras gentes virtute tibi prestita ad agnitionem veritatis[z] aduocare.

Sequitur oratio.

---

[v] *Sic,* for *sedere.*

[w] *inungi,* in AN, P 2288, p. 1315; for *immiti.*

[x] *Sic,* for *dicere.*

[y] *Sic,* for *quo possis.*

[z] Only in AN, P 2288, p. 1315; *virtutis,* in the other two copies.

Deus cuius est omnis potestas et dignitas, da famule[a] tue signo tue fidei prosperum sue dignitatis effectum in qua tibi semper firma maneat tibique iugiter placere concedat.[b] Per dominum.

Tunc debet ei imponi a solo archiepiscopo corona in capite ipsius, quam impositam sustentare debent vndique barones: archiepiscopus autem debet dicere in impositione orationem.

Accipe coronam glorie, honorem iocunditatis, vt splendida fulgeas et eterna exultatione coroneris.

Alia oratio.

Omnium domine fons bonorum et cunctorum dator prouectuum tribue famule tue N. adeptam bene regere dignitatem, et a te sibi prestitam in ea bonis operibus corrobora gloriam. Per dominum.

Post istam orationem barones qui coronam eius sustentant deducunt eam ad solium, vbi in sede parata collocatur circumstantibus eam baronibus et matronis nobilioribus. In oblatione, in pace ferenda, et in communicatione penitus est ordo regis superius adnotatus obseruandus.

Benedictio Vexilli.

Oratio.

Inclina domine aurem tuam ad preces nostras humilitatis, et per interuentum beati Michaelis archangeli tui et beati Dyonisii martiris omniumque celestium virtutum presta nobis auxilium dextere tue, vt sicut benedixisti Abraham aduersus quinque reges triumphantem atque Dauid regem in tui nominis laude triumphales congressus exercentem, ita benedicere et sanctificare digneris vexillum hoc quod ob defensionem sancte ecclesie contra hostilem rabiem defertur, quatenus in nomine tuo fideles et defensores populi dei illud consequentes per virtutem sancte Crucis triumphum et victoriam se ex hostibus acquisisse letentur. Qui cum patre, &c.

Ad tradendum autem vexillum domino regi, dicas ita.

Diex par sa grace et par les prieres nostre glorieux patron Monseigneur sainct Denis vous donne[c] auoir noble[d] victoire de tous vos ennemis. Amen.

---

[a] Only in AN, P 2288, p. 1315; *familie*, in the other two copies.
[b] *Sic*, for *contendat*.
[c] *doient*, in AN, P 2288, p. 1317; *sic*, in the two other copies.
[d] Only in AN, P 2288, p. 1317; *bonne*, in the two other copies.

D.

Coronation *Ordo* Included by Jean du Tillet in the *Recueil des Roys de France* Presented to Charles IX in 1566

All printed editions of this *ordo* differ significantly in orthography and punctuation from the presentation copy of the volume, BN, fr. 2848, fols. 167v-78r; see also SS, Fr. F. v. IV, No. 9, fols. 166v-77r;, and BPU, fols. 207r-20r.

This edition is based on the presentation copy. The scribe employed at least five forms of initial *l*, two forms of initial *e*, and four forms of initial *d*; he ordinarily distinguished between initial *I* and *J* by placing a bar across the stroke of the latter letter. The distinction between initial *I* and *J* is recorded here, since modern type makes this possible; the differences among the initial *e*'s and initial *d*'s generally seem to represent a distinction between capital and lower case letters and have been recorded as such; some initial *l*'s evidently designate capital letters. Marks at the ends of lines have not been recorded, except when they seem to have been used to indicate a break between sentences or phrases. The points which the scribe occasionally used are generally placed in the middle of the line of script. For the sake of clarity, paragraph divisions have been introduced.

Major variants and differences in orthography in SS, Fr. F. v. IV, No. 9, and in BPU, MS fr. 84, are given in the notes, where the different copies are referred to simply as BN, SS, and BPU. BPU, MS fr. 84, is generally far closer to the presentation copy in orthography, accenting, and punctuation than is SS, Fr. F. v. IV, No. 9.[1] This, like other evidence, suggests that the Geneva manuscript was copied directly from the presentation copy.

• • • • •

Parce que le vray office des Roy et Royne est declairé par les oraisons et ceremonies de leurs sacres & couronnemens ne sera Impertinent Inserer lordre commandé par ledict Roy Loys le Jeune Iusques a present obserué Auecques sumptuosités plus

[1] SS, fol. 166v, renders the king's name *Lois le Jenne*, the spelling usually found in the manuscript. The scribe often employs *i* where *y* is found in the presentation copy, as in *Roiaume, chanoine, fois, octroier, aussi, aidant, palais, trois, liesse, cheminent, voie, Golias, multiplie, tousiours, Moise, vnion, puis, laiz, histoire*. Conversely, the scribe uses *y* for the presentation copy's *i* in *ainsy, ensuyt*, (although this word is sometimes rendered *ensuit*), *mys, aussy*. These variants will not be noted below.

grandes / Car le dire de Sainct Iehan crisostome[2] est certain que les Roys complaisans a Dieu ont prosperé longuement et leurs ennemys ont esté humiliés soubz eulx / Ceulx quj ont mal Regné ont este humiliés soubz leurs ennemys et chastiés en leurs personnes et estat /

Premierement soit préparé vng trosne en maniere descharffauld[a] aucunement eminent Joignant par dehors au choeur de leglise mis ou mylieu[b] entre lun et lautre ouquel soit monté par degrés et y puissent estre auec[c] le Roy les pairs du Royaume[d] et autres si mestier est /

Ou Jour que ledict Roy viendra pour estre couronné, soit Receu a procession tant des chanoines que autres eglises conuentueles[e]/ Le samedy precedent le dimenche[f] du sacre et couronnement dudict Roy a lissue de complyes la garde de ladicte eglise soit commise aux gardes deputés par Jcelluy Roy auecques les propres gardes de ladicte eglise en laquelle ledict Roy ou silence[g] de celle nuict vienne faire son oraison et selon sa deuotion y veille vne piece en prieres / Quant matines sonnent les gardes dudict Roy soient appareillés[h] pour garder lentree de ladicte eglise et les autres portes dicelle[i] bien fermees et garnyes mettre[j] eus honnorablement et diligemment les chanoynes et clercz. de ladicte eglise toutes les foys quil leur sera besoing / Les matines soient chantees ainsi quil est accoustumé, lesquelles acheuees soit prime sonnee & chantee a laulbe du Jour / Apres vienne ledict Roy en leglise auecques les Archeuesques, Euesques, Barons & autres quil vouldra quj y entrent, Et ce auant que leaue beniste soit faicte / Les sieges soient disposés enuiron lautel d'une part & dautre esquelx les archeuesques et euesques soient assis par honneur / Les Euesques pairs celluy de Laon le premier, puys celluy de Langres, apres celluy de Beauuoys, puys celluy de Chaalons[k]/ et le Dernier celluy de Noyon auecques les autres euesques suf-

---

[2] *.i. homel. sur le .1. .S. Math,* marginal notation. Although this precise quotation does not occur in Chrysostom's first homily on Matt. 1, at the beginning of the sermon Chrysostom contrasts the true king (or God) and the tyrants who are bound under him: MPG, 57: 24-25.

[a] *vn . . . deschauffault,* in SS, fol. 167r.

[b] *meileu,* in SS, fol. 167r.

[c] *auecq,* in SS, fol. 167r, the usual spelling.

[d] *Roiaume,* SS, fol. 167r, the usual spelling.

[e] *conuentuelles,* in SS, fol. 167r, and in BPU, fol. 207r.

[f] *precedant le dimanche,* in SS, fol. 167r, and in BPU, fol. 207r.

[g] *seillence,* in SS, fol. 167r.

[h] *appareillées,* in SS, fol. 167r.

[i] *dicelles,* in SS, fol. 167r.

[j] *mectre,* in SS, fol. 166v, the usual spelling.

[k] *Challons,* in SS, fol. 167r.

fragans de larcheuesché de Reins estans assis a part entre l'autel et le Roy a lopposite dudict Autel non loing dudict Roy, Sans quil y ait entre eulx gueres de personnes pour euiter lindecence /

Conuient scauoir que le Roy doit[l] choisir de ses plus nobles & puissans Barons et les enuoyer a la poincte du Jour a Sainct Remy pour auoir la saincte empoule[m] / Et Ilx[n] doyuent Iurer aux abbé et eglise que de bonne foy Ilx conduiront et Reconduiront ladicte saincte empoule a[o] ladicte eglise sainct Remy /

Ce faict entre prime et tierce les moynes dudict[p] Sainct Remy viennent en procession auecques les croix et cierges et ladicte saincte empoule laquelle soit portee par labbé tresreueremment soubz vng poisle de soye duquel les quatre bastons soient portés par quatre Religieux vestuz en aulbes. Et quant Ilx seront arriués a leglise sainct Denis[q] ou pour la presse si elle estoit trop grande Iusques a la grande[r] porte dicelle / Larcheuesque accompaigné des autres archeuesques, euesques et barons et des chanoines si faire ce peult aille au deuant de ladicte saincte empoule / la Recoyue de la main dudict abbé et luy promecte de la luy Rendre de bonne foy / Ainsi la porte a lautel auecques grande Reuerence du peuple ledict abbé et aucuns desdictz moynes l'accompaignans / Semblablement les autres moynes attendent en. ladicte eglise sainct denys[s] ou en la chappelle sainct Nicolas[t] Iusques a ce que tout soit parfaict et que ladicte saince Empoule soit Rapportee / L'archeuesque lors s'appareille a la messe vestu des plus Insignes vestemens et du palle auecques les diacres et soubzdiacres et en ceste maniere vestu vienne a l'autel en procession selon quil est accoustumé Et le Roy se lieue et le Reuere venant /

Quand ledict archeuesque sera a l'autel demande au Roy pour toutes les eglises a luy subiectes ce quj ensuit /

Nous te Requerons nous octroyer que a nous et aux eglises a nous commises conserues le priuilege canonique,[u] loy et Iustice deue, nous gardes et defendes comme Roy est tenu en son Royaume a chacun euesque et eglise a luy commise,

---

[l] *doibt*, in SS, fol. 167v, the usual spelling; similarly, in this MS *doyuent* is spelled *doibuent*.

[m] *Sic*, in SS, fol. 167v, but occasionally *empoulle* below.

[n] *Ilz*, in SS, fol. 167v.

[o] *en*, in SS, fol. 167v.

[p] *dudit*, in SS, fol. 167v, the usual spelling.

[q] *denys* in BPU, MS fr. 84, fol. 208r.

[r] *grand;* at the end of the line, in SS, fol. 167v, with the following two words omitted.

[s] *denis*, in SS, fol. 167v, the usual spelling.

[t] *nicollas*, in SS, fol. 167v.

[u] *canonicque*, in SS, fol. 168r.

Et ledict Roy Responde aux euesques Je vous promectz et octroye[v] que a chacun de vous et aux eglises a vous commises Je garderay le priuilege canonique, loy et Iustice deue et a mon pouuoir (Dieu aydant) vous defendray comme Roy est tenu par droict en son Royaume a chacun euesque et a leglise a luy commise / Aussi ledict Roy promette[w] & Jure par serment ce quj ensuyt[x] /

Je promectz. ou nom de Jesuschrist au peuple crestien a moy subiect ces choses

Premierement que tout le peuple crestien gardera a leglise de dieu en tout tempz la vraye paix par vostre aduys[y] /

Jtem que Je defendray[z] toutes Rapines et Iniquités de tous degrés /

Jtem que en tous Iugemens Je commanderay equité et misericorde, affin[a] que dieu clement et misericordieux m'octroye et a vous sa misericorde /

Jtem que de bonne foy Je trauailleray a mon pouuoir mettre hors de ma terre et Iurisdiction a moy commise tous les heretiques declairés par leglise /

Toutes les choses susdictes Je confirme par serment /

mette lors la main sur le liure des euangiles[b] /

Ces promesses faictes soit Incontinant commencé a chanter le Te Deum, et deux Archeuesques ou euesques maynent ledict Roy par les mains a l'autel deuant lequel Il se prosterne Iusques a la fin dudict Te Deum, Apres se lieue /

Auparauant doyuent auoir este mises sur ledict autel les couronne Royale, son espee enclose dedans le fourreau, ses esperons d'or, le sceptre doré et la verge a la mesure d'une couldee ou plus ayant au dessus vne main d'iuoire[c] / Aussi les chausses appellées sendales[d] ou botines de soye de couleur de bleu azuré semees par tout de fleurs de lys d'or et la Tunique[e] ou dalmatique de mesmes couleur et euure faicte en la maniere de chazuble de laquelle les soubzdiacres sont vestuz a la messe / Et auec ce le surcot quj est le manteau Royal totalement de semblables couleur et euure[f] faict

---

[v] *vous octroye*, in SS, fol. 168r.
[w] *promect*, in SS, fol. 168r.
[x] *uyt*, written over erasure.
[y] *vray aduis*, in SS, fol. 168r.
[z] *defenderay*, in SS, fol. 168r.
[a] *Afin*, in SS, fol. 168r, the usual spelling.
[b] *euangilles*, in SS, fol. 168r, the usual spelling.
[c] *d'une main d'yuoire*, in SS, fol. 168v.
[d] *Sendalles*, in SS, fol. 168v.
[e] *Tunicque*, in SS, fol. 168v.
[f] *oeuure*, in SS, fol. 168v, the usual spelling.

a bien pres en maniere d'une chappe sans chaperon / Toutes lesquelles choses labbé de sainct Denys en france doit de son monastére apporter a Reins et estre a l'autel pour les garder / Lors le Roy estant deuant l'autel[g] despouille premierement ses vestemens fors la camisole de soye et sa chemise quj soient ouuertes bien a val deuant et derriere, scauoir est a la poictrine et entre les espaules[h] / Les ouuertures de ladicte camisole estans Recloses et Reioinctes ensemble par attaches d'argent / Adonc tout premier le grand chambellan de france chausse au Roy lesdictes botines que ledict abbé de sainct denis luy[i] aura baillees / Et apres le duc de Bourgoigne luy attache les esperons et Incontinant les luy oste / Puys larcheuesque seul luy ceigne son espee Et aussi tost la luy desceigne[j] et la tire hors du fourreau quj soit mis sur l'autel et ladicte espee nue mise par ledict archeuesque en la main du Roy en disant loraison quj ensuyt /

Prens ce glaiue a toy donné auecques la benediction de Dieu par lequel en la vertu du sainct esperit[k] tu puisse resister et Repoulser tous tes ennemys et les aduersaires de la saincte eglise, defendre le Royaume a toy commis et garder larmee de Dieu par laide de Nostre Seigneur Jesuscrist triumphateur Jnuincible lequel Regne auec le pere, et cetera.

Lors par le choeur soit chantée ceste anteyne[l] / Soye conforté et virile, Obserue les enseignemens du seigneur ton Dieu affin que tu chemynes en ses voyes et gardes ses ceremonies, commandemens, tesmoignages et Iugemens et quil te confirme en quelque endroict que tu te tournes /

Et larcheuesque dye ceste oraison, Dieu quj par ta prouidence gouuerne les choses celestes et terriennes ensemble / soye propice a nostre Roy trescrestien A ce que par la vertu du glaiue spirituel toute la force de ses ennemys soit Rompue et toy bataillant pour luy entierement brisee par nostre seigneur Jesuschrist, et cetera.

A lheure ledict Roy Recoyue en humilité ladicte espee de la main dudict archeuesque et loffre a l'autel, puys la Repreigne de la main dudict archeuesque et[m] sans demeure la baille au Connestable de france sil en a / Et sil n'en à a[n] celluy de ses barons

---

[g] *lhostel*, in SS, fol. 168v.
[h] *espaulles*, in SS, fol. 168v.
[i] Repeated, in SS, fol. 168v.
[j] *deceigne*, in SS, fol. 168v.
[k] *esprit*, in SS, fol. 168v, the usual spelling; *esperitz*, in BPU, fol. 209v.
[l] *antheyne*, in SS, fol. 169r.
[m] *loffre . . . et* omitted, in SS, fol. 169r.
[n] Omitted, in SS, fol. 169r.

quil luy plaira pour la porter deuant luy tant en leglise Iusques a la fin de la messe, que apres la messe Iusques au palays / Cela faict l'unction soit preparee en ceste maniere, Le cresme estant mys a l'autel sur vne patene consacrée Larcheuesque ouure la saincte empoule apportee par labbé sainct Remy, et estant sur ledict Autel et en tire auec[o] vne petite verge d'or vng peu de lhuille enuoyé du ciel et diligemment[p] auec le doigt le mesle ou cresme preparé en la patene pour oindre le Roy / lequel seul entre tous les Roys de la terre Resplendit de ce glorieux priuilege Quil est singulierement oinct de lhuille enuoyé du ciel / Ladicte vnction preparee soient par ledict archeuesque deffermées lesdictes attaches des ouuertures des vestemens du Roy deuant et derriere et ledict Roy mis a genoux deux archeuesques ou euesques commencent la letanye laquelle finye larcheuesque assys comme Il syet quand[q] Il consacre les Euesques Dye sur luy auant que loindre les troys oraisons quj ensuyuent

Nous tinuoquons[r] seigneur sainct pere tout puissant Dieu eternel qu'il te plaise cestuy ton seruiteur (Soit nomme) auquel par la prouidence de ta diuine dispensation cree des le commencement[s] as donné croistre Iusques a ce present Iour ResJouy de la fleur de Ieunesse / enrichy du Don de ta pieté et plain de la grace de verité faire de Jour en Jour tousJours proffiter en myeulx[t] deuant Dieu et les hommes, affin que par la largesse de la grace superieure Il preigne en grande lyesse le trosne du supreme[u] gouuernement et par le mur de ta misericorde couuert de toutes parts de laduersité des ennemys Il puisse eureusement[v] gouuerner le peuple a luy commis en la paix de propiciation et vertu de victoire par Nostre seigneur Jesuschrist,[w] et cetera,

Dieu quj par vertu conseille tes peuples et par amour les domine, Donne a cestuy ton seruiteur lesperit de ta sapience auec la Reigle de discipline / A ce que a toy deuot de tout son cueur Il soit tousJours Jdoyne ou gouuernement du royaume et par ton don en son tempz la seurté de leglise soit adressee et que la deuotion ecclesiastique soit permanente en tranquillité[x] / Et que luy perse-

[o] *auecq*, in SS, fol. 169r.
[p] *dilligemment*, in SS, fol. 169r.
[q] *quant*, in SS, fol. 169r.
[r] A small scrape on the parchment above *in*.
[s] *commencemant*, in SS, fol. 169v.
[t] *profficter en mieux*, in SS, fol. 169v.
[u] *supresme*, in SS, fol. 169v.
[v] *heureusement*, in SS, fol. 169v, the usual spelling.
[w] *Jhesuschrist*, in SS, fol. 169v, the usual spelling.
[x] *tranquilite*, in SS, fol. 169v.

uerant en bonnes oeuures puisse par ta conduicte paruenir au Royaume eternel Par nostre seigneur Jesuschrist, & cetera /.

En ses Jours naisse[y] a Tous equité et Iustice / aux amys secours / Aux ennemys obstacle / Aux affligés consolation / Aux eleuez[z] correction / Aux Riches enseignement / Aux pauures pityé / Aux pelerins pacification / Aux pauures subiectz paix et seurté en la patrie / Apreigne continuellement a se commander soy mesmes et moderément[a] gouuerner vng chacun selon son estat, affin que arrousé de ta compunction[b] Il puisse donner a tout le peuple exemples de vye a toy agreables et chemynant par la voye de verité auec le trouppeau a luy subiect acquiere[c] en abondance[d] frugales[e] richesses et percoyue ensemble tout ce quj est par toy[f] concedé pour le salut des ames & des corpz./ Et ainsi mettant en toy la cogitation de sa pensee et tout conseil soit veu Jnuenter tousiours les gouuernacles[g] du peuple en paix et sapience assemblees et par ton ayde ait la prolixité et prosperité de la presente vye et par tempz bons paruienne a grande vieillesse / et deliure des lyens de tous vices par la largesse de ta pieté obtienne parfaicte[h] fin de ceste fragilité et les perpetuelles Recompenses[i] de la felicité Infinye et societes eternelles des anges Par nostre seigneur Jesuschrist, & cetera /

Lesdictes troys oraisons acheuees Dye ledict archeuesque celle de la consecration du Roy quj ensuyt/.[j]

Dieu eternel tout puissant createur et gouuerneur du ciel et de la terre facteur et dispositeur des anges & des hommes Roy des Roys et seigneur des seigneurs quj feys Abraham ton fidele[k] seruiteur triumpher de ses ennemys / A moyse et Josué preposés[l] a ton peuple as donné plusieurs victoires / As eleué[m] a la haultesse du Royaume Dauid ton humble seruiteur et l'as deliuré de la gueule[n] du lyon et de la main de la beste et de Golyas et du

[y] *n'aisse*, in SS, fol. 169v.
[z] *elleuez*, in SS, fol. 169v.
[a] *modereement*, in SS, fol. 170r.
[b] *arousé de ta conpunction*, in SS, fol. 170r.
[c] *acquere*, in SS, fol. 170r.
[d] Corrected from *abundance*.
[e] *frugalles*, in SS, fol. 170r.
[f] *o* corrected by erasure.
[g] *a* corrected over an erasure.
[h] *obtienne parfaicte*, over an erasure.
[i] *Rescompences*, in SS, fol. 170r.
[j] *ensuict*, in SS, fol. 170r.
[k] *fidelle*, in SS, fol. 170r.
[l] *proposez*, in SS, fol. 170r; *proposes*, in BPU, fol. 211v.
[m] *elleué*, in SS, fol. 170r.
[n] *quelle*, in SS, fol. 170r.

maling glaiue de Saül et de tous ses ennemys / As enrichy Salomon du don Indicible de sapience et paix, Apaisé regarde aux prieres de nostre humilité et multiplye les dons de tes benedictions sur cestuy ton seruiteur (soit nomme) lequel par humble deuotion nous elisons par ensemble ou Royaume, et l'enuironne tousJours et en tous lieux de la dextre de ta puissance A ce que confirmé de la fidelité dudict Abraham, Joyssant de la mansuetude de moyse, garny de la fortitude de Josue, exalté de lhumilité de Dauid / Decoré de la sapience de Salomon, Il te soit en toutes choses complaisant, et marche tousiours de pas sans chopper par la voye de Iustice et tellement nourrisse, enseigne, garde, et Instruise doresnauant leglise de tout le Royaume et les peuples y annexés administre puissamment et regalement[o] le Regiment de ta vertu contre tous ennemys visibles et Inuisibles quil ne delaisse le trosne[p] Royal Scauoir est les sceptres des francoys, Bourguignons, et Aquitaniens mais Reforme par ton ayde leurs voluntés a la concorde des premiere foy et paix, Affin que clarifié de la deue subiection de tous ses peuples[q] et glorifié de lamour condigne Il puisse par ta miseration establir et gouuerner en vnyon le sommet de la gloire paternelle par long[r] espace de vye et garny du heaulme de ta protection tousiours couuert du bouclier Inuincible enuironné des armes celestes Il preigne[s] eureusement le triumphe de la victoire desirable de ses ennemys, face crainte de sa puissance aux Infideles,[t] et Rapporte en Joye la paix a ceulx quj militent soubz toy / et le decore par multipliee benediction d'honneur des vertus desquelles as decoré tes fideles susdictz / Le colloque haultement ou gouuernement du Royaume et loingz de lhuille de la grace du sainct esperit /

Ladicte oraison finye face ledict archeuesque l'onction[u] des cresme et huille enuoyé du ciel par luy meslé auparauant en la patene comme dict a esté et ce en cinq endroictz de la personne du Roy / Le premier au dessus du chief, Le second en la poictrine / Le tiers entre les espaules / Le quart esdictes deux espaules / Le quinct es Joinctures des deux bras disant a chacun endroict Je loingz de lhuille sanctifié ou nom du Pere, du filx et du sainct esperit / Et tous Respondent Ainsi soit Il / A prendre

---

[o] *regallement,* in SS, fol. 170v.
[p] *throsne,* in SS, fol. 170v.
[q] *pleuples,* in SS, fol. 170v.
[r] *longue,* in SS, fol. 170v.
[s] *prengne,* in SS, fol. 170v.
[t] *Jnfidelles,* in SS, fol. 170v, the usual spelling; similarly, *fidelle.*
[u] Corrected from *unction.*

les espaulles[v] pour deux Et bras pour deux lonction[w] seroit faicte en sept endroictz /

Pendant que ledict[x] archeuesque la faict soit chantee lanteyne / Le presbtre Sadoch et le prophete Nathan oignirent Salomon Roy en hierusalem,[y] et venans Joyeulx deyrent, viue le Roy eternellement,

Laquelle acheuee ledict archeuesque dye les oraisons quj ensuiuent /

Seigneur dieu oingtz ce Roy ou gouuernement de ce que as[z] oingtz les presbtres, Roys, prophetes et martirs quj par foy ont vaincu les Royaumes / ouuré la Iustice et obtenu les promissions / Ta tressacree vnction descoule sur son chief, descende Iusques audedans, penetre le profond de son[a] cueur et soit par ta grace faict digne des promesses qu'ont obtenues les tresvictorieux Roys affin quil Regne eureusement ou siecle present et paruienne a leur compaignee ou Regne celeste, par nostre seigneur Jesuschrist ton filx quj a este oinct de l'huille de Joye pardessus tous ses consors et en vertu de la croix a debellé les puissances de l'air, destruict les enfers, vaincu le Royaume du Diable, et victeur est monte aux cieulx en la main duquel consistent victoire toute gloire & puissance Vit auec toy et Regne Dieu en vnité du sainct esperit par tous les siecles des siecles /.

Dieu fortitude des eleuz et haultesse des humbles quj as ou commencement voulu chastier les pechés du monde par effusion du deluge et as demonstré par la columbe portant le Rameau d'oliue la paix estre Rendue aux terres et apres par vnction d'huille as ordonné presbtre Aaron ton seruiteur et puys par Infusion de cest vnguent[b] as Renduz parfaictz les presbtres, Roys et Prophetes pour Regir le peuple d'Israel et as par la voix prophetique de Dauid ton seruiteur predict que la face de leglise seroit Joyeuse en huylle / Ainsi nous te supplyons pere tout puissant que ton plaisir soit sanctifier de ta benediction cestuy ton seruiteur par la gresse de ceste creature / A ce quil apporte a la semblance de la columbe la paix de simplicité au peuple a luy commis, quil Imite diligemment ou seruice de Dieu les exemples d'Aaron et quil atteigne tousiours les haultesses du Royaume en conseilx de science et equité de Iugement et le faictz auoir par

---

[v] *espaulles*, in SS, fol. 171r, the usual spelling.

[w] Corrected from *unction*.

[x] Omitted, in SS, fol. 171r.

[y] *Jhierusalem*, in SS, fol. 171r; *Jherusalem*, in BPU, fol. 212v.

[z] *quas*, in SS, fol. 171r.

[a] *ton*, in SS, fol. 171r.

[b] *vngent*, in SS, fol. 171v.

ceste vnction d'huille (toy aydant) la face preparee a Joye a tout le peuple Par Jesuschrist nostre seigneur & cetera /

Jesuschrist nostre seigneur Dieu filx de Dieu quj par le Pere a este oinct de l'huille d'exultation pardessus tous ses participans par la presente Infusion du sacré vnguent du sainct Esperit Infonde sur ton chief la benediction et la face penetrer Iusques a linterieur de ton cueur / Affin que tu puisse par ce don visible et traictable perceuoir les choses Inuisibles / Et apres auoir par Iustes moderations accomply le Regne temporel Regner auec luy eternellement Par Jesuschrist nostre seigneur & cetera /

Lesdictes[c] oraisons acheuees, soient par ledict archeuesque presbtres ou diacres les attaches des ouuertures[d] des vestemens du Roy Refermees a cause de l'onction[e] / Et lors ledict grand chambellan de france veste audict Roy les dalmatique de bleu azuré et par dessus le manteau Royal de facon que la main dextre soit a deliure deuers louuerture dudict manteau lequel sur la senestre main soit eleué comme la chazuble d'un presbtre.[f] Et apres ledict Archeuesque luy mette lanneau ou doigt medicinal de la main[g] dextre disant

Prens l'anneau signacle de la saincte foy, solidité du Royaume, augmentation de puissance, par lesquelles choses tu sache[h] chasser les ennemys par puissance triumphale, exterminer les heresies / Revnir les subiectz et les annexer a la perseuerance de la foy catholique Par Jesuschrist nostre seigneur & cetera /

Apres ledict anneau baillé dye ledict archeuesque loraison quj ensuyt /.

Dieu duquel est toute puissance et dignité donne a ton seruiteur l'eureux effect de sa dignité en laquelle toy Remunerant Il soit permanent te craigne tousiours et s'efforce complaire Par Jesuschrist nostre seigneur & cetera /.

Puys ledict Archeuesque mette le sceptre en la main dextre dudict Roy en disant

Prens le sceptre enseigne de la puissance Royale[i] Scauoir est la droicte verge du Royaume verge de vertu par laquelle gouuerne bien toy mesmes[j] / Defendz des meschans par Royale puissance saincte eglise quj est le peuple crestien a toy commis de Dieu /

---

[c] *Les*, in SS, fol. 171v.
[d] *des ouuertures* omitted, in SS, fol. 171v.
[e] Corrected from *unction*.
[f] Erasure under the final *re*.
[g] Omitted, in SS, fol. 172r.
[h] *saches*, in SS, fol. 172r.
[i] *Roialle*, in SS, fol. 172r, the usual spelling.
[j] *toyemesmes*, in SS, fol. 172r.

Corrige les mauuais / pacifie les droicturiers, adresse les quilx puissent par ta[k] grace tenir la droicte voye / affin que du Royaume temporel tu paruienne au Royaume eternel aydant celluy duquel le Regne et empire est sans fin permanent es siecles des siecles /

Apres ledict sceptre baillé dye loraison quj ensuyt

Seigneur fontayne de tous biens Dieu aucteur[l] de tous bons effectz donne (nous te supplyons) a ton seruiteur bien gouuerner celle dignité quil a apprehendee / te plaise luy corroborer l'honneur ouquel l'as constitué, honorifie le pardessus tous les Roys de la terre / Enrichis le de benediction abondante / Consolide le de ferme stabilité ou trosne du Royaume, Visite le en lignee / Donne luy prolixité de vye / En ses Jours naisse[m] tousiours Iustice, affin que en Joye et liesse Il ait gloire ou Royaume eternel Par Jesuschrist & cetera,

Consequemment ledict archeuesque mette la main de Iustice en la main senestre dudict Roy en disant

Prens la verge de vertu et equité par laquelle tu sache asseurer les bons et faire[n] craindre les mauuais / Enseigne le chemyn aux desvoyés, Tendz la main aux tumbés, Rabaisse les orguilleux, Eleue les humbles affin que nostre seigneur Jesuschrist t'ouure l'huys ayant de luymesmes prononcé Je suys lhuys par lequel quj entrera sera sauué, et luy quj est la clef de Dauid et le sceptre de la maison d'Israel quj ouure / et nul ferme / qui ferme et nul ouure / celluy qui mect hors de la maison de prison lenchesné seant es tenebres et vmbre de mort te soit aydant a ce que tu puisse ensuyure en toutes choses celluy duquel le prophete Dauid a chanté Dieu ton siege[o] est ou siecle du siecle la verge d'equité est la verge de ton Regne et Jmiter celluy quj dict Ayme Iustice et hay Iniquité pource Dieu ton Dieu ta oingt de l'huille de lyesse a lexemple de celluy quil auoit oingt deuant les siecles pardessus tous ses participans Jesuschrist nostre seigneur /

Ladicte main de Iustice baillee audict Roy / le chancellier de france sil y est sy non ledict archeuesque, appelle par leurs noms et selon leur ordre les pairs de france les lays les premiers puys les clercz lesquelx estans alentour preigne ledict archeuesque[p] la couronne Royale de dessus l'autel et la mette seul sur le chief du Roy / et aussi tost tous lesdictz pairs tant clercz que lays y

[k] *a* written over erasure.
[l] *autheur,* in SS, fol. 172r.
[m] *n'aisse,* in SS, fol. 172v.
[n] *i* is corrected over an erasure.
[o] *siecle,* in SS, fol. 172v.
[p] *led' ar* corrected over erasure.

mectent les mains et eulx seulx la soustiennent de tous costés disant ledict archeuesque /

Dieu te couronne de la couronne de gloire et Iustice honneur et oeuure de constance, affin que par loffice de nostre benediction auecques droicte foy et fruict multiplié de bonnes euures tu paruienne au Royaume perpetuel par la largesse de celluy duquel le Regne et empire est permanent es siecles des siecles /

Ladicte couronne assize[q] sur ledict chief du Roy soustenue par lesdictz pairs ledict archeuesque dye les oraison et benediction suyuantes /

Dieu d'eternité duc des vertuz victeur de tous ennemys Beneys cestuy ton seruiteur a toy Inclinant son chief / conserue le en longue sante et prospere felicité / en quelque endroict quil Inuoque ton ayde assiste luy aussi tost, le garde et defendz / Octroye luy (nous te supplyons seigneur) les Richesses de ta grace / Accomplys en biens son desir / la couronne luy soit en miseration et misericorde et a toy seigneur serue continuellement en bonne deuotion Par nostre seigneur Jesuschrist & cetera /

Le Dieu tout puissant estende la dextre[r] de sa benediction et Infunde sur toy le don de sa protection / tenuironne du mur de felicité et garde de sa propiciation par lintercession des merites de la saincte vierge marie, des benoist sainct pierre prince des apostres[s] / Sainct Gregoire et tous les sainctz / Ainsi soit Il /

Le seigneur te pardonne tous les maulx[t] que tu as faictz, T'octroye la grace et misericorde que humblement tu luy demande et te deliure de toutes aduersites et de toutes embusches des ennemys visibles et Inuisibles / Ainsi soit Il /

Commette a ta garde ses bons anges lesquelx tousJours et en tous lieux te precedent Accompaignent & suyuent et sa puissance te deliure de peché, de glaiue et de malauenture de tous perilx Ainsi soit Il /

Conuertisse tes ennemys a la[u] benignité de paix et charité, te face gracieux et aymable a tous les bons / Remplisse de confusion a toy salutaire ceulx quj seront obstinés a te hayr & persecuter et sur toy florisse sanctification eternelle / Ainsi soit Il /

Te face tousJours victorieux et triumphateur[v] de tes ennemys visibles et Inuisibles / Infunde continuellement en ton cueur les craincte et amour conJoinctes de son sainct nom Te Rende perse-

---

[q] *assise,* in SS, fol. 173r.
[r] *extende la d'extre,* in SS, fol. 173r.
[s] *appostres,* in SS, fol. 173r.
[t] *maux,* in SS, fol. 173r.
[u] *ta,* in SS, fol. 173v.
[v] *triumpher,* in SS, fol. 173v.

uerant en droicte foy et bonnes euures[w] et la paix concedee en tes Jours te conduise auec la palme de victoire ou Regne perpetuel / Ainsi soit Il /

Et celluy quj ta voulu constituer Roy sur son peuple tayant faict eureux en ce present siecle T'octroye participation de la felicité eternelle Ce que veuille donner celluy quj Regne & cetera /

Seigneur quj de tout tempz gouuerne les Regnes de tous Roys Benys[x] ce present prince / Ainsi soit Il /

Et de telle benediction le glorifie quil tienne le sceptre de salut auec la sublimité de Dauid et soit enrichy du don de saincte propiciation / Ainsi soit Il /

Octroye luy par ton. Inspiration gouuerner le peuple comme as donné a Salomon le Regne pacifique Ce que veuille donner celluy quj Regne & cetera /

Apres ledict archeuesque adressant sa parolle audict Roy luy dye

Soye[y] stable et Retiens doresnauant lestat lequel as tenu Iusques a present par la suggestion de ton pere de droict hereditaire delegué par lauctorité de Dieu tout puissant et par nostre presente tradition Scauoir est de tous les euesques et autres seruiteurs de Dieu et aye souuenance departir en lieux conuenables autant plus grand honneur au clergé que tu le voy estre plus proche des sacrés Autelx / affin que le mediateur de Dieu et des[z] hommes te confirme mediateur du clergé et du peuple en ce trosne du Royaume et que nostre seigneur Jesuscrist Roy des Roys et seigneur des seigneurs quj Regne auec Dieu & cetera / te face auec luy Regner ou Royaume eternel[a] /

Et adiouste ledict archeuesque les oraisons ou benedictions[b] suyuantes /

Le Dieu tout puissant te donne de la Rosee du ciel et gresse de la terre / abondance de froment, vin et huille / Les peuples te seruent et les lignees te Reuerent / Soye seigneur de tes freres, et les filx de ta mere sagenoillent deuant toy / Quiconques te benira soit Remply de benedictions et Dieu soit a ton ayde par nostre seigneur Jesuschrist & cetera /

Le dieu tout puissant te benye des benedictions du ciel en hault es montaignes[c] et collines et des benedictions de labisme estans

[w] *bonnes meurs et oeuures,* in SS, fol. 173v.
[x] *Beneis,* in SS, fol. 173v.
[y] *Sois,* in SS, fol. 173v, the usual spelling.
[z] *d* corrected over erasure.
[a] *et* corrected over erasure.
[b] *benedictions ou oraisons,* in SS, fol. 174r.
[c] *montagnes,* in SS, fol. 174r.

ca bas benedictions des mamelles Raisins et pommes Les benedictions des anciens peres Abraham Jsaac et Jacob soient confortees sur toy Par nostre seigneur Jesuschrist & cetera .

Seigneur beney la fortitude du prince, Recoy les euures de ses mains Sa terre par ta benediction soit Remplye de pommes, du fruict du ciel Rosee et abisme quj est dessoubz / Du fruict des soleil et lune et du sommet des anciennes montaignes / Des pommes des collines eternelles des bledz de la terre et de sa plenitude / La benediction de celluy quj apparut ou buisson vienne sur son chief et la plaine[d] benediction du seigneur soit en ses filx / Son pied soit teinct en huille Ses corns[e] soient comme les cornes du Rinoceron. en eulx Il dechassera les gentilx Iusques aux Limites de la terre Car celluy quj a monté au ciel sera a tousiours son ayde /

Lesdictes oraisons ou benedictions acheuees ledict archeuesque accompaigné desdictz pairs soustenans ladicte couronne mene ledict Roy ainsi aorné ou trosne a luy preparé et le assiee[f] en sa chaise si eminente[g] quil puisse estre veu de tous / Ce faict sa mitre ostee l'aille baiser ainsi seant[h] et dye viue le Roy eternellement / Apres luy, les autres pairs euesques et lays soustenans sadicte couronne facent le semblable disans mesmes parolles / Et les premier chantre et soubzchantre gardans le choeur[i] commencent la messe quj soit chantee en son ordre et dicte loraison speciale pour ledict Roy quj ensuyt,

Nous te Requerons dieu tout puissant que nostre Roy (soit nommé) ton seruiteur lequel par ta miseration a Receu le gouuernement du Royaume percoyue aussi laccroissement[j] de toutes vertus desquelles decemment aorné Il puisse euiter les monstres des vices, vaincre les ennemys et paruenir agreable a toy quj es la voye verite et vye Par nostre seigneur Jesuscrist & cetera /.

Lors que leuangile est chanté ledict Roy se leue[k] de sa chaise et luy soit ostee sa couronne de dessus la teste / Apres leuangile le plus grand des archeuesques et euesques preigne le liure des euangiles et[l] le porte a baiser audict Roy puys audict archeuesque

---

[d] *pleine*, in SS, fol. 174r.
[e] *Sic; cornes*, in SS, fol. 174r, and in BPU, fol. 216v.
[f] *lassiée*, in SS, fol. 174v; in BPU, fol. 217r, *du luy prepare et le assiet*.
[g] *eminante*, in SS, fol 174v.
[h] *sceant*, in SS, fol. 174v.
[i] *cueur*, in SS, fol. 174v.
[j] *acroissement*, in SS, fol. 174v.
[k] *lieue*, in SS, fol. 174v.
[l] *le*, in SS, fol. 174v.

celebrant la messe / A loffrande soient portés vng pain / vng baril d'argent[m] plain de vin / et treize besans dor / Et ledict Roy y soit conduict et Ramené par lesdictz pairs soustenans sadicte couronne Son espee nue portee deuant luy allant a ladicte offrende[n] et Retournant /

En ses secretz dye ledict archeuesque ce quj ensuyt[o]

Nous te supplyons seigneur quil te plaise sanctifier les presens offertz et que par ta largesse Ilx proffictent a nostre Roy (soit nommé) pour obtenir le salut de lame et du corpz et paracheuer loffice enJoinct Par nostre seigneur Jhesuschrist & cetera /

Seigneur ceste oraison salutaire preserue nostre Roy (soit nomme) ton seruiteur de toutes aduersités affin quil obtienne la tranquilité[p] de la paix ecclesiastique / et apres le decours de ce tempz paruienne a lheritaige eternel Par nostre seigneur Jesuschrist & cetera ./

Auant que ledict archeuesque chante ; Pax domini sit semper vobiscum, Il dye sur ledict Roy et son peuple les benedictions suyuantes /

Le seigneur te benye et garde et ainsi quil luy a pleu te constituer Roy sur son peuple ainsi Il te face eureux en ce present siecle et compaignon[q] de leternelle felicite / Ainsi soit Il /

Les clergé et peuple quil a voulu par sa grace et ton commandement estre assemblés face estre eureusement gouuernés moyennant ta dispensation et son administration / Ainsi soit Il

Affin que obeissans aux diuins admonestemens vuydes de toutes aduersités abondans de tous biens seruans a ton ministere par amour fidele Ilx Joyssent en ce present siecle de la tranquilité de paix et apres auec toy de la societé des cytoiens eternelx Ce que veuille donner celluy quj Regne / Ainsi soit Il /

Apres ledict pax domini, Celluy quj aura porté baiser[r] audict Roy le liure des euangiles preigne la paix dudict archeuesque le baisant en la Joue / et la presente par le baiser audict Roy. et apres luy tous les autres archeuesques et euesques en leur ordre aillent baiser Jcelluy Roy seant en son trosne et la messe acheuee lesdictz pairs deRechef l'amenent deuant le grand autel ou Il Recoyue par la main dudict archeuesque la communion. des corps[s] et sang de

---

[m] *baril de Argent*, in SS, fol. 174v.
[n] The first *e* corrected over an erasure; *offrande*, in SS, fol. 174v, and in BPU, fol. 217v.
[o] *sensuit*, in SS, fol. 174v.
[p] *transquilite*, in SS, fol. 175r, as also below.
[q] *co* corrected over erasure.
[r] Omitted, in SS, fol. 175r.
[s] *s* corrected over erasure.

nostre seigneur[t] ./ Ce faict ledict archeuesque luy oste la grande couronne quil auoit sur la teste et a luy despouille de ses plus Insignes habillemens et Reuestu dautres mecte sur son chief vne autre couronne plus petite Et ainsi ledict Roy sen aille au palays,[u] Sadicte espee estant portee nue deuant luy Et soit sa chemise brullee[v] a cause de la saincte vnction

Apres lesdictz sacre & messe lesdictz[w] Barons Reconduisent la saincte Empoule Iusques a sainct Remy honorablement[x] et seurement et soit Remise en son lieu ./

Monsieur Iehan de france filx du Roy Iehan duc de berry ostaige en angleterre deliuré a tempz le premier feurier .M. iij[c]. lxv.[y] feyt promesse de Retourner en foy de vray filx de Roy sacré[3] quj monstre que le sacre du Roy trescrestien honnoroit ses filx et tesmoignoit leur foy[z] et loyaulté plus grande que de ceulx quj estoient filx de Roys non sacrés /

Au partir de Reins ledict[a] Roy a accoustumé aller a Sainct marcol et y faire faire sa neufeine / Apres et non plus tost Il touche les malades des escruelles[b] quj est chose ancienne[c] / Le Roy Philippes le bel approchant de sa mort feyt appeller le Roy Loys hutin son filx aisne linstruisit et apprint la maniere de[d] toucher lesdictz[e] malades[f] luy enseignant sainctes et deuotes paroles quil auoit accoustumé dire en les touchant, Le prescha de sainctete de vye pour faire cest attouchement luy Remonstrant que selon lescripture Dieu ne oyt ne exaulce les vicieux et par eulx ne faict miracles /.

Witikind en lhystoire saxonique[g4] Recite le sacre Dothon. premier empereur faict a Aix la chappelle par hildebert archeuesque de Maience assisté de ceulx de Treues et Cologne et quil print les Insignes[h] Imperiaulx de dessus lautel[i] luy baillant lespee luy deit[j]

---

[t] *Jhesuschrist* added, in SS, fol. 175r.
[u] *pallais,* in SS, fol. 175v.
[v] *bruslée,* in SS, fol. 175v.
[w] *Sic.*
[x] *honnorablement,* in SS, fol. 175v.
[y] *mil trois cens soixante cinq,* in SS, fol. 175v.
[3] See 71 above. For the oath, see *Fœdera,* ed. Rymer, 3[1]: 107.
[z] *f* corrected over erasure.
[a] *le,* in SS, fol. 175v.
[b] *u* written over erasure; *mallades des escrouelles,* in SS, fol. 175v.
[c] *antienne,* in SS, fol. 175v.
[d] *apprint a toucher,* in SS, fol. 175v.
[e] *Sic.*
[f] *mallades,* in SS, fol. 175v.
[g] *saxonnicque,* in SS, fol. 175v.
[4] *Liure .2.,* marginal notation. Witukind, *Rerum gestarum Saxonicarum,* 55-57.
[h] *enseignes,* in SS, fol. 176r.
[i] *lhostel,* in SS, fol. 176r.

prens ce glaiue par lequel tu dechasses tous les barbares ennemys de Jesuscrist et mauuays crestiens de tout l'empire des francoys par lauctorité diuine et puissance a toy donnee pour tresferme paix de tous les crestiens /[5]

Luy vestant le manteau luy deit

soye admonesté[k] par ces cornes demises Iusques aux espaules de quel zele de foy tu doy ardoir et[l] te conduire Iusques a la fin a garder la paix,[6]

Luy donnant les sceptre et main de Iustice luy deyt

par ces Insignes tu soye admonesté corriger tes subiectz de chastiement[m] paternel et tendre la main de misericorde, premierement aux ministres de Dieu, puys aux vefues et pupilles et que lhuille de miseration Jamais ne defaille de ton chief affin que soye ou present et futur siecles de premiation sempiternelle[n] couronné,[7]

Les ceremonies dudict sacre sont significatiues de loffice du prince /.

Quand[o] la Royne est sacree & couronnee auec le Roy[p] audict Reins luy soit preparé vng trosne moindre aucunement que celluy[q] dudict Roy lequel y seant Ja sacré et couronné la Royne soit amenée en[r] leglise et se prosterne deuant l'autel pour faire son oraison, laquelle acheuee soit Releuee[s] par les euesques sur ses genoux et encline son chef[t] pendant que ledict archeuesque dira loraison quj ensuyt,[u]

Seigneur entendz a noz supplications et ce quj est a faire par le ministere de nostre humilité soit Remply de leffect de ta vertu,

---

[j] *dist*, in SS, fol. 176r.

[5] " 'Accipe', inquit, 'hunc gladium, quo eicias omnes Christi adversarios, barbaros et malos Christianos, auctoritate divina tibi tradita omni potestate totius imperii Francorum, ad firmissimam pacem omnium Christianorum' ": Witukind, *Rerum gestarum Saxonicarum*, 56.

[k] *soye admonnesté*, in SS, fol. 176r.

[l] *doibtz ardoir de*, in SS, fol. 176r.

[6] "Deinde sumptis armillis ac clamide induit eum: 'His cornibus', inquit, 'humitenus demissis monearis, quo zelo fidei ferveas, et in pace tuenda perdurare usque in finem debere' ": Witukind, *Rerum gestarum Saxonicarum*, 56.

[m] *chastiment*, in SS, fol. 176r.

[n] An erasure follows this word.

[7] "Exinde sumpto sceptro baculoque: 'His signis', inquit, 'monitus paterna castigatione subiectos corripias, primumque Dei ministris, viduis ac pupillis manum misericordiæ porrigas; numquamque de capite tuo oleum miserationis deficiat, ut in presenti et in futuro sempiterno premio coroneris': Widukind, *Rerum gestarum Saxonicarum*, 56.

[o] *Quant*, in SS, fol. 176r.

[p] *le Roy* written over erasure.

[q] *u* corrected over erasure.

[r] *n* is corrected.

[s] *relleuée*, in SS, fol. 176r.

[t] *Sic.*

[u] *ensuict*, in SS, fol. 176r, and below.

Les tunique[v] et chemise de la Royne doyuent estre ouuertes[w] Iusques a la ceincture[x] et ledict archeuesque l'oigne du sainct huille au chief et en la poictrine disant

Ou nom du pere du filx et du sainct Esperit / Ceste vnction d'huille te proffite en honneur et confirmation eternelle /

Apres ladicte vnction Dye loraison quj ensuyt /

Dieu eternel tout puissant apaisé[y] par noz prieres Infunde l'abondant[z] esprit[a] de ta benediction sur ta seruante affin qu'elle ceJourdhuy Instituee Royne par limposition de nostre main demeure par ta sanctification digne et eleue Et que Jamais cy apres elle comme Indigne[b] ne soit separee de ta grace Par nostre seigneur Jhesuscrist & cetera /

Puys ledict archeuesque sans oraisons mette es mains de ladicte Royne le sceptre moindre & dautre maniere que celluy du Roy / et la main de Iustice semblable a celle dicelluy Roy / Et lors luy mette l'anneau ou doigt luy disant

Prens l'anneau de la foy signacle de la saincte trinité par lequel tu puisse[c] euiter toutes malices heretiques Et par la vertu quj test[d] donnee appeller les nations barbares a la cognoissance de la verité

Apres dye loraison suyuante /

Dieu duquel est toute puissance et dignité donne a ta seruante par ce signe de ta foy l'effect prospere de sa dignité En laquelle foy elle demeure tousiours ferme et continuellement elle s'efforce de te plaire Par nostre seigneur Jesuscrist & cetera /

Soit puys apres par le seul archeuesque Imposee la couronne sur le chief de ladicte Royne laquelle couronne soit soustenue de toutes partz par les Barons et la mectant[e] Dye ledict archeuesque

Prens la couronne de gloire, honneur de liesse affin que tu Reluyse splendide et soye couronnee de Joye pardurable /

Apres auoir mise ladicte couronne adJouste ledict archeuesque loraison quj ensuyt

Seigneur fontaine de tous biens et donneur[f] de tous honneurs

---

[v] *tunicque,* in SS, fol. 176v.

[w] *ouu* corrected over erasure.

[x] *seinture,* in SS, fol. 176v.

[y] *appaisé,* in SS, fol. 176v.

[z] *abundant,* in SS, fol. 176v.

[a] *Sic.*

[b] *eleue . . . Indigne* omitted, in SS, fol. 176v.

[c] *puisses,* in SS, fol. 176v.

[d] An apostrophe between *t* and *est* has been erased.

[e] *mettant,* in SS, fol. 176v.

[f] *dhonneur,* in SS, fol. 177r.

octroye a ta seruante bien Regir celle dignité qu'elle a prinse et fortifie en elle par bonnes euures la gloire que luy[g] as donnee Par nostre seigneur Jesuscrist & cetera /

Ce faict les barons soustenans sa couronne la menent et colloquent en son trosne estans lesdictz barons et les plus grandes et nobles Dames Joignant elle /

A loffrande de la messe la paix et la. communion lordre du sacre du Roy soit obserué en celluy de la Royne Et lordre susdict est gardé quant elle est sacree et couronnee ailleurs que audict Reins

Ceulx dudict feu Roy henry second et de la Royne Catherine[h] sa femme ont este amplement escriptz et publyés par Impression, par Jceulx sera cogneu quil y a eu[i] petite diuersité: / :

E.
The *Vexillum* and the *Benedictio Vexilli* in Du Tillet's Editions of the *Recueil des Roys de France* for Henry II and Charles IX

The text is drawn from the *Recueil* for Henry II; the edition is based on BN, fr. 2854, fol. 211r-v; important variants from SS, Fr. F. v. IV, No. 8/1, fol. 192r-92v, are given; see also BN, fr. 18653, fols. 91v-92r; *Recveil des Roys*, 234-35. The italicized portions are those that Du Tillet added to the second recension; they are taken from the presentation copy, BN, fr. 2848, fols. 208v-209v; see also SS, Fr. F. v. IV, No. 9, fols. 207v-208v, and BPU, MS fr. 84, fols. 259v-60v. The same principles observed in the edition of Du Tillet's *ordo* are followed here.

• • • • •

Loriflamme, ainsi que Recite Guillaume le breton. en lhistoire[a] du Roy Philippes auguste, estoit de simple cendal de couleur de flamme dor, qui a splendeur Rouge, et la forme semblable a celles des bannieres des eglises, que lon porte es processions[1] La Cronique de france, descripuant[b] loriflamme porté en la bataille du[c]

---

[g] *l* corrected over erasure.

[h] *Catharine*, in SS, fol. 177r.

[i] Omitted, in SS, fol. 177r.

[a] *l'hystoire*, in SS, fol. 192r.

[1] "Ast regi satis est tenues crispare per auras / Vexillum simplex, cendato simplice textum, / Splendoris rubei, lethania qualiter uti / Ecclesiana solet certis ex more diebus; / Quod cum flamma habeat vulgariter aurea nomen, / Omnibus in bellis habet omnia signa preire, / Quod regi prestare solet Dionysius abbas, / Ad bellum quoties sumptis proficitur armis": *Œuvres de Rigord et de Guillaume le Breton*, 2: 319 (*Philippidos libri XII*, 11: lines 32-39). See Contamine, "L'oriflamme," 189.

[b] *descuiuant*, in SS, fol. 192v.

[c] *de*, in SS, fol. 192v.

mont de Cassel, deuant le Roy philippes de valoys dict qu'il estoit attache au bout dune lance, dun vermeil fort, aguyse de gonfanon, a deux queues, ayant alentour houppes de soye verde.[2] Cela manifeste quil y en a eu plusieurs de diuerses formes, qui Rend doubteuse la voix commune quil ayt este enuoye du ciel au Roy Clouis premier, apres son baptesme. Aussi deux tiltres declairent loriflamme, lun du Roy Robert estant en ladicte abbaye, dacte du vingtcinqiesme Januier, lan premier de son Regne, qui fut neuf cens quatre vingtz dix sept, d'aucuns biensfaictz dudict Roy a ladicte abbaye, en esperance que par lintercession desdictz Sainctz martyrs[d] Il ayt victoire de ses ennemys, et quil puisse apres Rapporter en ladicte eglise loriflamme, bannyere dela subiection desdictz martirs Jnuincible par layde de dieu.[3] *Le Sieur de Joinuille en l'histoire sainct loys ne l'appelle autrement que la banniere sainct denys*[e] / *Elle fut portee*[f] *ou premier voyage*[g] *que ledict*[h] *Roy feit oultremer* /[4] Lautre tiltre est dudict Roy Loys le gros, *daté a paris lan .M.C.xxiiij*[i] *estant ou tresor des chartres ouquel ledict Roy*[j] narre que le conte du vexin est tenu a hommaige desdictz martyrs, et que les contes dudict vexin souloient & auoient droict[k] porter loriflamme

---

[2] ". . . et tenoit en sa main une lance en laquelle l'oriflame estoit attachié, qui estoit d'un vermeil samit a guise de gonfanon à ii queues, et avoit entour houpes de soye vert": *Grandes Chroniques*, ed. Viard, 9: 88; ed. Paris, 5: 317.

[d] *martirs*, in SS, fol. 192v, and in BN, fr. 18653, fol. 92r.

[3] Robert's charter is ed. in Felibien, *Histoire de l'Abbaye Royale, preuves*, lxxxij-iv, no. CIX. Du Tillet's statement seems to be based on his misconstruction of a sentence in the king's description of the conflict between the abbey and Burchard le Barbu that he had tried unsuccessfully to stop by ordering the destruction of Burchard's fortress, "unde gravissimam irarum flammam adversus ecclesiam Domni nostri Dionysii conflavimus." In the charter the king announced a solution to the resulting hostilities, "[u]t autem sub pacis vinculo posset recurrere ab utraque parte facta dissentio": ibid., lxxxiij. Evidently, neither of these statements alludes to the *oriflamme* and its return to the church, but rather to the "most serious flame of wrath" that the king's action had kindled, and his desire to end the resulting dissension. Neither includes any reference to God or to Saint Denis and his companions, although earlier in the act the king alluded to "God's help" (to him as defender of the needs of the churches and servants of God) and the assistance of Denis, "cujus protectionum alis evecti, & quamplurima jam pericula superavimus, & ad hæc regni fastigia nos ascendisse confidimus": ibid., lxxxij. Such misinterpretations are rarely found in Du Tillet's works.

[e] *denis*, in SS, fol. 208r. The same orthographical idiosyncracies found in the copy of du Tillet's *ordo* in this MS, which are noted in Appendix I, D, 117-31 above, recur in this text.

[f] Written over erasure.

[g] *voiage*, in SS, fol. 208r.

[h] *le*, in SS, fol. 208r.

[4] Joinville, *Œuvres* (*L'Histoire de saint Louis*), 102 ("l'ensaigne Saint-Denis"), 106 ("l'enseigne Saint-Denis"), 154 ("gonfanon Saint-Denis").

[i] *mil C xxiiij*, in SS, fol. 208r.

[j] In place of this phrase the first recension reads *qui*.

[k] *auoient droict et souloient*, in the second recension.

appartenant a l'autel d'iceulx, Ledict[l] Roy, comme conte dudict vexin, print dudict autel loriflamme par les mains dudict abbe Suggier, qui estoit de son conseil.[5] Par la est appertement cogneu que loriflamme estoit la banniere[m] Sainct denys (comme toutes eglises en ont) Et que les Roys, allans en[n] guerre par deuotion & confiance de l'intercession desdictz Sainctz, Silz marchoient soubz leur bannyere,[o] pour auoir victoire, la leuoient de ladicte eglise

la prenans des mains de l'abbé qui la benissoit de la benediction quj ensuyt /

Jncline seigneur tes oreilles[p] aux prieres de nostre humilité et par l'intercession du benoist michel ton archange et de toutes les vertus celestes Donne nous l'aide de ta dextre affin que comme tu as benis[q] Abraham triumphant contre les cinq Roys Et le Roy Dauid exerceant les progrez[r] triumphaulx en la louange de ton nom Ainsi Il te plaise benire[s] et sanctifier ceste enseigne laquelle est portee pour la defense de[t] saincte eglise contre la Raige des ennemys A ce que en ton nom les fideles & defenseurs du peuple de Dieu qui la suyuront se ResJouyssent auoir acquis triumphe & victoire des aduersaires par vertu de la saincte croix de celluy qui Regne auec le pere et cetera.

Apres ladicte benediction ledict abbé la baillant audict Roy luy disoit /

Dieu par sa grace et par les prieres[u] vostre glorieux patron. mon seigneur Sainct Denis[v] vous doint auoir noble victoire de tous voz ennemys Ainsi soit Il /

---

[l] The second recension replaces *Ledict* with *Jcelluy*.

[5] "Præsenti itaque venerabili Abbate præfatæ ecclesiæ Sugerio, quem fidelem & familiarem in consiliis nostris habebamus in præsentia Optimatum nostrorum, Vexillum de altario beatorum martyrum, ad quod Comitatus Vilcassini quem nos ab ipsis in feodum habemus spectare dinoscitur, morem antiquum antecessorum nostrorum servantes & imitantes, signiferi jure, sicut Comites Vilcassini soliti erant, suscepimus": Felibien, *Histoire de l'Abbaye Royale, preuves*, xciij, no. CXXIV. See Suger, *Vie de Louis VI*, ed. Waquet, 220-21; Contamine, "L'oriflamme," 181-83; Barroux, "L'Abbé Suger," 1-26; Bournazel, "Suger and the Capetians," in *Abbot Suger*, ed. Gerson, 61, 63; Brown, "Saint-Denis and the Turpin Legend," 53-54, n. 9.

[m] *bannyere*, in SS, fol. 192v.

[n] The second recension replaces *en* with *a la*.

[o] *banniere*, in SS, fol. 192v.

[p] The first three letters are inserted over an erasure; *aureilles*, in SS, fol. 208r.

[q] *Sic; begny*, in SS, fol. 208r.

[r] *proprez*, in SS, fol. 208r.

[s] *Sic*.

[t] *la defense de*, omitted in SS, fol. 208r.

[u] *de* added, in SS, fol. 208r.

[v] *denys*, in SS, fol. 208r.

Ce faict ledict Roy la faisoit porter par ledict[w] *conte du vexin*[x] ayant ce droict, comme lun des principaulx vassaulx desdictz martirs. Apres que le[y] conte fut escheu a la couronne, les Roys commirent[z] pour porter en leur[a] lieu loriflamme quelque cheualier de grand Renom, et estime, de preudhommye & vaillance, lequel, auant le Receuoir se mectoit en bon estat de sa conscience, Receuoit son createur et faisoit les sermens accoustumez.

---

[w] *le*, in SS, fol. 208v.

[x] The first recension reads, following "la leuoient de ladicte eglise," "La faisoient porter par le conte du vexin."

[y] The second recension replaces *le* with *ledict*.

[z] The second recension replaces *les Roys commirent* with *le Roy commist*.

[a] The second recension replaces *leur* with *son*.

II.
The *Ordo Maior* of *Croix*

Register *Croix* of the Chambre des comptes contained two versions of the royal coronation ceremonial. Some consideration has already been given to the second and longer of these, a recension of the last direct Capetian *ordo* of 1250-70, which I have dubbed the *Ordo maior* of *Croix*. Particular attention has been paid to the phrases and passages that Du Tillet modified and altered when he prepared a translated version for his second *Recueil des Roys*. This appendix deals in greater detail with the *Ordo maior* itself, and its relationship to the last direct Capetian *ordo* and the *ordo* of Charles V.

In the absence of the edition of the last direct Capetian *ordo* that Richard A. Jackson is now preparing, the only easily accessible edition is that published by Edmond Martène. Comparison of the *Ordo maior* with this edition poses some problems. Minor variations may result from scribal errors; at this stage they are hardly worth enumerating or analyzing.[1] There are, however, many substantial differences, which are unlikely to result from scribal idiosyncracies or *lapsus*. These variants suggest that the *Ordo maior* of *Croix* was redacted after the recension of the last direct Capetian *ordo* for Charles IV and Jeanne d'Evreux (1326) and before the composition of the *ordo* of Charles V of 1364-65. In some cases the *Ordo maior* includes changes that appeared in the *ordo* of Charles IV and Jeanne d'Evreux; other alterations in the *Ordo maior* are found in the *ordo* of Charles V, whose redactors seem to have consulted the *Ordo maior* as they worked. This sequence suggests that the *ordo* was drawn up in connection with the coronation of Philip VI of Valois in 1328, but there seems to be no way to establish that this was the case.

---

[1] One important minor variant is the *Ordo Maior*'s addition of *domine* in the prayer *Te invocamus* ("Te invocamus domine sancte pater omnipotens eterne Deus . . ."), omitted by Godefroy, but found in Du Tillet's translation and in the *ordo* of Charles V: *De antiquis ritibus*, ed. Martène, 2: 225; *Coronation Book*, ed. Dewick, 25; Appendix I C and D, 106 and 122 above; cf. *Ceremonial*, ed. Godefroy, 1: 4. The sections containing this prayer are missing from the Urbana-Champaign *ordo*, which begins in the middle of the prayer *Deus qui providentia*, preceding the king's offering of the sword at the altar: cf. *De antiquis ritibus*, ed. Martène, 2: 224.

A major difference occurs at the beginning of the *Ordo maior,* in the section dealing with the monks of Saint-Remi and the holy ampulla. In the last direct Capetian *ordo* the description of the procedures to be followed is uneasily divided between an early section, "Quando sacra ampulla debet venire," and the paragraph on the return of the ampulla, at the end of the order for the king's coronation.[2] Recognizing the confusion, the redactor of the *Ordo maior* transferred to the early section the first sentence of the *De reductione ampulle,* "Sciendum est quod rex debet accipere de baronibus suis nobilioribus et fortioribus et eos in aurora diei mittere apud sanctum Remigium pro sancta ampulla, et isti debent iurare abbati et ecclesie quod dictam sanctam ampullam bona fide ducent et reducent ad ipsam ecclesiam beati Remigii." The later section on the ampulla is correspondingly shortened.[3]

This alteration is not found in the *ordo* of Charles V, although others are. Immediately before the discussion of the ampulla, the *Ordo maior* substitutes *magna populi reuerentia* for *magna reverentia,* a reading that appears in the *ordo* of Charles V. Similarly, the *ordo* of Charles V resembles the *Ordo maior* in omitting the phrase "dum cantatur Tertia, facta aqua benedicta" from the section dealing with the arrival of the ampulla.[4] Later, in describing the king's preparation for vesting, the *ordo* of Charles V contains the *Ordo maior*'s phrase "qui prosternit se ante altare."[5] The *ordo* of Charles V does not, however, follow the *Ordo maior*'s omission of the superfluous and awkward "Huc usque de gladio" before the description of the preparation of the unction.[6] Nor does it change the words *cum acu aurea* to *cum aurea virgula* in describing the archbishop's preparation of the chrism and holy oil.[7] Like the *Ordo maior,* however, the *ordo* of Charles V omits the last direct Capetian *ordo*'s commentary on the royal unction, "Alii enim reges, inunguntur solum in humero, ille vero in capite, & in aliis membris sicut inferius distinguetur," a statement found in the *ordo* of Charles IV and Jeanne d'Evreux.[8] The *Ordo maior*'s deletion of the litany also broke with the tradition established in the

[2] *De antiquis ritibus,* ed. Martène, 2: 223, 227.

[3] Appendix I C and D, 103 and 115 above; *Ceremonial,* ed. Godefroy, 1: 2, 11; cf. *De antiquis ritibus,* ed. Martène, 2: 227; and *Coronation Book,* ed. Dewick, 17-18, 43.

[4] *De antiquis ritibus,* ed. Martène, 2: 223; *Coronation Book,* ed. Dewick, 18.

[5] *Coronation Book,* ed. Dewick, 20.

[6] *De antiquis ritibus,* ed. Martène, 2: 224.

[7] *De antiquis ritibus,* ed. Martène, 2: 224. Du Tillet translated the phrase (122 above) as "vne petite verge d'or"; cf. *vergette d'or* in the coronation *ordo* in Foulquart's treatise, ed. in *Archives administratives de la ville de Reims,* ed. Varin, 2^1: 579, n. 1 continued from 559.

[8] *De antiquis ritibus,* ed. Martène, 2: 224; Urbana-Champaign *Ordo,* fol. 1v; *Coronation Book,* ed. Dewick, 25.

last direct Capetian *ordo* and perpetuated in the *ordo* of Charles IV and Jeanne d'Evreux. Again, in this respect the *ordo* of Charles V resembles the *Ordo maior.*[9] In the instructions for the robing of the king following the unction, the *Ordo maior* rejected the tradition of the last direct Capetian *ordo* and the *ordo* of Charles IV and Jeanne d'Evreux in deleting *saltem* from the phrase "ab archiepiscopo uel sacerdotibus uel saltem dyachonibus," and in omitting *propter munditiam consecrationis;* in these cases as well the *ordo* of Charles V agrees with the *Ordo maior.*[10] Similarly, like the *Ordo maior,* it lacks the traditional phrase associated with the summoning of the peers after the king's investiture with the rod, "eo ordine quo dictum est superius de sedendo."

Most—but not all—of the changes introduced in the *Ordo maior* of *Croix* improved the text of the last direct Capetian *ordo.* The most awkward addition in the *Ordo maior* is the statement inserted before the prayer on the bestowal of the ring: "et in datione sceptri et virge dicuntur iste orationes. Sed notandum est quod antequam dentur sceptrum et virga datur anulus et in datione anuli dicitur hec oratio." Despite its clumsiness, the *ordo* of Charles V includes this phrase.[11]

The *Ordo maior* of *Croix* made alterations in two benedictions, *Omnipotens Deus benedicat tibi* and *Benedic domine fortitudinem,* and these changes are also found in the *ordo* of Charles V. In the first benediction, the additional phrase "abissi iacentibus deorsum benedictionibus uberum et" appears in the *ordo* of Charles IV and Jeanne d'Evreux[12]; in the second, the changes *de fructu celi* (for *de fructu cælesti*) and *de vertice antiquorum montium* (for *de virtute antiquorum montium*) do not.[13] The minor alterations that the *Ordo maior* introduces in the description of the royal offering, alterations that are not found in the *ordo* of Charles IV and Jeanne d'Evreux, for the most part appear in the *ordo* of Charles V. That

---

[9] *De antiquis ritibus,* ed. Martène, 2: 224-25; Urbana-Champaign *Ordo,* fols. 2r-4v. See *Coronation Book,* ed. Dewick, 51-53, and the notes, for the litany, which is not included in the *ordo* itself. Godefroy based his ed. of Charles V's *ordo* on that of John Selden, who included the litany in its proper place in the service: *Ceremonial,* ed. Godefroy, 1: 36-37; Selden, *Titles of Honor,* 231, and 231-33, for the litany; see 81 n. 313 above.

[10] *De antiquis ritibus,* ed. Martène, 2: 225 (*per diaconum*); Urbana-Champaign *Ordo,* fol. 10v; *Coronation Book,* ed. Dewick, 30; see 109 above.

[11] *Coronation Book,* ed. Dewick, 34; cf. *De antiquis ritibus,* ed. Martène, 2: 226; Urbana-Champaign *Ordo,* fol. 11r; see 109 above; it is omitted in Du Tillet's *ordo,* 126 above; *Ceremonial,* ed. Godefroy, 1: 7.

[12] Cf. *De antiquis ritibus,* ed. Martène, 2: 226; Urbana-Champaign *Ordo,* fol. 16v; *Coronation Book,* ed. Dewick, 39-40; *Ceremonial,* ed. Godefroy, 1: 9; see 113 above.

[13] Cf. *De antiquis ritibus,* ed. Martène, 2: 226; Urbana-Champaign *Ordo,* fol. 16v (where a fourteenth-century corrector expuncted *virtute* and wrote *vertice* above); *Coronation Book,* ed. Dewick, 40; *Ceremonial,* ed. Godefroy, 1: 9; see 113 above.

ordo agrees with the *Ordo maior* in adding the phrase *cum oris osculo,* absent from the *ordo* of Charles IV and Jeanne d'Evreux, to the description of the presentation of the *pax* to the king and queen.[14]

The most radical alteration in the *Ordo maior* of *Croix* is the insertion into the body of the service (following the royal offering) of the benedictions preceding the *Pax domini.* In the last direct Capetian *ordo,* the *ordo* of Charles IV and Jeanne d'Evreux, and the *ordo* of Charles V, these benedictions are found after the service for the queen's coronation. The *Ordo maior* places them earlier, before the transmission of the *pax* to the king and queen.[15]

Many changes, major and minor, that appear in the *Ordo maior* of *Croix* are found in the *ordo* of Charles V, although in a number of cases the redactors of that *ordo* followed the traditional phraseology and order of the last direct Capetian *ordo,* generally as modified in the *ordo* of Charles IV and Jeanne d'Evreux. But the parallels between the *Ordo maior* and the *ordo* of Charles V are too striking to leave any serious doubt that the redactors working under Charles V knew and used the fuller and better *ordo* that was registered in the Chambre des comptes.

---

[14] *Coronation Book,* ed. Dewick, 41-43; cf. *De antiquis ritibus,* ed. Martène, 2: 227; Urbana-Champaign *Ordo,* fol. 19r; see 114 above.

[15] Cf. *De antiquis ritibus,* ed. Martène, 2: 227; Urbana-Champaign *Ordo,* fol. 23r-v; *Coronation Book,* ed. Dewick, 49-50. In Du Tillet's translation, the benedictions preceding the *Pax domini* follow the *Postcommunio* since, as has been noted (see 70 above), the translation transfers the *Secreta* and the *Postcommunio* from the position at the beginning of the mass that they occupy in the *Ordo maior* to the section following the offering. In the last direct Capetian *ordo* (*De antiquis ritibus,* ed. Martène, 2: 227) the benedictions terminate "Quod vivit"; in the *Ordo maior,* "amen quod ipse prestare"; in the Urbana-Champaign *Ordo,* "amen. Quod prestare dignetur qui uiuit et regnat"; in the *ordo* of Charles V, "Amen. Quod ipse prestare dignetur cuius regnum et imperium sine fine permanet in secula seculorum. Amen. Et benediccio dei omnipotentis patris et filij et spiritus sancti super uos descendat et maneat semper. Amen."

BIBLIOGRAPHY

MANUSCRIPTS

Arras, Bibliothèque municipale
MSS 1051 (140), 1062 (222) (Seventeenth-century copies on parchment of the *Liber* of Bishop Lambert of Arras [1093-1115], from the library of Saint-Vaast of Arras)

Auxerre, Bibliothèque municipale
MS 123 (Annotated autograph manuscript of the Chronicle of Robert of Auxerre from the beginning of the world to 1211)

Cambridge, Eng., Caius College
MS 177/210 (Mid-twelfth-century historical miscellany from the house of the Blessed Virgin, Reading)

Chantilly, Institut de France, Musée Condé, Cabinet des livres
MS 1149 (XIX D 17) (Seventeenth-century copies of documents relating to royal ceremonies including coronations, funerals, processions, and marriages, made for the princes of Condé, *grands-maîtres* of France; vol. 356 of their collection of copies of documents concerning ceremonial)

Geneva, Bibliothèque publique et universitaire
MS 84 (Sixteenth-century copy on paper of the presentation copy of Jean du Tillet's *Recueil des Roys* for Charles IX)

London, British Library
Cotton Tiberius B. viii (Coronation Book of Charles V, 1365)

Paris, Archives nationales
KK 1439 (*Cérémonial* of Godefroy; collection of material relating to coronations)
KK 1440 (*Cérémonial* of Godefroy; index)
KK 1442 (*Cérémonial* of Godefroy; collection of documents relating to coronations, 1059-1610)
P 2288 (Eighteenth-century copies of documents from the Chambre des comptes)

Paris, Bibliothèque de l'Arsenal
MS 2590 (Seventeenth-century manuscript containing extracts from registers of the Parlement by Pierre Pithou)

Paris, Bibliothèque de l'Assemblée nationale (Chambre des députés)

MS 195 (B 105^{i}, vol. 68) (Seventeenth-century copy of BN, n. a. f. 7232; Brienne collection)

Paris, Bibliothèque de l'Institut de France

MS Godefroy 184 (Seventeenth-century extracts from Register *Croix* of the Chambre des comptes, 1223-1337)

MS Godefroy 294 (Seventeenth-century copies of documents relating to royal rights)

MS Godefroy 380 (Seventeenth-century copies of documents concerning coronations)

MS Godefroy 382 (Seventeenth-century copies of documents concerning coronations)

MS Godefroy 384 (Sixteenth- and seventeenth-century copies of documents concerning French and other coronations, from the early thirteenth through the seventeenth century)

MS Godefroy 520 (Seventeenth-century copies of material relating to nobility and genealogy)

MS Godefroy 532 (Seventeenth-century copies of miscellaneous documents, most relating to apanages)

MS Godefroy 533 (Seventeenth-century copies of miscellaneous documents, some relating to royal rights)

Paris, Bibliothèque Mazarine

MS 2013 (543) (Twelfth-century historical miscellany from the abbey of Saint-Denis)

MS 3039 (1810) (Seventeenth-century copy of tables and extracts from *Mémoriaux*, registers, and charters of the Chambre des comptes)

Paris, Bibliothèque nationale

Collection Baluze, MS 379 (Seventeenth-century collection of copies of and extracts from charters, ceremonials, and other manuscripts)

Collection de Champagne, MS 33 (Reims VII, part 2) (Collection of material relating to the history of Reims, copied in the sixteenth, seventeenth, and eighteenth centuries, including [fols. 14r-114v] notes for Antoine Colard's *Annalium Rhemensium libri septem quibus Antistium vrbis Rhemorum gesta Explicantur*)

Collection Duchesne, MS 74 (Extracts from cartularies and compendia collected by André du Chesne [1584-1614])

Collection Dupuy, MS 142 (Sixteenth-century inventory of and extracts from registers of the Chambre des comptes)

Collection Mélanges de Colbert, MS 46, part 2 (miscellaneous collection of papers belonging to Jean-Baptiste Colbert

[1619-83], including [fols. 390r-401v] Antoine Colard's *Commentaria rerum Remensium*)

MS fr. 2755 (Seventeenth-century copies of extracts from the registers of the Chambre des comptes)

MS fr. 2847 (Sixteenth-century copy on paper of Jean du Tillet's *Recueil des Roys* for Charles IX)

MS fr. 2848 (Presentation copy on parchment of Jean du Tillet's *Recueil des Roys* for Charles IX)

MS fr. 2854 (Presentation copy on parchment of Jean du Tillet's *Recueil des Roys* for Henri II)

MS fr. 2859 (Sixteenth-century copy on paper of Jean du Tillet's *Recueil des Roys* for Charles IX)

MS fr. 4411 (Seventeenth-century copies of extracts from Registers *Saint-Just* and *Croix* of the Chambre des comptes)

MS fr. 4596 (Sixteenth-century copies of extracts from registers of the Chambre des comptes, 1256-1328)

MS fr. 5000 (Sixteenth-century copy on paper of Jean du Tillet's *Recueil des Roys* for Charles IX)

MS fr. 5290 (Fifteenth-century copies of royal financial ordonnances and extracts from registers of the Chambre des comptes, from Philip III [1270-85] to Louis XI [1461-83])

MS fr. 5317 (Sixteenth-century copies of extracts and tables from registers of the Chambre des comptes)

MS fr. 5784 (Presentation copy on parchment of Jean du Tillet's *Recueil des honneurs et rangs des grands*)

MS fr. 6491 (Sixteenth-century copy on paper of Jean du Tillet's *Recueil des Roys* for Charles IX)

MS fr. 16600 (Seventeenth-century copies of extracts from Registers *Pater* and *Noster* of the Chambre des comptes, with notes by Achille III du Harlay, first president of the Parlement of Paris [1689-1707])

MS fr. 16924 (Sixteenth- and seventeenth-century copies of memoranda and documents concerning the rights of the French crown, 1125-1599; Harlay collection)

MS fr. 17294 (Miscellaneous papers, mostly belonging to Jean du Tillet)

MS fr. 18513 (Theodore Godefroy, collection of material relating to *Le Ceremonial François*, 1323-1654)

MS fr. 18437 (Record of the suit and trial of Robert of Artois, 1329-37)

MS fr. 18653 (Presentation copy on parchment of Jean du Tillet's *Recueil des Roys* for Henri II)

MS n. a. f. 7232 (Brienne 263) (Mid-seventeenth century copies of documents relating to French coronations, 1059-1610; commissioned by Antoine de Loménie, lord of La Ville-aux-Clercs, *secrétaire d'Etat* to Henri IV and Louis XIII [d. 1638])

MS lat. 1126 (Evangeliary of Gaignières, late-ninth or early-tenth century)

MS lat. 1930 (Twelfth-century manuscript of works of Saint Augustine, from Saint-Etienne of Caen)

MS lat. 2893 (Twelfth-century manuscript of the letters of Ivo of Chartres; Colbert collection)

MS lat. 5991A (Sixteenth-century inventory of and extracts from registers of the Chambre des comptes; Colbert collection)

MS lat. 9436 (Eleventh-century missal from Saint-Denis)

MS lat. 12006 (Twelfth-century commentary on Psalms)

MS lat. 12814 (*Liber parvus viridus* [*Noster*[1]] of the Chambre des comptes)

MS lat. 13315 (Late-eleventh- or early-twelfth-century pontifical from northern France, acquired by Saint-Germain-des-Prés)

MS lat. 14192 (Miscellaneous collection of booklets)

MS n. a. f. 7232 (Brienne 263) (Seventeenth-century collection of materials relating to the coronations of French kings and queens, 1059-1610)

Reims, Bibliothèque municipale

MS 225 (Twelfth-century missal, use of Saint-Remi of Reims)

MS 342 (Twelfth-century pontifical, use of Notre-Dame of Reims)

MS 1765 (Eighteenth-century collection of notes and documents concerning the archbishops of Reims by Canon Jean Lacourt)

MS 1769 (Nineteenth-century copy of Antoine Colard's *Annalium Remensium archiepiscoporum libri VII*, made by A. Duchénoy from BN, Champagne 33)

MS 1770 (Eighteenth-century notice on the archbishops of Reims, based on Guillaume Marlot's history of Reims)

Rouen, Bibliothèque municipale

MS 1173 (Y 11) (Twelfth-century historical miscellany from the abbey of Jumièges)

Saint Petersburg, National Library of Russia

MS Fr. F. v. IV, No. 8/1 (Presentation copy on parchment of Jean du Tillet's *Recueil des Roys* for Henri II)

MS Fr. F. v. IV, No. 9 (Presentation copy on parchment of Jean du Tillet's *Recueil des Roys* for Charles IX)

Urbana-Champaign, Rare Book and Special Collections Library of the University of Illinois

Coronation Book of Charles IV and Jeanne d'Evreux

Vatican City, Biblioteca Apostolica Vaticana

MS Ottobon. lat. 811 (Miscellaneous collection of booklets owned by Paul Petau [1568-1614])

MS Reg. lat. 574 (Fourteenth-century manuscript of works of Guillaume de Nangis and the *ordo* of Reims, owned by Paul Petau [1568-1614])

MS Lat. 4733 (Fourteenth-century pontifical with a copy of the last direct Capetian *ordo* and Louis IX's instructions to his son)

PUBLISHED SOURCES

Abbo. *Le siége de Paris par les Normands. Poème du IXe siècle.* Edited and translated by Henri Waquet. Les classiques de l'histoire de France au Moyen Age, 20. Paris: "Les Belles Lettres," 1942.

Abbot Suger and Saint-Denis: A Symposium. Edited by Paula Lieber Gerson. New York: The Metropolitan Museum of Art, 1985.

Adalbero of Laon. *Poème au roi Robert.* Edited by Claude Carozzi. Les classiques de l'histoire de France au Moyen Age, 32. Paris: "Les Belles Lettres," 1979.

———. *See also Carmen Panegyricvm*

Agathias. *Agathvs De Bello Gotthorum Et aliis Peregrinis Historiis Per Christophorum Persona Romanum Priorem Sanctæ Balbinæ e Græco in Latinum traductus.* Translated by Christopher Persona. Rome: Iacobus Mazochius, 1516.

Aguesseau, Henri-François. *Œuvres de M. le Chancelier d'Aguesseau.* 13 vols. Paris: Libraires associés, 1759-89.

Alletz, Pons Augustin ["M. A. de M."]. *Cérémonial du sacre et couronnement des rois et reines de France, précédé d'un discours préliminaire démontrant l'ancienneté et les motifs de cet acte de religion, et le majestueux appareil avec lequel il est célébré; suivi de la traduction de toutes les prières de cette auguste cérémonie; et d'une table chronologique et historique du sacre et couronnement des rois de France de la deuxième et de la troisième race.* 2nd ed. Paris: F. Denn, 1825.

Annales monastici. Edited by Henry Richard Luard. 5 vols. Rolls Series, 36. Vol. 1. *Annales de Margan. (A.D. 1066-1232); Annales de Theokesberia. (A.D. 1066-1263); Annales de Burton. (A.D. 1004-1263).* Vol. 2. *Annales Monasterii de Wintonia. (A.D. 518-1277);*

Annales Monasterii de Waverleia. (A.D. 1-1291). London: Her Majesty's Stationery Office, 1864-69.

Anselme de la Vierge Marie, le Père [Pierre Guibours]. *Histoire genealogique et chronologique de la Maison Royale de France, des Pairs, Grands Officiers de la Couronne & de la Maison du Roy: & des anciens Barons du Royaume: Avec les Qualitez, l'Origine, le Progrés & les Armes de leurs Familles; Ensemble les Statuts & le Catalogue des Chevaliers, Commandeurs, & Officiers de l'Ordre du S. Esprit. Le tout dressé sur Titres originaux, sur les Registres des Chartes du Roy, du Parlement, de la Chambre des Comptes, & du Châtelet de Paris, Cartulaires, Manuscrits de la Bibliotheque du Roy, & d'autres Cabinets curieux.* 3rd ed. Edited by Honoré Caille, lord of Le Fourny, and les Pères Ange de Sainte Rosalie [François Raffard] and Simplicien. 9 vols. Paris: La Compagnie des libraires, 1726-33. Rprt. Paris: Editions du Palais Royal, 1967.

———. *Le Palais de l'Honnevr, contenant les Genealogies historiqves des illvstres Maisons de Lorraine et de Savoye, & de plusieurs nobles Familles de France. Ensemble l'Origine & explication des Armes, Deuises & Tournois; l'Institution des Ordres militaires, & des principales Charges & Dignitez de la Couronne. Les Ceremonies qui s'obseruent en France aux Sacres des Roys & Reynes; leurs Entrées solemnelles, les Baptesmes des Fils & Filles de France; les Pompes funebres qui se sont faites aux Obseques de nos Roys. Auec vn Traitté fort curieux pour apprendre parfaitement la Science du Blazon; Enrichies des Armes & Figures en Taille-douce.* Paris: Estienne Loyson, 1663.

Arbellot, François. "Etude historique et bibliographique sur Geoffroy de Vigeois." *Bulletin de la Société archéologique et historique du Limousin,* 36 (2nd ser., 14) (1888), 135-61.

Archives administratives de la ville de Reims. Collection de pièces inédites pouvant servir à l'histoire des institutions dans l'intérieur de la cité. Edited by Pierre-Joseph Varin. 3 vols. in 5. Collection de documents inédits sur l'histoire de France, 1st ser., Histoire politique. Paris: Crapelet, 1839-48.

Aubert, Félix. *Histoire du Parlement de Paris de l'origine à François Ier, 1250-1515.* 2 vols. Paris: Alphonse Picard, 1894.

Auteuil, Charles de Combault, baron d'. *See* Combault, Charles de, baron d'Auteuil

Balayé, Simone. *La Bibliothèque Nationale des origines à 1800.* Geneva: Droz, 1988.

Baldwin, John W. *The Government of Philip Augustus: Foundations of French Royal Power in the Middle Ages.* Berkeley: University of California Press, 1986.

Baluze, Etienne. *See Miscellaneorum liber sextus*

Barlow, Frank. "The King's Evil." *English Historical Review,* 95 (1980), 3-27.

———. *Thomas Becket.* Berkeley: University of California Press, 1986.

Barroux, Robert. "L'Abbé Suger et la vassalité du Vexin en 1124. La levée de l'oriflamme, la Chronique du pseudo-Turpin et la fausse donation de Charlemagne à Saint-Denis de 813." *Le Moyen Age,* 64 (4th ser., 13) (1958), 1-26.

Barthélemy, Anatole de. "Essai sur l'origine des armoiries féodales et sur l'importance de leur étude au point de vue de la critique historique." *Mémoires de la Société des antiquaires de l'Ouest,* 35 (1870-71), 35-76.

Bautier, Robert-Henri. "La place de l'abbaye de Fleury-sur-Loire dans l'historiographie française du IXe au XIIe siècle." In *Etudes ligériennes d'histoire et d'archéologie médiévales. Mémoires et exposés présentés à la semaine d'études médiévales de Saint-Benoit-sur-Loire du 3 au 10 juillet 1969.* Edited by René Louis. Auxerre: Société des fouilles archéologiques et des monuments historiques de l'Yonne, 1975. Pp. 25-33.

———. "Sacres et couronnements sous les Carolingiens et les premiers Capétiens." *Annuaire-Bulletin de la Société de l'histoire de France, année 1987,* (1989), 7-56.

———. *See also Chronique de Saint-Pierre-le-Vif, Recueil des actes d'Eudes*

Bedos Rezak, Brigitte. *See* Rezak, Brigitte Bedos

Benoist, René. *L'Ordre et les Ceremonies dv Sacre et Covronnement dv tres-Chrestien Roy de France, Latin & François, traduict par M. René Benoist Angeuin, Docteur en Theologie, & Curé de Sainct Eustache à Paris.* Paris: Nicolas Chesneau, 1575.

Benton, John F. "Introduction: Suger's Life and Personality." In *Abbot Suger,* ed. Gerson. Pp. 3-15.

Berger, Elie. "Annales de Saint-Denis, généralement connues sous le titre de Chronicon sancti Dionysii ad cyclos paschales." *Bibliothèque de l'Ecole des chartes,* 40 (1879), 261-95.

Bernardi, Joseph-Elzéar-Dominique. "Mémoire sur l'origine de la pairie en France et en Angleterre." *Mémoires de l'Institut royal de France, Académie des Inscriptions et Belles-Lettres,* 10 (1833), 579-665. Read on 21 March 1827, after Bernardi's death on 25 October 1824.

Beugnot, Arthur-Auguste. *See Les Olim*

[Bévy, Charles-Joseph de]. *Histoire des inaugurations des Rois, Empereurs, et autres Souverains de l'univers; depuis leur origine jusqu'a présent. Suivie d'un précis de l'état des Arts & des Sciences sous chaque Regne: des principaux faits, mœurs, coutumes & usages les plus remarquables des François, depuis Pepin jusqu'à Louis XVI.* Paris: Moutard, 1776.

Bie, Jacques de, and Hilarion de Coste. *Les vrais Portraits des Rois de France. Tirez de ce qvi novs reste de leurs Monumens, Sceaux, Medailles, ou autres Effigies, conseruées dans les plus rares & plus curieux Cabinets du Royaume. Av Tres-Chrestien Roy de France et de Navarre Lovis XIII. Par Iacqves de Bie, Chalcographe. Seconde Edition. Augmentée de nouueaux Portraits, & enrichie Des Vies des Rois, par le R. P. H. de Coste, Paris. Relig. de l'Ordre des Peres Minimes.* Paris: Iean Camusat, 1636.

Bloch, Marc. *Les rois thaumaturges: étude sur le caractére surnaturel attribué à la puissance royale particulièrement en France et en Angleterre.* Publications de la Faculté des lettres de l'Université de Strasbourg, 19. Strasbourg et al.: Istra et al., 1924. Rprt. Paris: Armand Colin, 1961.

Bober, Harry. "The Coronation Book of Charles IV and Jeanne d'Evreux." In *Rare Books: Notes on the History of Old Books and Manuscripts published for the Friends and Clients of H. P. Kraus.* Vol. 8^3. New York: H. P. Kraus, November 1958.

Bodin, Jean. *Les Six Livres de la Repvbliqve de I. Bodin Angeuin.* Paris: Iacques du Puys, 1579, 1583.

Bonnefon, Paul. "L'historien Du Haillan." *Revue d'histoire littéraire de la France,* 15 (1908), 642-96 (sub-titled, "Lettres et documents inédits"); 22 (1915), 453-92.

Bouchel, Laurent [Bochellus, Laurentius]. *See Decretorvm Ecclesiæ Gallicanæ*

Boulainvilliers, Henri, count of. *Abregé chronologique de l'histoire de France.* 3 vols. The Hague [Paris]: Gesse et Neaulme, 1733.

———. *Histoire de l'ancien gouvernement de la France. Avec XIV. Lettres Historiques sur les Parlemens ou Etats-Generaux.* 3 vols. The Hague and Amsterdam: Aux dépends de la Compagnie, 1727.

Bouman, Cornelius A. *Sacring and Crowning: The Development of the Latin Ritual for the Anointing of Kings and the Coronation of an Emperor before the Eleventh Century.* Bijdragen van het Instituut voor Middeleeuwse Geschiedenis der Rijks-Universiteit te Utrecht, 30. Groningen: J. B. Wolters, 1957.

Bournazel, Eric. "Suger and the Capetians." In *Abbot Suger,* ed. Gerson. Pp. 55-72.

———, and Jean-Pierre Poly. "Couronne et mouvance: institutions et représentations mentales." In *La France de Philippe Auguste,* ed. Bautier. Pp. 217-34, with discussion on 235-36.

Brial, Michel-Jean-Jacques. "Anonyme. Auteur du formulaire pour le sacre de Philippe-Auguste." *Histoire littéraire de la France,* 14 (1817), 22-26.

———. "Guillaume de Champagne, archevêque de Reims." *Histoire littéraire de la France,* 15 (1820), 505-24.

Briquet, Charles Moïse. *Les filigranes. Dictionnaire historique des marques du papier dès leur apparition vers 1282 jusqu'en 1600, avec 39 figures dans le texte et 16,112 fac-similés de filigranes.* 4 vols. Geneva et al.: A. Jullien et al., 1907. Rprt. New York: Hacker, 1966. Rprt., with supplement. Edited by Allan Stevenson. Amsterdam: Paper Publications Society, Labarre Foundation, 1968.

Brown, Elizabeth A. R. "Eleanor of Aquitaine: Parent, Queen, and Duchess." In *Eleanor of Aquitaine, Parent and Politician.* Edited by William W. Kibler. Symposia in the Arts and the Humanities, 3. Austin: University of Texas Press, 1976. Pp. 9-34.

———. *Jean du Tillet and his* Recueils *for the Kings of France.* Forthcoming.

———. *Jean du Tillet and the French Wars of Religion: Five Tracts, 1562-1569.* Medieval and Renaissance Texts and Studies. Binghamton: Medieval and Renaissance Texts and Studies, 1993.

———. "Kings Like Semi-Gods: The Case of Louis X of France." Forthcoming.

———. "La notion de la légitimité et la prophétie à la cour de Philippe Auguste." In *La France de Philippe Auguste,* ed. Bautier. Pp. 77-110, with discussion on 111.

———. "Saint-Denis and the Turpin Legend." Forthcoming in *The* Codex Calixtinus *and the Shrine of Saint James.* Edited by John Williams and Alison Stones. Tübingen: Gunter Narr Verlag, 1992. Pp. 51-88.

———, and Michael W. Cothren. "The Twelfth-Century Crusading Window of the Abbey of Saint Denis: *Praeteritorum enim Recordatio Futurorum est Exhibitio.*" *Journal of the Warburg and Courtauld Institutes,* 49 (1986), 1-40, and pls. 1-12.

———, and Richard C. Famiglietti. *The Lit de Justice: Semantics, Ceremonial, and the Parlement of Paris, 1300-1600.* Beihefte der Francia (Deutsches Historisches Institut Paris). Sigmaringen: Jan Thorbeke, 1993.

Bruel, Alexandre. "Notes de Vyon d'Hérouval sur les baptisés et les convers et sur les enquêteurs royaux au temps de saint Louis et de ses successeurs (1234-1334)." *Bibliothèque de l'Ecole des chartes,* 28 (6th ser., 3) (1867), 609-21.

Brühl, Carlrichard. "Fränkischer Krönungsbrauch und das Problem der 'Festkrönungen.' " *Historische Zeitschrift,* 194 (1962), 265-326.

Brussel, Nicolas. *Nouvel examen de l'usage général des Fiefs en France pendant le XI. le XII. le XIII. et le XIVe. siécle, pour servir à l'intelligence des plus anciens Titres du domaine de la Couronne.* 2 vols. Paris: Claude Prud'homme and Claude Robustel, 1727.

Bryant, Lawrence M. *The King and the City in the Parisian Royal Entry Ceremony: Politics, Ritual, and Art in the Renaissance.* Travaux d'Humanisme et Renaissance, 216. Geneva: Droz, 1986.

Buchner, Max. "Nochmals die Krönungsordnung Ludwigs VII. von Frankreich: Eine Erwiderung." *Zeitschrift der Savigny Stiftung für Rechtsgeschichte, Germanistische Abteilung,* 33 (1912), 328-89.

——— [Maximilian]. "Zur Datierung und Characteristik altfranzösischer Krönungsordnungen mit besonderer Berücksichtigung des 'angeblichen' ordo Ludwigs VII." *Zeitschrift der Savigny-Stiftung für Rechtsgeschichte, Germanistische Abteilung,* 31 (1910), 360-423.

Bur, Michel. *Suger, abbé de Saint-Denis, régent de France.* Paris: Perrin, 1991.

Bzovius, Abraham. *Annalivm ecclesiasticorvm post Illvstriss. et Reverend. Dominvm, D. Cæsarem Baronivm, S. R. E. Cardinalem Bibliothecarivm.* Vol. 14. *Rervm in orbe Christiano ab Anno Domini 1300 vsque ad Annum Dom. 1378. gestarum narrationem complectens.* Cologne: Antonius Boetzerus, 1618.

———. *Historiæ Ecclesiasticæ ex Illvstriss. Cæsaris Baronii S. R. E. Cardinalis Bibliothecarii Annalibvs, Aliorvmq. Viror. Illvst. Ecclesiasticis Historicisque Monumentis.* 2 vols. Cologne: Antonius Boetzerus, 1617.

Bzowski, Abraham. *See* Bzovius, Abraham

Cameron, Averil. *Agathias.* Oxford: Clarendon Press, 1970.

Camps, François de. *Dissertation historique du Sacre et Couronnement des Rois de France Depuis Pepin jusqu'à Louis le Grand inclusivement, &c.* N.pl.: n.pub., 1722.

Carloix, Vincent. *Mémoires de la vie de François de Scepeaux, sire de Vieilleville et Comte de Duretal, maréchal de France; Contenants plusieurs Anecdotes des Regnes de François I, Henri II, François II, & Charles IX.* 5 vols. Paris: H. L. Guerin et L. F. Delatour, 1757. Rprt. in *Nouvelle collection des mémoires pour servir à l'histoire de France depuis le XIIIe siècle jusqu'à la fin du XVIIIe siècle.* Edited by Joseph-François Michaud and J.-J.-F. Poujoulat, et al. 34 vols. Paris: Didier, 1854-57. 1st ser. Vol. 9. Pp. 1-400.

Carmen Panegyricvm de Lavdibvs Berengarii Avg. et Adalberonis Episcopi Lavdvnensis ad Rotbertvm Regem Francorvm Carmen. Edited by Adrien de Valois. Paris: Jean du Puis, 1663. *Carmen Adalberonis* rprt. without dedication. MPL. Vol. 141. Cols. 787-822.

Carolus-Barré, Louis. "Pillage et dispersion de la bibliothèque de l'abbaye de Saint-Denis." *Bibliothèque de l'Ecole des chartes,* 138 (1980), 97-101.

Carozzi, Claude. *See* Adalbero of Laon

Cartellieri, Alexander. *Philipp II August, König von Frankreich.* 4 vols. Leipzig: Dyk, 1899-1922.

Cartellieri, Otto. *Abt Suger von Saint-Denis, 1081-1151.* Historische Studien, 11. Berlin: E. Ebering, 1898. Rprt. Vaduz: Kraus, 1965.

Cérémonial du sacre des rois de France, avec le formulaire en latin et en français, Tel qu'il fut suivi au Sacre de Louis XVI et modifié pour le Sacre de Charles X. Edited by Charles Millon. La Rochelle: Editions Rupella, Charles Millon, 1931.

Ceremonial de France, ov Description des Ceremonies, Rangs, & Seances obseruées aux Couronnemens, Entrées, & Enterremens des Roys & Roynes de France, & autres Actes et Assemblées solemneles. Recueilly des Memoires de plusieurs Secretaires du Roy, Herauts d'armes, & autres. Edited by Theodore Godefroy. Paris: Abraham Pacard, 1619.

Le Ceremonial François, ov Description des Ceremonies, Rangs et Seances, observées en France en diuers Actes, & Assemblées solennelles. Edited by Theodore Godefroy and Denys Godefroy. 2 vols. Paris: Sebastien Cramoisy et Gabriel Cramoisy, 1649.

Chantilly, Le Cabinet des livres, Manuscrits. Institut de France. Musée Condé. Vol. 3. *Histoire.* Paris: Plon-Nourrit, 1911.

Chéruel, Adolphe. *Dictionnaire historique des institutions, mœurs et coutumes de la France.* Part 2. 5th ed. Paris: Hachette, 1880.

Chichon, Jacques. *De adeptione Regni, consecratione & coronatione Henrici Secundi, Francorum Regis inuictissimi, deque ingressu illius in ciuitate Rhemensi Ecphrasis.* Paris: Mathieu David, 1547.

La chronique de Morigny (1095-1152). Edited by Léon Mirot. Collection de textes pour servir à l'étude et à l'enseignement de l'histoire, 41. 2nd ed. Paris: Alphonse Picard, 1909.

———. *Ex Historia Mauriniacensis Monasterii* (excerpts). Preface by Georg Waitz. *Monumenta Germaniae Historica. Scriptorum.* Vol. 26. Hannover: Hahn, 1882. Pp. 37-45.

Chronique de Saint-Pierre-le-Vif de Sens, dite de Clarius. Chronicon Sancti Petri Vivi Senonensis. Edited and translated by Robert-Henri Bautier and Monique Gilles, with Anne-Marie Bautier.

Paris: Editions du Centre National de la Recherche Scientifique, 1979.

Clark, Willene. "Art and Historiography in Two Thirteenth-Century Manuscripts from Northern France." *Gesta,* 17 (1978), 37-48.

Combault, Charles de, baron of Auteuil. *Histoire des Ministres d'Estat, qvi ont servi sovs les Roys de France de la troisiesme lignee. Avec le Sommaire des Regnes ausquels ils ont vescv. Le tovt ivstifié par les Chroniqves des Auteurs Contemporains; Chartes d'Eglises; Lettres & Memoires des Affaires d'Estat; Registres anciens, & autres bonnes preuues.* Paris: Antoine de Sommaville, 1642.

Conciliorvm antiqvorvm Galliæ A Iac. Sirmondo S. I. Editorvm Svpplementa Nvnc Prodevnt. Edited by Pierre Delalande. Paris: Societas Typographica Librorum Officii Ecclesiastici, 1666.

Constable, Giles. *See* Peter the Venerable

Contamine, Philippe. "L'oriflamme de Saint-Denis aux XIVe et XVe siècles. Etude de symbolique religieuse et royale." *Annales de l'Est,* 5th ser., 25 (1973), 179-244.

——— . "Les pairs de France au sacre des rois (XVe siècle). Nature et portée d'un programme iconographique." *Bulletin de la Société nationale des antiquaires de France,* (1988), 321-47, with discussion on 347-48.

The Coronation Book of Charles V. of France (Cottonian Ms. Tiberius B. VIII.). Edited by Edward Samuel Dewick. Publications of the Henry Bradshaw Society, 16. London: Harrison and Sons, 1899.

Corpus iuris canonici. Editio Lipsiensis secunda post Aemilii Ludouici Richteri curas ad librorum manu scriptorum et editionis Romanae fidem recognouit et adnotatione critica instruxit. Edited by Emil Friedberg. 2 vols. Leipzig: Bernhard Tauchnitz, 1879-1881.

Cossart, Gabriel. *See Sacrosancta Concilia*

Coste, Hilarion de. *See* Bie, Jacques de

Cothren, Michael W. *See* Brown, Elizabeth A. R., and Michael W. Cothren

Couderc, Camille. "Note sur le manuscrit latin 12814 de la Bibliothèque nationale." *Bibliothèque de l'Ecole des chartes,* 49 (1888), 645-53.

David, Marcel. "Le serment du sacre du IXe au XVe siècle. Contribution à l'étude des limites juridiques de la souveraineté." *Revue du Moyen Age latin,* 6 (1950), 1-272.

De antiquis ecclesiæ ritibus libri tres. Edited by Edmond Martène. New ed. 4 vols. Antwerp and Venice: Jo. Bapt. Novelli, 1763-64.

Decretorvm Ecclesiæ Gallicanæ, ex Conciliis eivsdem œcumenicis, Statutis Synodalibus, Patriarchicis, Prouincialibus, ac Diœcesanis, Regijs Constitutionibus, Senatusconsultis, Episcoporum Galliæ scriptis, al-

ijsque cum veterum, tum recentiorum pietatis eximiæ virorum monimentis collectorum. Libri VIII. Edited by Laurentius Bochellus [Laurent Bouchel]. Paris: Barthelemy Macé, 1609. Rprt. Paris: Nivelle, Sebastian Cramoisy, 1621.

Delaborde, H.-François. *See Œuvres de Rigord et de Guillaume le Breton*

Delalande, Pierre. *See Conciliorvm antiqvorvm Galliæ*

Delisle, Léopold. *Le Cabinet des Manuscrits de la Bibliothèque impériale. Etude sur la formation de ce dépôt comprenant les éléments d'une histoire de la calligraphie, de la miniature, de la reliure, et du commerce des livres à Paris avant l'invention de l'imprimerie.* Histoire générale de Paris, 10. 3 vols. Paris: Imprimerie impériale/nationale, 1868-81.

———. *Catalogue des actes de Philippe-Auguste, avec une introduction sur les sources, les caractères et l'importance historiques de ces documents.* Paris: Auguste Durand, 1856.

———. "Le psautier de saint Louis et les deux manuscrits de Guillaume de Jumièges conservés à l'Université de Leyde." In idem, *Mélanges de paléographie et de bibliographie.* Paris: Champion, 1880. Pp. 167-94.

———. "Recherches sur l'ancienne bibliothèque de Corbie." *Bibliothèque de l'Ecole des chartes,* 21 (5th ser., 1) (1860), 393-439.

De Meyier, Karel Adriaan. *See* Meyier, Karel Adrian de

Desjardins, Gustave. *Histoire de la cathédrale de Beauvais.* Beauvais: Victor Pineau, 1865.

Dictionnaire universel françois et latin, vulgairement appellé Dictionnaire de Trevoux. New ed. 5 vols. Nancy: Pierre Antoine, 1734.

Doublet, Jacques. *Histoire de l'Abbaye de S. Denys en France. Contenant les Antiqvitez d'icelle, les Fondations, Prerogatiues & Priuileges. Ensemble les Tombeavx et Epitaphes des Roys, Reynes, Enfans de France, & autres signalez Personnages qui s'y treuuent iusques à present. Le tovt recveilly de plvsievrs Histoires, Bulles des Papes, & Chartes des Roys, Princes, & autres documens Autentiques.* Paris: Iean de Heuqueville, 1625.

Du Cange, Charles du Fresne, sieur. "Dissertation V. Des cours et des festes solennelles des Roys de France." In idem, *Histoire de S. Lovys.* Part 2. Pp. 157-65. Also in idem, *Glossarium,* 7: 19-23 (at end).

———. *Glossarium mediæ et infimæ Latinitatis.* Edited by G. A. L. Henschel et al. 7 vols. Paris: Firmin Didot, 1840-50.

———. *Glossarium ad scriptores mediæ et infimæ latinitatis.* New ed. Edited by the Benedictine monks of the Congregation of Saint Maur. 6 vols. Paris: Charles Osmont, 1733-36.

——— . *Histoire de S. Lovys, IX. dv nom, roy de France, ecrite par Iean Sire de Ioinville, senéchal de Champagne: enrichie de nouuelles Obseruations & Dissertations historiques. Avec les etablissemens de S. Lovys, le conseil de Pierre de Fontaines, & plusieurs autres pieces concernant ce regne, tirées des manuscrits.* Paris: S. Mabre-Cramoisy, 1668.

Du Chesne, André. *Les Antiqvitez et Recherches de la Grandeur et Maiesté des Roys de France. Diuisees en trois livres, Le premier, De la Religion, Foy, Vaillance, Autorité, Pieté, Iustice, Clemence, & Preseance des Roys de France sur tous les Roys de la Terre. Le second, Des Habillemens royavx, et Ceremonies gardees de tout temps, tant aux Sacres, Couronnemens, Entrees, & Lits de Iustice, qu'autres Solemnitez publiques, & Funerailles de leurs Maiestez. Le troisiesme, De la Cour et svite royalle, Excellences & Grandeurs des Roynes, Prerogatiues des Enfans de France, & Ceremonies pratiquées de toute Ancienneté à leurs Naissances & Baptesmes: Priuileges des Princes du Sang, Institution des Cheualiers des Ordres, & premiere Origine des grands Officiers de la Maison de France. A Monseignvr le Davphin.* Paris: Iean Petit-Pas, 1609.

——— . *See also Historiæ Francorum scriptores*

Duft, Johannes. *Hochfeste im Gallus-Kloster: Die Miniaturen im Sacramentarium Codex 341 (11. Jahrhundert) mit Texten aus der Stiftsbibliothek Sankt Gallen.* Beuron and Constance: Beuroner Kunstverlag, Jan Thorbecke, 1973.

Du Haillan, Bernard de Girard, seigneur de. *See* Girard, Bernard de, lord of Le Haillan

Dupleix, Scipion. *Histoire Generale de France. Avec l'Estat de l'Eglise & de l'Empire.* 3 vols. Paris: Laurent Sonnius, 1621-28. 3rd ed. 3 vols. Paris: Claude Sonnius, 1630-31. 5th ed. 4 vols. Paris: Claude Sonnius, 1637-41.

Du Pouget, Marc. "Recherches sur les chroniques latines de Saint-Denis: édition critique et commentaire de la Descriptio Clavi et Corone Domini et de deux séries de textes relatifs à la légende carolingienne." Thèse, Ecole nationale des Chartes, 1978. Summarized in *Positions des thèses de l'Ecole des chartes,* (1978), 41-46.

Du Tillet, Jean. *Commentariorum & disquisitionum de rebus Gallicis libri duo, nunc primum Latine redditi. Quibus accesserunt Vincentii Lupani de Magistratibvs et præfectvris Francorum Lib. III. Adjectus in fine Index rerum verborumque notatu digniorum.* Translated by Lotarius Philoponus. Frankfurt am Main: Andreas Wechelus, 1579.

——— . *Institvtion dv Pere Chrestien a ses Enfans.* Paris: Guillaume Morel, 1563. Paris, Bibliothèque Mazarine: 12601.

———. *Les Memoires et Recerches de Iean dv Tillet greffier de la cour de Parlement à Paris. Contenans plvsievrs choses memorables pour l'intelligence de l'estat des affaires de France.* Rouen: Philippe de Tours, 1578. 2nd ed. Troyes: Philippe des Chams, 1578.

———. *Portraits des rois de France du Recueil de Jean du Tillet. Reproduction réduite des 32 miniatures du manuscrit français 2848 de la Bibliothèque nationale.* Edited by Henri Omont. Paris: Berthaud Frères, 1908.

———. *De Rebvs Gallici Liber.* In *Respublica sive Status.* Pp. 135-381.

———. *Recveil, Des Gverres et Traictez d'entre les Roys de France et d'Angleterre.* Also published as *To. II. Contenant les Gverres et Traictez de paix, Trefves, et Alliances d'entre les Roys de France & d'Angleterre.* Paris: Iaques du Puys, 1588.

———. *Recveil des Roys de France, levrs Covronne et Maison. Ensemble, le rang des grands de France, par Iean du Tillet, Sieur de la Bussiere, Protenotaire & Secretaire du Roy, Greffier de son Parlement. Plus vne Chronique abbregee contenant tout ce qui est aduenu, tant en fait de guerre, qu'autrement, entre les Roys & Princes, Republiques & Potentats Estrangers: Par M. I. du Tillet, Euesque de Meaux, freres. En outre les Memoires dudit Sieur sur les Priuileges de l'Eglise Gallicane, & plusieurs autres de la Cour de Parlement, concernant lesdits priuileges. En ceste derniere Edition a esté adiousté les Inuentaires sur chasque Maison des Roys & grands de France: & la Chronologie augmentee iusques à ce temps.* Paris: Abel l'Angelier; Barthelemy Macé; Pierre Mettayer, [1606]-1607. Rprt. Paris: Pierre Mettayer, 1618.

———. *Recveil des Roys de France, Levrs Couronne et Maison, Ensemble, le rengs des grands de France, par Iean du Tillet, Sieur de la Bussiere, Protenotaire & Secretaire du Roy, Greffier de son Parlement. Plvs, Vne Chronique abbregee contenant tout ce qui est aduenu, tant en fait de Guerre, qu'autrement, entre les Roys & Princes, Republiques & Potentats estrangers: Par M. I. du Tillet, Euesque de Meaux freres.* Paris: Iaques du Puys, [1579]-1580. Rprt. Paris: Iaques du Puys, 1586, 1587.

———. *Regum et Reginarum Coronatio.* In *Respublica sive Status* (without attribution to Du Tillet). Pp. 579-606.

Eadmer. *Historia novorum in Anglia et Opuscula duo de vita sancti Anselmi et quibusdam miraculis ejus.* Edited by Martin Rule. Rolls Series, 82. London: Her Majesty's Stationery Office, 1884.

Ecles, Francis Carolus. *The Coronation Service: Its Meaning and History.* London: A. R. Mowbray, 1952.

Ehlers, Joachim. "Die *Historia Francorum Senonensis* und der Aufstieg des Hauses Capet." *Journal of Medieval History,* 4 (1978), 1-26.

"Eloge de Monsieur Vion Seigneur d'Herouval, Auditeur des Comptes." *Journal des sçavans, pour l'Année M.DC.LXXXIX,* 17 (1695), 348-52. Presented on 23 May 1689.

Elze, Reinhard. "Königskrönung und Ritterweihe. Der Burgundische Ordo für die Weihe und Krönung des Königs und der Königin." In *Institutionen, Kultur und Gesellschaft im Mittelalter: Festschrift für Josef Fleckenstein zu seinem 65. Geburtstag.* Edited by Lutz Fenske, Werner Rösener, and Thomas Jotz. Sigmaringen: Jan Thorbecke, 1984. Pp. 327-42.

———. "Ein Krönungsordo aus Portugal." In *Memoriam Sanctorum Venerantes: Miscellanea in onore di Mons. Victor Saxer.* Studi di Antichità Cristiana, 48. Vatican City: Pontificio Istituto di Archeologia Cristiana, 1992. Pp. 323-34.

Euw, Anton von, and Joachim M. Plotzek. *Die Handschriften der-Sammlung Ludwig.* 4 vols. Cologne: Schnütgen Museum, 1979-85.

Famiglietti, Richard C. *See* Brown, Elizabeth A. R., and Richard C. Famiglietti

Favyn, André. *Histoire de Navarre, Contenant l'Origine, les Vies et conquestes de ses Roys, depuis leur commencement iusques a present. Ensemble ce qui c'est* [sic] *passé de plus remarquable durant leurs regnes en France, Espagne, et ailleurs.* Paris: Laurent Sonnius, Pierre Mettayer, Pierre Cheualier, 1612.

———. *Le Theatre d'Honnevr et de Cheualerie, ov l'Histoire des ordres militaires des Roys, & Princes de la Chrestienté, & leur Genealogie: De l'Institution des Armes, & Blasons; Roys, Heraulds, & Poursuiuants d'Armes; Duels, Ioustes, & Tournois; & de tout ce qui concerne le faict du Cheualier de l'Ordre. Auec les Figures en taille douce naïuement representées. Et Deux Tables: L'Vne des choses remarquables: & l'Autre des Armes des Illustres Familles de la Chrestienté.* 1 vol. in 2. Paris: Robert Foüet, 1620.

———. *Traictez des premiers Officiers de la Coronne de France, sovbz noz Roys de la premiere, seconde & troisiesme lignée.* Paris: Fleury Bouriquant, 1613.

Felibien, Michel. *Histoire de l'Abbaye Royale de Saint-Denys en France, contenant La vie des abbez qui l'ont gouvernée depuis onze cens ans: les Hommes Illustres qu'elle a donnez à l'Eglise & à l'Etat: les Privileges accordez par les Souverains Pontifes & par les Evêques: les Dons des Rois, des Princes & des autres Bienfacteurs. Avec la Description de l'Eglise & de tout ce qu'elle contient de remarquable. Le tout justifié par des Titres authentiques & enrichi de Plans, de Figures & d'une Carte Topographique.* Paris: Frederic Leonard, 1706. Rprt. Paris: Editions du Palais Royal, 1973.

Fœdera, Conventiones, Litteræ, et cujuscunque generis Acta Publica inter Reges Angliæ et alios quosvis Imperatores, Reges, Pontifices, Principes, vel Communitates ab ingressu Gulielmi I. in Angliam, A.D. 1066. ad nostra usque tempora habita aut tractata. Edited by Thomas Rymer and Robert Sanderson, and Adam Clarke and Frederick Holbrooke. 4 vols. in 7 parts. London: Record Commission, 1816-69.

La France de Philippe Auguste: le temps des mutations. Actes du Colloque international organisé par le C.N.R.S. (Paris, 29 septembre - 4 octobre 1980). Edited by Robert-Henri Bautier. Colloques internationaux du Centre National de la Recherche Scientifique, 602. Paris: Editions de la Centre National de la Recherche Scientifique, 1982.

Franklin, Alfred Louis Auguste. *Les anciennes bibliothèques de Paris, églises, monastères, colléges, etc..* 3 vols. Histoire générale de Paris, 12. Paris: Imprimerie impériale/nationale, 1867-73.

———. *Les sources de l'histoire de France. Notices bibliographiques et analytiques des inventaires et des recueils de documents relatifs à l'histoire de France.* Paris: Firmin-Didot, 1877.

Freeman, Edward A. *The History of the Norman Conquest of England, its Causes and its Results.* 2nd ed. 6 vols. Oxford: Clarendon Press, 1870-79.

Gaborit-Chopin, Danielle. "La plaque d'Hervé et Roger, évêques de Beauvais." *Bulletin de la Société nationale des antiquaires de France,* (1989), 279-89, with discussion on 289-90.

Gallia Christiana, in Provincias ecclesiasticas distributa; qua series et historia Archiepiscoporum, Episcoporum, et Abbatum Franciæ vicinarumque ditionum ab origine Ecclesiarum ad nostra tempora deducitur, & probatur ex authenticis Instrumentis ad calcem appositis. Edited by Denis de Sainte-Marthe et al. 16 vols. Paris: Jean-Baptiste Coignard, Imprimerie royale, 1715-1865.

Garand, Monique-Cécile. "Manuscrits monastiques et scriptoria aux XIe et XIIe siècles." In *Codicologica.* Vol. 3. *Essais typologiques.* Edited by A. Gruys and J. P. Gumbert. Leiden: E. J. Brill, 1980. Pp. 9-33.

Garnier, Jean-Paul. *Le Sacre de Charles X et l'opinion publique: contribution à l'histoire des idées constitutionnelles sous la Restoration.* Thèse pour le doctorat, Faculté de droit de l'Université de Paris. Paris: Jouve, 1927.

Gervase of Canterbury. *The Historical Works of Gervase of Canterbury.* Edited by William Stubbs. 2 vols. Vol. 1. *The Chronicle of the Reigns of Stephen, Henry II., and Richard I.* Rolls Series, 73. London: Her Majesty's Stationery Office, 1879-80.

Gesta Regis Henrici secundi Benedicti abbatis. The Chronicle of the Reigns of Henry II. and Richard I. A.D. 1169-1192; Known Commonly under the Name of Benedict of Peterborough. Edited, from the Cotton. MSS. Edited by William Stubbs. 2 vols. Rolls Series, 49. London: Her Majesty's Stationery Office, 1867.

Giesey, Ralph E. *The Royal Funeral Ceremony in Renaissance France.* Travaux d'Humanisme et Renaissance, 37. Geneva: Droz, 1960. Translated as *Le roi ne meurt jamais: les obsèques royales dans la France de la Renaissance.* Translated by Dominique Ebnöther. Paris: Flammarion, 1987.

Gilles, Monique. *See Chronique de Saint-Pierre-le-Vif*

Girard, Bernard de, lord of Le Haillan. *De l'estat et svccez des affaires de France. Œuure contenant les choses plus singulieres & plus remarquables, aduenuës durant les regnes des Rois de France, depuis Pharamond premier Roy des Francs, Francons, ou Françoys, iusques au Roy Loys vnziesme. Ensemble vne sommaire histoire des Seigneurs, Comtes, & Ducs d'Aniou.* Paris: [Pierre] l'Huillier, 1570. Rprt. Paris: [Pierre] l'Huillier, 1571.

———. *De l'estat et svccez des affaires de France. Œuure despuis les precedentes Editions, augmenté, enrichy, & illustré, contenant sommairement l'Histoire des Roys de France, & les choses plus remarquables par eux instituées pour l'ornement & grandeur de leur Royaume. Ensemble vne sommaire Histoire des Seigneurs, Contes, & Ducs d'Anjou.* Paris: Pierre l'Huillier, 1572.

———. *De l'estat et svccez des affaires de France. Œuure despuis les precedentes editions augmenté, enrichi, & illustré de plusieurs belles recherches, contenant sommairement l'Histoire des Roys de France, & les choses plus remarquables par eux instituees pour l'ornement, grandeur, & establissement de leur Royaume & authorité. Ensemble Vne Sommaire Histoire des Seigneurs, Comtes, & Ducz d'Anjou.* Paris: P[ierre] l'Huillier, 1580.

———. *L'Histoire de France.* Paris: Michel Sonnius, 1576.

———. *L'Histoire de France, Par Bernard de Girard, Seigneur du Haillan, Historiographe de France. Contenant, outre ce qui est aduenu en ce Royaume, les choses plus memorables passees en Allemagne, Flandres, Angleterre, Italie, Sicile, & pays de Leuant.* 2 vols. [Geneva]: Pierre de Saint-André, 1577.

——— [to the reign of Charles VII], Arnaud le Ferron, et al. *Histoire generale des Roys de France, contenant les choses memorables, advenues tant au Royaume de France, qu'és Provinces estrangeres sous la domination des François, durant douze cens ans*. 2 vols. Paris: Sebastien Cramoisy, 1615.

Gislebert of Mons. *Chronicon*. Edited by Wilhelm Arndt. *Monumenta Germaniae Historica. Scriptorum*. Vol. 21. Hannover: Hahn, 1899. Pp. 481-601.

Godefroy, Denys. *See Le Ceremonial François*

Godefroy, Theodore. *See Ceremonial de France, Le Ceremonial François*

Godefroy-Ménilglaise, Denis-Charles, marquis of. *Les savants Godefroy. Mémoires d'une famille pendant les XVIe, XVIIe et XVIIIe siècles*. Paris: Didier, 1873. Rprt. Geneva: Slatkine, 1971.

Goldsilber, E.-A. "Courrier allemand." *Revue des questions historiques*, 90 (n. s., 46) (1911), 212-39.

Golein, Jean. "The *Traité du sacre* of Jean Golein." Edited by Richard A. Jackson. *Proceedings of the American Philosophical Society*, 113^4 (1969), 305-24.

Les Grandes Chroniques de France. Edited by Jules Viard. 10 vols. Publications de la Société de l'histoire de France, 395, 401, 404, 415, 418, 423, 429, 435, 438, 457. Paris: Honoré Champion and C. Klincksieck, 1920-53.

Les Grandes Chroniques de France, selon que elles sont conservées en l'église de Saint-Denis en France. Edited by Paulin Paris. 6 vols. Paris: Techener, 1836-38.

Gransden, Antonia. *Historical Writing in England* c. *550 to* c. *1307*. London: Routledge & Kegan Paul, 1974.

Guillaume le Breton. *See Œuvres de Rigord et de Guillaume le Breton*

Guillaume de Nangis. *Chronique latine de Guillaume de Nangis de 1113 à 1300, avec les continuations de cette chronique de 1300 à 1368*. Edited by Hercule Géraud. 2 vols. Publications de la Société de l'histoire de France, 33, 35. Paris, Jules Renouard, 1843.

Guillot, Olivier. "Les étapes de l'accession d'Eudes au pouvoir royal." In *Media in Francia. . . . Recueil de mélanges offert à Karl Ferdinand Werner à l'occasion de son 65e anniversaire par ses amis et collègues français*. Maulévrier: Hérault-Editions, 1989. Pp. 199-223.

Halphen, Louis. "Histoire de France, époques franque et des Capétiens directs." *Revue historique*, 108 (1911), 131-47.

Hampe, Karl. "Reise nach Frankreich und Belgien im Frühjahr 1897." *Neues Archiv*, 23 (1898), 375-417.

Hanning, Robert M. "Suger's Literary Style and Vision." In *Abbot Suger*, ed. Gerson. Pp. 145-50.

Haueter, Anton, *Die Krönungen der französischen Könige im Zeitalter des Absolutismus und in der Restoration.* Abhandlung zur Erlangung der Doktorwürde der Philosophischen Fakultät I der Universität Zürich. Zürich: Juris Druck, 1975.

Hauser, Henri. "Un récit catholique des trois premières guerres de religion: les Acta Tumultuum Gallicanorum." *Revue historique,* 108 (1911), 59-74, 294-318; 109 (1912), 75-84.

Havet, Julien. "Questions mérovingiennes: II. Les découvertes de Jérôme Vignier. Testament et épitaphe de Perpétue, évêque de Tours; Diplôme de Clovis pour Micy (Saint-Mesmin); Colloque de Lyon, 499; Cinq lettres d'évêques et de papes, 462-501; Fragment d'une vie de Sainte Odile." *Bibliothèque de l'Ecole des chartes,* 46 (1885), 205-71.

Hedeman, Anne D. "The Commemoration of Jeanne d'Evreux's Coronation in the *Ordo ad Consecrandum* at the University of Illinois." *Essays in Medieval Studies: Proceedings of the Illinois Medieval Association,* 7 (1990), 13-28.

Hénault, Charles-Jean-François. *Nouvel abrégé chronologique de l'histoire de France. Contenant les événemens de notre histoire depuis Clovis jusqu'à la mort de Louis XIV. les guerres, les batailles, les siéges, &c.* 3rd ed. Paris: Prault, 1749.

Heslin, Anne. "The Coronation of the Young King in 1170." In *Studies in Church History.* Vol. 2. *Papers Read at the Second Winter and Summer Meetings of the Ecclesiastical History Society.* Edited by G. J. Cuming. London: Nelson, 1968. Pp. 165-78.

Hinkle, William M. *The Fleurs de Lis of the Kings of France, 1285-1488.* Carbondale: Southern Illinois University Press, 1991.

———. *The Portal of the Saints of Reims Cathedral: A Study in Mediaeval Iconography.* Monographs on Archaeology and Fine Arts Sponsored by the Archaeological Institute of America and the College Art Association of America, 13. New York: College Art Association of America in conjunction with The Art Bulletin, 1965.

———. *Historiæ Francorum scriptores coætanei, Ab ipsivs gentis origine [vsqve ad R. Philippi IV. dicti Pvlchri Tempora]. Quorum plurimi nunc primum ex Variis Codicibus MSS. in lucem prodeunt: alij vero auctiores & emendatiores. Cvm Epistolis Regvm, Reginarvm, Pontificvm, Ducum, Comitum, Abbatum, & aliis veteribus Rerum Francicarum Monumentis.* 5 vols. Edited by André du Chesne and (vols. 3-5) François Duchesne. Paris: Sebastian Cramoisy [and Gabriel Cramoisy, vol. 5], 1636-49.

Hobson, Anthony. *Humanists and Bookbinders. The Origins and Diffusion of the Humanistic Bookbinding, 1459-1559, with a Census of Historiated Plaquette and Medallion Bindings of the Renaissance.* Cambridge, Eng.: Cambridge University Press, 1989.

Hohler, Christopher. "Some Service-Books of the Later Saxon Church." In *Tenth-Century Studies: Essays in Commemoration of the Millenium of the Council of Westminster and* Regularis Concordia. Edited by David Parsons. London: Phillimore, 1975. Pp. 60-83, 217-27.

Holtzmann, Robert. "Der Prozeß gegen Johann ohne Land und die Anfange des französischen Pairshofes." *Historisches Zeitschrift*, 95 (n. s., 59) (1905), 29-57.

Howden (Hoveden). *See* Roger of Howden

Hugues of Fleury. *Hvgonis Floriacensis Monachi Benedictini Chronicon, qvingentis ab hinc annis & quod excurrit, conscriptum. Hactenvs a mvltis desideratvm, nunc tandem postliminio ex membranis antiquissimis erutum, ac publicis vsibus transcriptum. Ex mvsæo Bernhardi Rottendorffi, Com. Pal. Cæs. ac Reipub. Monast. Archiatri, Qui & subbreues Notas attexuit.* Edited by Bernhard Rottendorff. Münster: Bernard Ræsfeld, 1538.

———. *Hugonis Floriacensis Opera Historica. Accedunt aliae Francorum historiae.* Edited by Georg Waitz. *Monumenta Germaniae Historica. Scriptorum.* Vol. 9. Hannover: Hahn, 1851. Pp. 337-406.

Jackson, Richard A. "Anzeichen der Vergötterung des französischen Königs." In *Herrscherweihe und Königskrönung im frühneuzeitlichen Europa.* Edited by Heinz Duchhardt. Schriften der Mainzer Philosophischen Fakultätsgesellschaft, 8. Wiesbaden: Franz Steiner, 1983. Pp. 96-102, with discussion on 123-24.

———. "The Composition and Transmission of Medieval Coronation *Ordines.*" Unpublished paper. Presented at the International Conference on Coronations, Toronto, 1985.

———. "De l'influence du cérémonial byzantin sur le sacre des rois de France." *Byzantion*, 51 (1981), 201-10.

———. "Elective Kingship and *Consensus Populi* in Sixteenth-Century France." *Journal of Modern History*, 44 (1972), 155-71.

———. "Manuscripts, Texts and Enigmas of Medieval French Coronation *Ordines.*" *Viator*, 23 (1992), 35-71.

———. "Les manuscrits des *ordines* de couronnement de la bibliothèque de Charles V, roi de France." *Le Moyen Age*, 82 (1976), 67-88.

———. "Les *Ordines* des couronnements royaux au Moyen Age." In *Le sacre des rois. Actes du Colloque international d'histoire sur les sacres et couronnements royaux (Reims 1975)*. Paris: Les Belles Lettres, 1985. Pp. 63-74.

———. "Peers of France and Princes of the Blood." *French Historical Studies*, 7 (1971), 27-46.

———. *Vive le Roi!: A History of the French Coronation from Charles V to Charles X*. Chapel Hill and London: University of North Carolina Press, 1984. Translated as *Vivat Rex: histoire des sacres et couronnements en France (1364-1825)*. Translated by Monique Arav. Strasbourg: Association des publications près les Universités de Strasbourg, 1984.

———. *See* Golein, Jean

Joinville, Jean, lord of. *Œuvres de Jean sire de Joinville, comprenant: L'Histoire de saint Louis, le Credo et la lettre à Louis X, avec un texte rapproché du français moderne mis en regard du texte original, corrigé et complété à l'aide des anciens manuscrits et d'un manuscrit inédit*. Edited by Natalis de Wailly. Paris: Adrien Le Clere, 1867.

Kienast, Walther. "Die französischen Stämme bei der Königswahl." Originally published 1968. In idem, *Studien über die Französischen Volksstämme des Fruhmittelalters*. Pariser historische Studien, 7. Stuttgart: Anton Hiersemann, 1968. Pp. 130-50.

Labbe, Philippe. *Nova Bibliotheca MSS. Librorvm, sive Specimen Antiqvarvm Lectionvm Latinarvm et Græcarvm In quatuor partes tributarum, Cum Coronide dvplici, poetica et libraria, Ac Supplementis decem*. Paris: Jean Henault, 1653.

———. *See also Sacrosancta Concilia*

Laffitte, Marie-Pierre. "D'autres reliures à attribuer à l'incomparable doreur?" *Revue française d'histoire du livre*, 36 (1982), 435-40.

Lair, Jules. "Fragment inédit de la vie de Louis VII préparée par Suger." *Bibliothèque de l'Ecole des chartes*, 34 (1873), 583-96.

———. "Mémoire sur deux chroniques latines composées au XIIe siècle à l'abbaye de Saint-Denis." *Bibliothèque de l'Ecole des chartes*, 35 (1874), 543-80.

Landsberger, Franz. *Der St. Gallen Folchart-Psalter im Auftrage des Historischen Vereins des Kantons St. Gallen*. Saint Gall: Fehr, 1912.

Lanoë, Guy. "Définition du pouvoir royal dans les rites de couronnement." Unpublished paper. Presented at the Colloque sur Henri II Plantagenêt et son temps, Abbaye royale de Fontevraud, 29 September-1 October 1990.

———. "Un *ordo* de couronnement carolingien inconnu." Unpublished paper. Presented at the International Conference on Kings and Kingship in Medieval Europe, London, 1992.

———. "Quelques manuscrits liturgiques de Beauvais (IXe-XIIe siècles) d'après les anciens catalogues et les 'papiers' des érudits modernes." Forthcoming in *Studies for Keith Val Sinclair.* Edited by Peter Rolfe Monks and D. D. R. Owen. Townsville: University of Saint Andrews, 1992.

Langlois, Charles-Victor. *See* Petit, Joseph

La Planche, Louis Regnier, lord of. *See* Regnier, Louis, lord of La Planche

Layettes du Trésor des chartes. Edited by Alexandre Teulet, Joseph de Laborde, Elie Berger, and H.-François Delaborde. 5 vols. Paris: Henri Plon, E. Plon, and Plon-Nourrit, 1863-1909. Rprt. Nendeln/Liechtenstein: Kraus, 1977.

Leber, Jean-Michel-Constantin. *Des cérémonies du sacre, ou Recherches historiques et critiques sur les mœurs, les coutumes, les institutions, et le droit public des Français dans l'ancienne monarchie.* Paris: Baudouin Frères; Reims: Frémau, 1825.

Lehoux, Françoise. *Jean de France, duc de Berri, sa vie, son action politique (1340-1416).* 4 vols. Paris: A. et J. Picard, 1966-68.

[Le Laboureur, Jean]. *Histoire de la Pairie de France et du Parlement de Paris, Où l'on traite aussi des Electeurs de l'Empire, & du Cardinalat. Par Monsieur D. B. On y a joint des Traités touchant les Pairies d'Angleterre, & l'origine des Grands d'Espagne.* New ed. 2 vols. London: Samuel Harding, 1753.

Lelong, Jacques. *Bibliothèque historique de la France, Contenant Le Catalogue des Ouvrages, imprimés & manuscrits, qui traitent de l'Histoire de ce Royaume, ou qui y ont rapport; Avec des notes critiques et historiques: Par feu Jacques Lelong, Prêtre de l'Oratoire, Bibliothécaire de la Maison de Paris.* New ed. Edited by Fevret de Fontette. 5 vols. Paris: Jean-Thomas Herissant, 1768-78.

Lemarignier, Jean-François. "Autour de la royauté française du IXe au XIIe siècle." *Bibliothèque de l'Ecole des chartes,* 113 (1955), 5-36.

Leroquais, Victor. *Les pontificaux manuscrits des bibliothèques publiques de France.* 3 vols. Paris and Mâcon: Protat Frères, 1937.

Lestrange, François and Claude. *See Orationes duæ*

Levillain, Léon. "Le sacre de Charles le Chauve à Orléans." *Bibliothèque de l'Ecole des chartes,* 64 (1903), 31-53.

Lewis, Andrew W. *Royal Succession in Capetian France. Studies on Familial Order and the State.* Harvard Historical Studies, 100. Cambridge, MA: Harvard University Press, 1981. Translated as *Le sang royal: la famille capétienne et l'Etat, France, X^{e}-XIVe siècle.* Translated by Jeannie Carlier. Bibliothèque des histoires. Paris: Gallimard, 1986.

———. "Suger's Views on Kingship." In *Abbot Suger,* ed. Gerson. Pp. 49-54.

Liebman, Charles J., Jr. "Un sermon de Philippe de Villette, abbé de Saint-Denis, pour la levée de l'oriflamme (1414)." *Romania,* 68 (1944-45), 469-70.

Loisel [L'oisel], Antoine. *Memoires des Pays, Villes, Comté et Comtes, Evesché et Evesqves, Pairrie, Commvne, et Personnes de renom de Beavvais et Beavvaisis.* Paris: Samuel Thiboust, 1617.

Lombard-Jourdan, Anne. *Fleur de lis et Oriflamme. Signes célestes du royaume de France.* Paris: Presses du CNRS, 1991.

Lot, Ferdinand. "Quelques mots sur l'origine des pairs de France." *Revue historique,* 54 (1894), 34-59.

Louvet, Pierre. *Histoire et Antiqvitez dv Pais de Beavvaisis. A Monseignevr Messire Avgustin Potier, Euesque, Comte & Chastelain de Beauuais, Prince & Dame de Gerbray, Pair de France, & grand Aumosnier de la Reine, &c. Et a Messievrs les venerables Doyen, Chanoines & Chapitre dudit lieu.* 2 vols. (Vol. 2, as *Histoire et Antiqvitez dv Diocese de Beavvais. A Monseignevr Messire Charles de Monceaux, Conseiller & Aumosnier du Roy, ancien Abbé de S. Germer, & Seign. de Marticourt.*) Beauvais: La vefue Valet [Vallet], 1631-35.

Luchaire, Achille. *Etudes sur les actes de Louis VII.* Paris: Alphonse Picard, 1885.

———. *Histoire des institutions monarchiques de la France sous les premiers Capétiens.* 2 vols. Paris: Imprimerie nationale, 1883.

———. *Louis VI le Gros. Annales de sa vie et de son règne (1081-1137).* Paris: Alphonse Picard, 1890. Rprt. Geneva: Mégariotis, 1979.

Mabillon, Jean. *See Ouvrages posthumes*

Marlot, Guillaume. *Histoire de la ville, cité et université de Reims, métropolitaine de la Gaule belgique, divisée en douze livres, contenant l'estat ecclésiastique et civil du païs.* 4 vols. Reims: L. Jacquet, 1843-46.

———. *Metropolis Remensis Historia, A Frodoardo primum arctius digesta, nunc demum aliunde accersitis plurimum aucta, et illustrata, et ad nostrvm hoc sæcvlvm fideliter deducta.* 2 vols. Lille: Nicolas de Rache; Reims: Protase Lelorain, 1666-79.

———. *Le Theatre d'Honnevr, et de Magnificence, preparé av Sacre des Roys. Auquel il est traité de l'Inauguration des Souuerains; du lieu où elle se fait, & par qui; de la Verité de la Sainte Ampoule; des Roys qui en ont été Sacrez; du Couronnement des Reynes; des Entrées Royales, & Ceremonies du Sacre; & de la Dignité de nos Roys.* Reims: François Bernard, 1643.

Mayer, Ernst. "Die Pairs am französischen Königsgericht." *Mitteilungen des Instituts für österreichische Geschichtsforschung* [Vienna], 32 (1911), 435-58.

Ménin, Nicolas. *Cérémonies et prières du sacre des rois de France, accompagnées de recherches historiques*. Edited by Charles Motteley. Paris: Firmin Didot, 1825.

———. *Traité Historique et Chronologique du Sacre et Couronnement des Rois et des Reines de France: Depuis Clovis I. jusqu'à present. Et de tous les Princes Souverains de l'Europe. Augmenté de la Relation exacte de la Cérémonie du Sacre de Louis XV. Dedié au Roy.* Paris: Jean-Baptiste-Claude Bauche, Jean Pepingué, 1723.

Merton, Adolf. *Die Buchmalerei in St. Gallen vom neunten bis zum elften Jahrhundert*. 2nd ed. Leipzig: Karl W. Hiersemann, 1923.

Meyier, Karel Adriaan de. *Paul en Alexandre Petau en de Geschiedenis van hun Handschriften (Voornamelijk op Grond van de Petau-Handschriften in de Universiteitsbibliotheek te Leiden)*. Dissertationes inaugurales Batavae ad res antiquas pertinentes, 5. Leiden: E. J. Brill, 1947.

Mezeray, François Eudes de. *Abbregé chronologique, ou Extrait de l'histoire de France*. 3 vols. Paris: Denys Thierry, Jean Guignard, Claude Barbin, 1690.

Michaud, Joseph-François. *Biographie universelle ancienne et moderne*. New ed. 45 vols. Paris: Delagrave, 1870-73.

Millon, Charles. *See Cérémonial du sacre*

Miscellaneorum liber sextus, hoc est, Collectio veterum monumentorum quæ hactenus latuerant in variis codicibus ac bibliothecis. Edited by Etienne Baluze. Paris: Per Bibliopolarum Societatem, 1713.

Molinier, Auguste. *See* Vic, Claude de, and Jean-Joseph Vaissete. *Histoire générale de Languedoc*. 2nd ed.

———, and Louis Polin. *Les sources de l'histoire de France des origines aux guerres d'Italie*. 6 vols. Manuels de bibliographie historique, 3. Paris: Alphonse Picard, 1901-06. Rprt. Burt Franklin: Bibliography and Reference Series, 80. New York: Burt Franklin, n.d.

Monumenta Germaniae Historica. Legum. Vol. 2. *Constitutiones Imperii inde ab occasu Karolorum usque ad obitum Heinrici VII. imperatoris* [916-1313]. Edited by Georg Heinrich Pertz. Hannover: Hahn, 1837.

Monumenta Germaniæ Historica. Legum Sectio II. Capitularia Regum Francorum. Vol. 2. Edited by Alfred Boretius, Victor Krause, et al. Hannover: Hahn, 1890-93.

Morembert, T. de. "Godefroy (Theodore)." In *Dictionnaire de biographie française*, 92 (1983), 448-49, no. 40.

———. "Godefroy (Denis), dit Denis le Jeune ou Denis II." In *Dictionnaire de biographie française*, 92 (1983), 438, no. 16.

Moréri, Louis. *Le Grand Dictionnaire Historique, ou Le Mêlange curieux de l'Histoire sacrée et profane, qui contient en abrégé l'Histoire fabuleuse des Dieux & des Héros de l'Antiquité Païenne: Les Vies et les Actions remarquables des Patriarches; des Empereurs; des Rois; des Princes illustres; des Grands Capitaines; des Papes; des saints Martyrs & Confesseurs; des Peres de l'Eglise; des Evêques; des Cardinaux & autres Prélats célébres; des Hérésiarques & des Schismatiques: L'Histoire des Religions & Sectes des Chrétiens, des Juifs & des Païens: Des Conciles généraux & particuliers: Des Auteurs anciens & modernes; des Philosophes; des Inventeurs des Arts, & de ceux qui se sont rendus recommandables en toute Sorte de Professions, par leur Science, par leurs Ouvrages, & par quelque action éclatante: L'Etablissement et le Progres des Ordres Religieux & Militaires; & la Vie de leurs Fondateurs: Les Généalogies des Familles illustres de France, & des autres Pays de l'Europe: La Description des Empires, Royaumes, Républiques, Provinces, Villes, Isles, Montagnes, Fleuves & autres lieux considérables de l'ancienne & de la nouvelle Géographie, où l'on remarque la situation, l'étendue & la qualité du Pays; la Religion, le Gouvernement, les Mœurs & les Coutumes des Peuples.* New ed. Edited by Claude-Pierre Goujet and Etienne-François Drouet. 10 vols. Paris: Les libraires associés, 1759.

Nebbiai-Dalla Guarda, Donatella. *La bibliothèque de l'abbaye de Saint-Denis en France du IXe au XVIIIe siècle.* Paris: Editions du Centre National de la Recherche Scientifique, 1985.

Nelson, Janet L. *Charles the Bald.* The Medieval World. London: Longman, 1992.

———. "The Earliest Surviving Royal *Ordo:* Some Liturgical and Historical Aspects." Originally published 1980. In eadem, *Politics.* Pp. 341-60.

———. *Politics and Ritual in Early Medieval Europe.* London: Hambledon Press, 1986.

———. "The Rites of the Conqueror." Originally published 1982. In eadem, *Politics.* Pp. 375-401.

———. "Ritual and Reality in the Early Medieval *Ordines.*" Originally published 1975. In eadem, *Politics.* Pp. 329-39.

———. "The Second English *Ordo.*" In eadem, *Politics.* Pp. 361-74.

Nordenfalk, Carl. "Miniatures ottoniennes et ateliers capétiens." *Art de France*, 4 (1964), 44-59.

Œuvres de Rigord et de Guillaume le Breton, historiens de Philippe-Auguste. Edited by H.-François Delaborde, 2 vols. Publications de la Société de l'histoire de France, 210, 224. Paris: Renouard, 1882-85.

Oexle, Otto Gerhard. "Adalbero von Laon und sein 'Carmen ad Rotbertum Regem': Bemerkungen zu einer neuen Edition." *Francia*, 8 (1980), 629-38.

Les Olim, ou registres des arrêts rendus par la cour du roi, sous les règnes de Saint Louis, de Philippe le Hardi, de Philippe le Bel, de Louis le Hutin et de Philippe le Long. Edited by Arthur-Auguste Beugnot. 4 vols. Collection de documents inédits sur l'histoire de la France. 1st ser. Histoire politique, 29. Paris: Imprimerie royale/nationale, 1839-48.

Omont, Henri. "Recherches sur la bibliothèque de l'église cathédrale de Beauvais." *Mémoires de l'Institut national de France, Académie des Inscriptions et Belles-Lettres*, 40 (1916), 1-93.

———. *See also* Du Tillet, Jean. *Portraits*

Orationes duæ de Regis consecratione, à duobus nobilissimis adolescentibus, Francisco & Claudio Lestrangiis fratribus habitæ Lutetiæ in gymnasio Prælatorum, septimo Calend. August. 1547. Paris: Mathieu David, 1547.

Ordericus Vitalis. *Historia Æcclesiastica. The Ecclesiastical History.* Edited and translated by Marjorie Chibnall. 6 vols. Oxford Medieval Texts. Oxford: Clarendon Press, 1968-80.

Ouvrages posthumes de D. Jean Mabillon, et de D. Thierri Ruinart. Vol. 3. *Contenant la Vie d'Urbain II. les Preuves & le Voiage d'Alsace & de Lorraine, par D. T. Ruinart.* Paris: François Babuty et al., 1724.

Pange, Jean de. *Le Roi Très-Chrétien.* 2nd ed. Paris: Arma Artis, 1985.

Parent, Annie. *Les métiers du livre à Paris au XVIe siècle (1535-1560).* Centre de recherches d'histoire et de philologie de la IVe Section de l'Ecole Pratique des Hautes Etudes, VI. Histoire et civilisation du livre, 6. Geneva: Droz, 1974.

Pastoret, Claude-Emmanuel-Joseph-Pierre, marquis of. "Louis VII, le Jeune." *Histoire littéraire de la France*, 14 (1817), 41-88.

Patrologiæ cursus completus . . . Series græca, in qua prodeunt patres, doctores scriptoresque ecclesiæ graecæ, a S. Barbaba ad Photium. Ed. Jacques-Paul Migne. 161 vols. in 166. Paris: J.-P. Migne, 1857-80.

Patrologiæ cursus completus . . . Series prima . . . ecclesiæ latinæ. Ed. Jacques-Paul Migne. 221 vols. Paris: J.-P. Migne, 1844-55.

Pellegrin, Elisabeth, et al. *Les manuscrits classiques latins de la Bibliothèque vaticane.* Documents, études et répertoires publiés par l'Institut de Recherche et d'Histoire des Textes, 21. 2 vols. in 3. Paris: Editions du Centre National de la Recherche Scientifique, 1975-82.

Péré, Georges. *Le sacre et le couronnement des rois de France dans leurs rapports avec les lois fondamentales.* Thèse pour le doctorat [Sciences politiques], Université de Toulouse, Faculté de droit, année scolaire 1920-1921. Bagnères-de-Bigorre: Péré, 1921.

Peter the Venerable. *The Letters of Peter the Venerable.* Edited by Giles Constable. 2 vols. Harvard Historical Studies, 78. Cambridge, MA: Harvard University Press, 1967.

Petit, Joseph, Michel Gavrilovitch, Maury, and Téodoru; preface by Charles-Victor Langlois. *Essai de restitution des plus anciens mémoriaux de la Chambre des comptes de Paris.* Bibliothèque de la Faculté des lettres de l'Université de Paris, 7. Paris: F. Alcan, 1899.

Petit-Dutaillis, Charles-Edmond. *Etude sur la vie et le règne de Louis VIII (1187-1226).* Bibliothèque de l'Ecole des Hautes Etudes, Sciences philologiques et historiques, 101. Paris: Emile Bouillon, 1894.

Pinoteau, Hervé. "Quelques réflexions sur l'œuvre de Jean du Tillet et la symbolique royale français." Originally published 1957. In idem, *Vingt-cinq ans.* Pp. 114-40.

———. "La tenue de sacre de saint Louis IX, roi de France: son arrière-plan symbolique et la 'Renovatio regni Juda.' " Originally published 1972. In idem, *Vingt-cinq ans.* Pp. 447-504.

———. *Vingt-cinq ans d'études dynastiques.* Paris: Editions Christian, 1982.

Pithou, Pierre. *Opera, Sacra, Ivridica, Historica, Miscellanea.* Paris: Officina Nivelliana, Sebastien Cramoisy, 1609.

———. *Le premier Livre des Memoires des comtes hereditaires de Champagne et Brie.* Paris: Robert Estienne, 1572.

———. *Preuves des libertez de l'eglise gallicane.* 3rd ed. 4 parts in 1 vol. Paris: Sebastien Cramoisy et Gabriel Cramoisy, 1651 [1731].

Poly, Jean-Pierre. "La gloire des rois et la parole cachée ou l'avenir d'une illusion." In *Religion et culture autour de l'an Mil. Royaume capétien et Lotharingie. Actes du colloque Hugues Capet, 987-1987. La France de l'an Mil. Auxerre, 26 et 27 juin 1987 - Metz, 11 et 12 septembre 1987.* Edited by Dominique Iogna-Prat and Jean-Charles Picard. Paris: Picard, 1990. Pp. 167-88.

———. *See also* Bournazel, Eric, and Jean-Pierre Poly

Poole, Austin Lane. *From Domesday Book to Magna Carta, 1087-1216*. Vol. 3 of *The Oxford History of England*. Edited by G. N. Clark. Oxford: Clarendon Press, 1951.

Powicke, Maurice. *The Thirteenth Century, 1216-1307*. 2nd ed. Vol. 4 of *The Oxford History of England*. Edited by G. N. Clark. Oxford: Clarendon Press, 1962.

Prevost, Michel. "Boulainvilliers, Henri de." In *Dictionnaire de biographie française*, 6 (1954), 1338-39.

Prières et cérémonies du sacre de S. M. Charles X, publiées par ordre de M. l'archevêque de Reims. Paris: J. Didot Aîné, 1825.

Quéant, Constant-C. *Etude sur le Sacre*. Paris: J.-B. Dumoulin, 1868.

Quellensammlung zur kirchlichen Rechtsgeschichte und zum Kirchenrecht. Edited by Eduard Eichmann. 3 vols. Paderborn: Ferdinand Schöningh, 1912-16.

Quignon, G.-Hector. *La Bibliothèque de la ville de Beauvais (1789-1903) (Anciens Fonds, etc.)*. Petites études locales. Paris: Honoré Champion, 1904. Also in *Annuaire de l'Oise*, 79 (1904).

Ranum, Orest. *Artisans of Glory: Writers and Historical Thought in Seventeenth-Century France*. Chapel Hill: University of North Carolina Press, 1980.

Ralph Diceto. *Radulfi de Diceto decani Lundoniensis Opera Historica. The Historical Works of Master Ralph de Diceto, Dean of London*. Edited by William Stubbs. 2 vols. Vol. 1. *Abbreviationes chronicorum; Capitula Ymaginum historiarum; Ymagines historiarum*. Vol. 2. *Ymagines historiarum, Opuscula*. Rolls Series, 68. London: Her Majesty's Stationery Office, 1876.

Rasmussen, N. K. "Le 'Pontifical' de Beauvais (IXème-Xème siècles)." In *Studia Patristica*. Vol. 10. *Papers Presented to the Fifth International Conference on Patristic Studies Held in Oxford 1967*. Part 1. *Editiones, Critica, Philologica, Biblica, Historica, Liturgica et Ascetica*. Edited by F. L. Cross. *Texte und Untersuchungen zur Geschichte der altchristlichen Literatur*. Vol. 107. Berlin: Akademie-Verlag, 1970. Pp. 413-18.

Recueil des actes de Charles II le Chauve, roi de France. Edited by Georges Tessier, 3 vols. Académie des Inscriptions et Belles-Lettres, Chartes et diplômes relatifs à l'histoire de France, 8^2, 9^2, 10. Paris: Imprimerie nationale, 1943-55.

Recueil des actes d'Eudes, roi de France (888-898). Edited by Georges Tessier and Robert-Henri Bautier. Académie des Inscriptions et Belles-Lettres, Chartes et diplômes relatifs à l'histoire de France. Paris: Imprimerie nationale and C. Klincksieck, 1967.

Recueil des actes de Robert Ier et de Raoul, rois de France (922-936). Edited by Robert-Henri Bautier and Jean Dufour. Académie des Inscriptions et Belles-Lettres, Chartes et diplômes relatifs à l'histoire de France. Paris: Imprimerie nationale and C. Klincksieck, 1978.

Recueil des historiens des Gaules et de la France. Edited by Martin Bouquet et al. 24 vols. Paris: Victor Palmé, H. Welter, Imprimerie nationale, 1738-1904.

Regnier, Louis, lord of La Planche. "Histoire de l'estat de France tant de la république que de la religion sous le règne de François II" (1576). In *Choix de chroniques et mémoires sur l'histoire de France. [XVIe siècle] avec notices biographiques.* Edited by J. A. C. Buchon. Panthéon littéraire; Littérature française; Histoire. Paris: A. Desrez, 1836. Pp. 202-421.

———. *Histoire de l'estat de France, tant de la république que de la religion, sous le règne de François II.* Edited by Edouard Mennechet. 2 vols. Paris: Techener, 1836.

Respublica, Sive Status regni Galliæ diuersorum autorum. Lyon: Elzévir, 1626.

Rezak, Brigitte Bedos. *Anne de Montmorency, seigneur de la Renaissance.* La France au fil des siècles. Paris: Publisud, 1990.

———. "Suger and the Symbolism of Royal Power: The Seal of Louis VII." In *Abbot Suger,* ed. Gerson. Pp. 95-103.

Richard, Alfred. *Histoire des comtes de Poitou, 778-1204.* 2 vols. Paris: Picard, 1903.

Rigord. *See Œuvres de Rigord et de Guillaume le Breton*

Rivain, Camille. *Table générale par ordre alphabétique des matières contenues dans les quinze premiers volumes de l'Histoire littéraire de la France. Dictionnaire encyclopédique de l'état des sciences des lettres depuis les temps les plus reculés, jusqu'au XIIIe siècle exclusivement.* Paris: Firmin Didot, 1875.

Robert of Auxerre. "Chronicon." Edited by O. Holder-Egger. In *Monumenta Germaniae Historica. Scriptorum.* Vol. 26. Hannover: Hahn, 1882. Pp. 219-87.

Robert of Torigny. *The Chronicle of Robert of Torigni, Abbot of the Monastery of St. Michael-in-Peril-of-the-Sea.* Edited by Richard Howlett. Vol. 4 of *Chronicles of the Reigns of Stephen, Henry II., and Richard I.* Rolls Series, 82. London: Her Majesty's Stationery Office, 1882.

———. *Chronique de Robert de Torigni, abbé du Mont-Saint-Michel, suivie de divers opuscules historiques de cet Auteur et de plusieurs Religieux de la même Abbaye.* Edited by Léopold Delisle. 2 vols. Publications de la Société de l'histoire de Normandie, 3. Rouen: A. le Brument, 1872-73.

Robinson, P. R. "The 'Booklet,' a Self-Contained Unit in Composite Manuscripts." In *Codicologica*. Vol. 3. *Essais typologiques*. Edited by A. Gruys and J. P. Gumbert. Leiden: E. J. Brill, 1980. Pp. 46-69.

Roger of Howden. *Chronica Magistri Rogeri de Houedene*. Edited by William Stubbs. 4 volumes. Rolls Series, 51. London: Her Majesty's Stationery Office, 1868-71.

Roman d'Amat, Jean-Charles. "Du Tillet (Jean Ier)." In *Dictionnaire de biographie française*, 67 (1968), 915-16, no. 3.

———. "Du Tillet (Jean II)." In *Dictionnaire de biographie française*, 67 (1968), 916-17, no. 4.

Ruinart, Thierry. *See Ouvrages posthumes*

Le Sacre et covronnement du Roy Henry deuxieme de ce nom. Paris: Robert Estienne, n. d. [1547].

Sacrosancta Concilia ad Regiam Editionem exacta quæ olim quarta parte prodiit auctior Studio Philip. Labbei, & Gabr. Cossartii, Soc. Jesu Presbyterorum; Nunc vero integre insertis Stephani Baluzii, & Joannis Harduini additamentis, plurimis præterea undecunque conquisitis monumentis, notis insuper ac observationibus, firmiori fundamento Conciliorum epochas præcipue fulcientibus, longe locupletior, & emendatior exhibetur. Edited by Nicolas Colet. 21 vols. Venice: Sebastianus Colet et Johannes Baptista Albrizzi q. Hieron., 1728-33.

Schimmelpfennig, Bernhard. *Die Zeremonienbücher der römischen Kirche im Mittelalter.* Bibliothek des Deutschen Historischen Instituts in Rom, 40. Tübingen: Max Niemeyer, 1973.

Schneidmüller, Bernd. *Die Entstehung Frankreichs in der politisch-geographischen Terminologie (10.-13. Jahrhundert).* In *Nationes: Historische und philologische Untersuchungen zur Entstehung der europäischen Nationen im Mittelalter.* Edited by Helmut Beumann and Werner Schröder. Vol. 7. Sigmaringen: Jan Thorbecke, 1987.

———. "Französisches Sonderbewu[ß]tsein in der politisch-geographischen Terminologie des 10. Jahrhunderts." In *Nationes: Historische und philologische Untersuchungen zur Entstehung der europäischen Nationen im Mittelalter.* Edited by Helmut Beumann and Werner Schröder. Vol. 4. *Beiträge zur Bildung der französischen Nationen im Früh- und Hochmittelalter.* Edited by Helmut Beumann. Sigmaringen: Jan Thorbecke, 1983. Pp. 49-91.

Schramm, Percy Ernst. *Kaiser, Könige und Päpste. Gesammelte Aufsätze zur Geschichte des Mittelalters.* 4 vols. in 5. Stuttgart: Anton Hiersemann, 1968-71.

———. *Der König von Frankreich: Das Wesen der Monarchie vom 9. zum 16. Jahrhundert. Ein Kapitel aus der Geschichte des abendländischen Staates.* 2nd ed. 2 vols. Weimar: Hermann Böhlaus, 1960.

———. "Die Krönung bei den Westfranken und Angelsachsen von 878 bis um 1000." *Zeitschrift der Savigny-Stiftung für Rechtsgeschichte, Kanonistische Abteilung*, 54 (1934), 117-242.

———. "Ordines-Studien II: Die Krönung bei den Westfranken und den Französen." *Archiv für Urkundenforschung und Quellenkunde des Mittelalters. Beihefte zum Deutschen Archiv für Geschichte des Mittelalters*, 15 (1938), 3-55.

———. "Ordines-Studien III: Die Krönung in England." *Archiv für Urkundenforschung und Quellenkunde des Mittelalters. Beihefte zum Deutschen Archiv für Geschichte des Mittelalters*, 15 (1938), 305-91.

Schreuer, Hans. "Nachtrag zu der Abhandlung: Noch einmal über altfranzösische Krönungsordnungen." *Zeitschrift der Savigny-Stiftung für Rechtsgeschichte, Germanistische Abteilung*, 32 (1911), 312-15.

———. "Noch einmal über altfranzösische Krönungsordnungen." *Zeitschrift der Savigny-Stiftung für Rechtsgeschichte, Germanistische Abteilung*, 30 (1909), 142-92.

———. *Die rechtlichen Grundgedanken der französischen Königskrönung. Mit besonderer Rüchsicht auf die deutschen Verhältnisse*. Weimar: Hermann Böhlaus, 1911.

———. "Über altfranzösische Krönungsordnungen." *Zeitschrift der Savigny Stiftung für Rechtsgeschichte, Germanistische Abteilung*, 32 (1911), 1-40.

Selden, John. *Titles of Honor.* 2nd ed. London: William Stansby for Richard Whitakers, 1631.

Sherman, Claire Richter. "The Queen in Charles V's 'Coronation Book': Jeanne de Bourbon and the 'Ordo ad Reginam Benedicendam.' " *Viator*, 8 (1977), 255-98.

Simon, Renée. *A la recherche d'un homme et d'un auteur. Essai de bibliographie des ouvrages du comte de Boulainviller.* Paris: Boivin, [1941].

———. *Henry de Boulainviller: historien, politique, philosophe, astrologue (1658-1722).* Gap: Imprimerie Louis-Jean, 1940 (Thèse pour le Doctorat-ès-lettres présentée devant la Faculté des lettres de Lille). Paris: Boivin, [1941].

———. *Un révolté du grand siècle, Henry de Boulainviller. Avec un portrait, un autographe, un horoscope et quatre traités inédits.* Garches: Editions du Nouvel Humanisme, 1948.

Sirmond, Jacques. *Opera varia. Nunc primum collecta, ex ipsius schedis emendatiora, notis posthumis, epistolis, et opusculis aliquibus auctiora. Accedunt S. Theodori Studitæ epistolæ, aliaque scripta dogmatica, nunquam antea Græce vulgata, pleraque Sirmondo interprete.* 5 vols. Venice: Bartolomæus Javarina, 1728.

Soman, Alfred. "The London Edition of De Thou's *History:* A Critique of Some Well-Documented Legends." *Renaissance Quarterly,* 24 (1971), 1-12.

Spicilegium, sive Collectio veterum aliquot Scriptorum qui in Galliæ Bibliothecis delituerant. Edited by Luc d'Achery. New ed. Edited by Etienne Baluze, Edmond Martène, and Louis-François-Joseph de La Barre. 3 vols. Paris: Montalant, 1723.

Spiegel, Gabrielle M. *The Chronicle Tradition of Saint-Denis: A Survey.* Medieval Classics: Texts and Studies, 10. Brookline and Leyden: Classical Folia Editions, 1978.

———. "History as Enlightenment: Suger and the *Mos Anagogicus.*" In *Abbot Suger,* ed. Gerson. Pp. 151-58.

Stahl, Harvey. "The Problem of Manuscript Painting at Saint-Denis During the Abbacy of Suger." In *Abbot Suger,* ed. Gerson. Pp. 163-81.

Stein, Henri. *Bibliographie générale des cartulaires français ou relatifs à l'histoire de France.* Manuels de bibliographie historique, 4. Paris: Alphonse Picard, 1907.

Stubbs, William. *See* Roger of Howden

Suger. *Œuvres complètes de Suger.* Edited by A. Lecoy de La Marche. Publications de la Société de l'histoire de France, 139. Paris: Mme Vve Jules Renouard, 1867.

———. *Vie de Louis le Gros par Suger, suivie de l'Histoire du roi Louis VII.* Edited by Auguste Molinier. Collection de textes pour servir à l'étude et à l'enseignement de l'histoire, 4. Paris: Picard, 1887.

———. *Vie de Louis VI le Gros.* Edited and translated by Henri Waquet. Les classiques de l'histoire de France au Moyen Age, 11. Paris: "Les Belles Lettres," 1964.

Sutherland, Nicola Mary. "Was There an Inquisition in Renaissance France?" In eadem, *Princes, Politics and Religion, 1547-1589.* Historical Series, 30. London: Hambledon Press, 1984. Pp. 13-29.

Tessier, Georges. *See Recueil des actes de Charles le Chauve, Recueil des actes d'Eudes*

Texera, Joseph. *Rervm ab Henrici Condæi Franciæ Protoprincipis Majoribus gestarum, Epitome. Ejusdemque Henrici Genealogiæ Explicatio, A Divo Ludovico per Borbonios, atque ab Imbaldo Trimollio ad utrumque dicti Henrici parentem repetitæ.* Paris: Leodegarius Delaz, 1598.

Trenard, Louis. "Godefroy (Denis II)." In *Dictionnaire de biographie française,* 92 (1983), 438, no. 16.

Turner, Cuthbert Hamilton. "The Bibliography of Jean du Tillet." *Journal of Theological Studies,* 12 (1910), 128-33.

———. "Jean du Tillet: A Neglected Scholar of the Sixteenth Century." Appendix V. In *The Bodleian Manuscript of Jerome's Version of the Chronicle of Eusebius Reproduced in Collotype*. Introduction by John Knight Fotheringham. Oxford: Clarendon Press, 1905. Pp. 48-63.

Valensise, Marina. "Le sacre du roi: stratégie symbolique et doctrine politique de la monarchie française." *Annales. Economies—Sociétés—Civilisations*, 41 (1986), 543-77.

Valladier, André. *Paranese royale: Sur les Ceremonies du Sacre du Tres-Chrestien Lovys XIII. Roy de France & Navarre. Pour le lendemain du Sacre, iour de S. Luc, & de la ceremonie des Cheualiers du S. Esprit, faicte en l'Eglise Cathedralle de nostre Dame de Rheims*. Paris: Pierre Chevalier, 1611.

Valois, Adrien de. *Rervm Francicarvm vsqve ad Chlotharii Senioris Mortem Libri VIII*. 3 vols. Paris: Sebastien Cramoisy et Gabriel Cramoisy, 1646-58.

———. *Valesiana ou les pensées critiques, historiques et morales, et les poesies latines de Monsieur de Valois, Conseiller du Roi & Historiographe de France. Recueillies par Monsieur de Valois son Fils*. Paris: Florentin & Pierre Delaulne, 1694. BN: Z 1884.

———. *See also Carmen Panegyricvm*

Valon, François de. *Les pairs de France primitifs et leur cour*. Thèse pour le doctorat, Université de Toulouse, Faculté de droit, année 1930-1931. Toulouse: Henri Cléder, 1931.

Vic, Claude de, and Jean-Joseph Vaissete. *Histoire générale de Languedoc, Avec des notes & les Piéces justificatives: Composée sur les Auteurs & les Titres originaux, & enrichie de divers Monumens. Par un religieux Bénédictin de la Congregation de S. Maur*. 5 vols. Paris: Jacques Vincent, 1730-45.

———. *Histoire générale de Languedoc, avec des notes et les pièces justificatives*. 2nd ed. Edited by Auguste Molinier. 15 vols. Toulouse: E. Privat, 1872-93.

Vignier, Nicolas. *La Bibliotheqve Historiale, de Nicolas Vignier de Bar svr Seine, Medecin et Historiographe dv Roy. Contenant la disposition & concordance des temps, des histoires, & des historiographes, ensemble l'estat des principales & plus renomees Monarchies selon leur ordre & succession*. 4 vols. Paris: Abel L'Angelier, and La Veuve Iean Camusat et Pierre Le Petit, 1587-1650.

Von Euw, Anton. *See* Euw, Anton von

Vyon d'Herouval, Antoine. *See* Bruel, Alexandre

Waitz, Georg. "Die Formeln der deutschen Königs- und der römischen Kaiser-Krönung vom zehnten bis zum zwölften Jahrhundert." *Abhandlungen der Historisch-Philologischen Classe der Königlichen Gesellschaft der Wissenschaften zu Göttingen*, 18 (1873), 3-92.

———. *See also* Hugues of Fleury. *Hugonis Floriacensis Opera Historica*

Waldman, Thomas G. "Abbot Suger and the Nuns of Argenteuil." *Traditio*, 41 (1985), 239-72.

Waquet, Henri. *See* Suger. *Vie de Louis VI le Gros*

Ward, Paul L. "The Coronation Ceremony in Mediaeval England." *Speculum*, 14 (1939), 160-78.

———. "An Early Version of the Anglo-Saxon Coronation Ceremony." *English Historical Review*, 57 (1942), 345-61.

Warren, Wilfred Lewis. *King John*. New York: W. W. Norton, 1961.

Werner, Karl Ferdinand. "Avant les Capétiens." In *L'élection du chef de l'Etat en France de Hugues Capet à nos jours. Entretiens d'Auxerre 1987*. Edited by Léo Hamon and Guy Lobrichon. Paris: Beauchesne, 1988. Pp. 13-23.

Widukind. *Annales Witichindi Monachi Corbiensis, familiæ Benedictinæ: Editi de fide codicis manuscripti, & e publicato exemplari alicubi aucti. Addita est breuis appendix de familia & rebus gestis Palatinorum Saxoniæ, e Chronico Gozecensi. Item historia Henrici Leonis, Ducis Saxoniæ & Bauariæ, excerpta de Annalibus Helmoldi, Arnoldi, & Saxonia Krancij*. Edited by Reinerus Reineccius. Frankfurt-am-Main: Andreas Wechelus, 1755.

———. *Widukindi Monachi Corbeiensis Rerum gestarum Saxonicarum libri tres*. Edited by Georg Waitz and Carl Andreas Kehr. 4th ed. Scriptores rerum Germanicarum in usum scholarum ex Monumentis Germaniae Historicis separatim editi. Hannover and Leipzig: Hahn, 1904.

INDEX

www.ingramcontent.com/pod-product-compliance
Lightning Source LLC
LaVergne TN
LVHW081339110826
845153LV00010B/437

* 9 7 8 0 8 7 1 6 9 8 2 7 8 *